# THE GREAT AMERICAN BANK ROBBERY

# THE GREAT AMERICAN BANK ROBBERY

## THE UNAUTHORIZED REPORT ABOUT WHAT REALLY CAUSED THE GREAT RECESSION

by PAUL SPERRY

THOMAS NELSON
*Since 1798*

NASHVILLE DALLAS MEXICO CITY RIO DE JANEIRO

Published in Nashville, Tennessee, by Thomas Nelson. Thomas Nelson is a registered trademark of Thomas Nelson, Inc.

Thomas Nelson, Inc., titles may be purchased in bulk for educational, business, fund-raising, or sales promotional use. For information, please e-mail SpecialMarkets@ThomasNelson.com.

**Library of Congress Cataloging-in-Publication Data**

Sperry, Paul (Paul E.)

The great American bank robbery : the unauthorized report about what really caused the great recession / by Paul Sperry.

p. cm.

Includes bibliographical references and index.

ISBN 978-1-59555-270-9

1. Mortgage loans—United States. 2. Banks and banking—United States. 3. Housing policy—United States. 4. Global Financial Crisis, 2008–2009. 5. United States—Economic policy—2001-2009. I. Title.

HG2040.5.U5S64 2010

330.973—dc22 2010046011

*Printed in the United States of America*

11 12 13 14 15 RRD 6 5 4 3 2 1

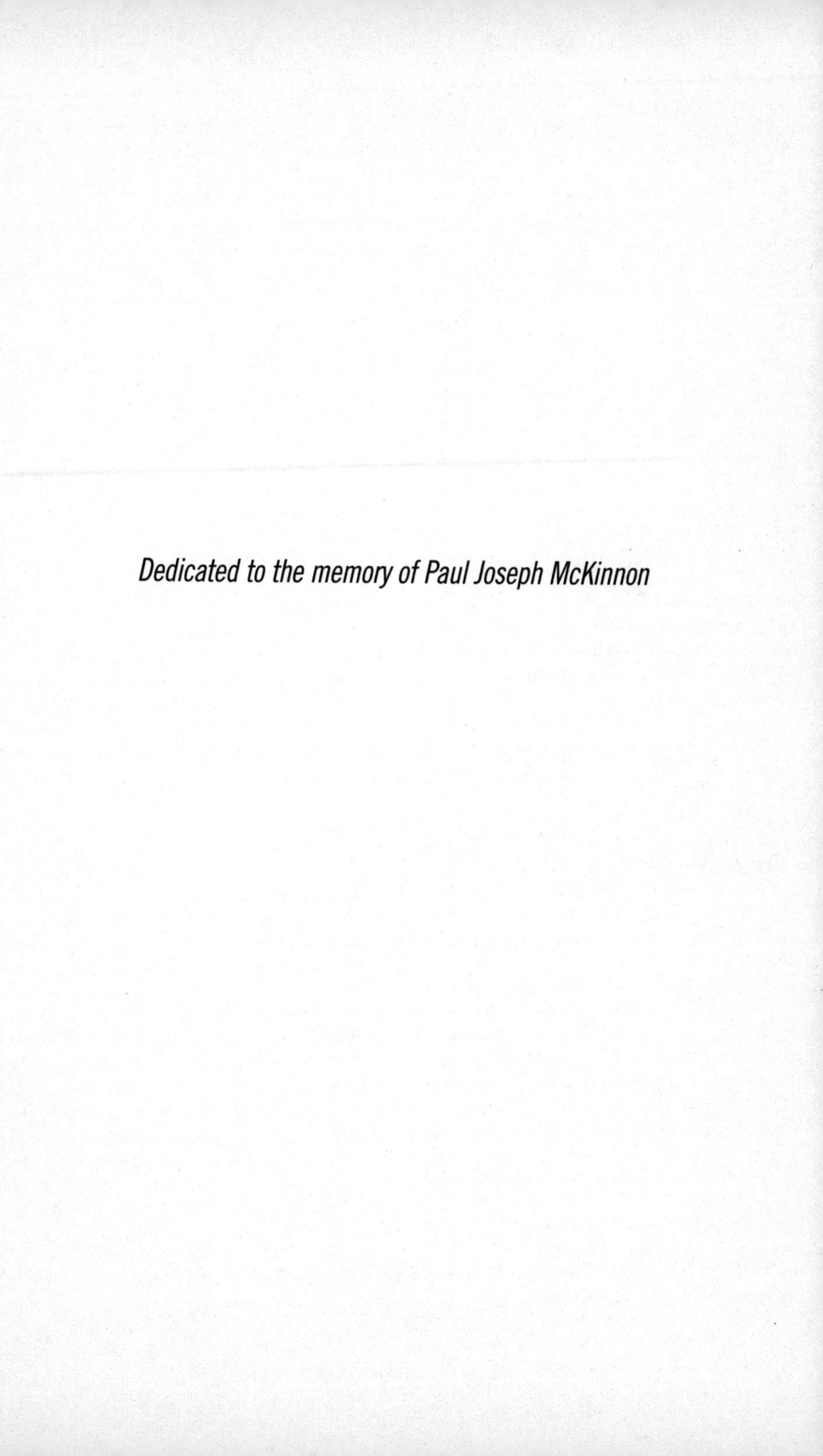

*Dedicated to the memory of Paul Joseph McKinnon*

# CONTENTS

# A NOTE OF CAUTION TO READERS

This book, at bottom, is an indictment. It does not seek to condemn the uncreditworthy minority borrowers who pursued the American dream of owning a home, even if prematurely. Rather, it accuses those who make a living exploiting these protected classes. Yes, the hardest-hit victims of the "subprime sub-crime," as Jesse Jackson has dubbed it, are indeed low- and moderate-income minorities, who were trapped in home loans beyond their means and have now lost everything. But they were not victimized as much by "predatory lenders" as by Washington social engineers and housing-rights activists who used lenders to integrate them into the economic mainstream—regardless of their financial wherewithal.

In the final analysis, they merely resegregated poor minorities into neighborhoods that are now more blighted than ever.

As these housing-rights zealots watch their multicultural experiment self-destruct from the safety of their ivory tower and government corner offices, minority borrowers are watching their homes get boarded up, their credit and borrowing power go from bad to worse, and their dreams of viable homeownership crumbling. It will be years before they can qualify again.

This is the real scandal and tragedy of the subprime credit crisis. For as well-intentioned as they may have been, the zealots failed—and are failing again—to recognize the long-term benefit of prudent underwriting standards: greater assurance that a homeowner who buys a home, stays in the home.

PAUL SPERRY

# PREFACE

It is now official: According to the Federal Reserve Board, the financial crisis has wiped out $14 trillion in American household wealth—an amount equal to the entire gross domestic product, and the worse loss of wealth since the Great Depression. This equates to an average loss of more than $123,000 per household. Yet Americans didn't *lose* it. It was taken.

Who took it?

The president blames "fat cat bankers." Michael Moore and others on the left want them locked up. The filmmaker even wrapped crime-scene tape around landmark investment banks on Wall Street.

President Obama recently paid a visit to the famous Manhattan financial district and gave its denizens a tongue-lashing. "The people on Wall Street still don't get it," he said. "You guys caused the problem."

But the real scene of the "subprime sub-crime"—the biggest robbery in history—is Washington.

This book is the first careful and thorough analysis of public policy's role in the crisis. It presents fresh new evidence that government social engineers—from both the Democrat and the Republican Parties—masterminded a massive bank heist with help from accomplices in the nonprofit sector. And now, under Obama, they are planning an even bigger heist. A 9/11-type commission has been impaneled to investigate.

But it's a frame-up. Commissioners have set up Wall Street bankers to take the fall.

This book is the report they won't release, the truth they don't want you to know.

## INTRODUCTION

# THE ANGELIDES COMMISSION

Old civic activists never die, we just get recycled.

— Philip Angelides, chairman of the Financial Crisis Inquiry Commission

In 1933, during the trough of the Great Depression, Senate Banking Committee chief counsel Ferdinand Pecora led congressional hearings to examine the root causes of the epochal financial crisis. The aggressive, cigar-chomping ex–New York prosecutor used the high-profile platform to demonize Wall Street bankers and agitate for New Deal financial reforms.

Commonly known as the Pecora Commission, his panel exercised subpoena power to drag "fat cat" bankers such as J. P. Morgan Jr. before Congress for public whippings. It pinned the stock market crash and Depression on Wall Street greed rather than bad Central Bank and other government policy, where many economists today believe it belongs.

The following year, President Roosevelt appointed Pecora commissioner of the newly formed Securities and Exchange Commission. "Bitterly hostile was Wall Street to the enactment of the regulatory legislation," Pecora later wrote.

Fast-forward three-quarters of a century.

A new commission has put Wall Street on trial for market "excesses." And the Obama administration is expected to use its findings to justify a new round of banking regulations—including another expansion of the Community Reinvestment Act, the controversial anti-redlining law—that threaten to take the financial industry—and possibly the economy—back to the 1930s.

On January 13, 2010, the Financial Crisis Inquiry Commission kicked off its yearlong hearings by promising a "thorough examination of the root causes" of the Great Recession. It has conducted more than 500 interviews and presumably sifted through the full body of evidence. Now it is set to release its final report, which promises to hold the guilty accountable and recommend reforms to prevent another crisis.

But don't hold your breath.

The commission is supposedly modeled after the blue-ribbon panel that looked into the 9/11 terrorist attacks. But it looks more like the Pecora Commission.

While commission chairman Philip Angelides has pledged "a full and fair inquiry," detractors say his hearings resembled more of an inquisition. They have a strong case: the "bipartisan" panel is made up of a majority of Democrats who clearly have it in for Wall Street.

Setting the tone was their witness list for the hearing curtain-raiser. Wall Street honchos from JPMorgan, Goldman Sachs, Morgan Stanley, and Bank of America landed in the pillories first, instead of Washington executives from Fannie Mae (Federal National Mortgage Association) and Freddie Mac (Federal Home Loan Mortgage Corporation) and officials from their federal regulator, the U.S. Department of Housing and Urban Development, who have far more to answer for. Under pressure from Washington, the congressionally chartered and taxpayer-subsidized agencies underwrote $1.8 trillion of the subprime and other toxic home loans that nearly KO'd the financial system. ("Subprime" refers to home loans made to borrowers with relatively poor or unproven credit histories. These loans are therefore riskier than prime loans, which are made to borrowers with stronger credit.)

Fannie and Freddie, which together provide funding for more than half the nation's mortgages, guaranteed more bad loans than anyone—much more than the combined holdings of the four bankers featured—yet they were missing from the opening witness list. So, too, were their HUD regulators, who pushed them to make the bad loans. Bankers took their place in the police lineup, and Angelides wasted no time pointing the finger at them.

He accused them of acting like unscrupulous used-car salesmen when they sold subprime mortgage-backed securities to investors. "It sounds like selling a car with faulty brakes," an imperious Angelides scolded.

While Wall Street contributed to the subprime feeding frenzy, it simply marketed the subprime securities that Washington mandated Fannie and Freddie to securitize and guarantee in order to earn Affordable Housing Goals credits from its mission regulator, HUD. Even so, Angelides demanded that bankers take the blame; and then, when they refused to be scapegoated, he grumbled that he was "troubled by the inability to take responsibility." Clearly frustrated, he later suggested everybody on Wall Street deserved blame. "Maybe this is like 'Murder on the Orient Express'" (the Agatha Christie murder mystery), he cracked. "Everybody did it."

Angelides appeared to have reached his conclusion on day one of the investigation.

For another indication that the fix was in, his star policy witness was Mark Zandi, who happens to be Democratic congressman Barney Frank's favorite economist. As head of the House Financial Services Committee, Frank protected Fannie and Freddie from oversight as they took on more and more bad loans in the name of Frank's hobbyhorse, "affordable housing." Yet in his 2008 book, *Financial Shock*, Zandi gave Frank a pass, while laying blame at the feet of Wall Street executives. Frank, in turn, wrote a blurb for the dust jacket of Zandi's book and praised it during his 2009 hearings to craft tough new banking regulations.

Asked by a reporter whether he and Zandi, a registered Democrat who has advised President Obama, disagree about anything, Frank replied, "Not really."

Also appearing in the inaugural hearing was a housing-rights activist for the Center for Responsible Lending, which helped pressure Fannie and Freddie to ease credit rules by accusing the mortgage giants of racial discrimination. The group, like scores of other community organizers, pushed for risky loans to uncreditworthy borrowers in a quest to end what it calls "financial apartheid" in the inner cities. Now that those loans have gone bust, they are accusing banks of "predatory lending."

The bespectacled Angelides brings his own strong bias to the table. A former Democratic state treasurer of California, he is a big fan of the Community Reinvestment Act, or CRA, and other federal regulations policing bank lending in poor and minority neighborhoods. He backed the Clinton administration's move in the mid-1990s to strengthen the CRA and other anti-redlining rules, which had the effect of watering down underwriting standards, socializing mortgages, and helping create the subprime market we all know so painfully well today.

In fact, Angelides himself helped fuel the crisis by pumping some $3 billion in California state funds into risky mortgage-backed securities based on urban home loans made under CRA guidelines and backed by Freddie Mac. He also plunged state pensions into the subprime market.

His initial 1999 investment marked the first time a state had bought such securities—a move that private economists at the time warned against, arguing his plan might be taking undue risk in pursuit of a social objective.

In a 1999 speech celebrating Community Banking Month, Angelides praised the CRA for pushing banks to invest "socially," while adding that "more financial resources should be targeted to underserved communities." He also vowed in a letter to the *Los Angeles Times* to use the CRA to help close "the gap between America's rich and poor." "The time has come . . . to mount a new march forward," Angelides wrote. "Fighting for the CRA is a good start."

His crusade to redistribute California wealth through CRA-eligible reinvestment did not end until 2007, the year the subprime bubble burst, when he stepped down as the state's treasurer. Now California is reeling from a wave of subprime mortgage defaults and losses on the mortgage-backed securities that Angelides pushed. In fact, his policies helped push the Golden State to the brink of bankruptcy.

Yet this is who is leading the investigation of the subprime crime. How did this happen? Angelides was handpicked by Democratic House Speaker Nancy Pelosi, an old crony from San Francisco.

More scandalous, Pelosi's lead detective has been in cahoots with the hold-up men. While in Sacramento, then treasurer Angelides worked closely with affordable-housing activists who prey on banks for multicultural loans. The San Francisco–based Greenlining Institute, for one, helped him steer state tax dollars to lenders that gave in to the radical group's demands and were deemed minority friendly. One of its favored lenders at the time was Los Angeles–based Countrywide Financial, America's biggest subprime lender and one of the first casualties of the financial crisis.

Angelides has also partnered with the radical (and criminal) inner-city group ACORN, which over the years has used the CRA to shake down banks for billions of dollars in minority loan set-asides and other concessions.

The 57-year-old Angelides promised hearings free of "the opinion or political leanings of any member of the Commission." That is a tall order for himself, never mind commissioners such as former Democratic senator Bob Graham, whose mind is already made up that government had no hand in the subprime scandal. As Graham stated in the opening round of hearings, "I don't think banks were pressured into doing this."

Angelides, for his part, is a longtime Democratic Party functionary. He served as former chairman of the California Democratic Party—a fact missing from his commission bio—and now chairs the San Francisco–based Apollo Alliance, a haunt of liberal Democrat activists. He sits on Apollo's board with former Clinton chief of staff John Podesta, who led Barack Obama's presidential transition team after the election; and Van Jones, a black nationalist and self-declared "communist," who landed a top job in the Obama White House before resigning amid a flurry of controversy over his past radical statements and activities.

Make no mistake: Angelides is no cold-eyed, dispassionate investigator. He is an activist with an ax to grind. As he shared with old Democrat pal Bill Press on Press's radio show, "Old civic activists never die, we just get recycled." What's more, Angelides has stacked his investigative team with old Democrat cronies and political donors from California, including a San Francisco trial lawyer who specializes in bringing class-action lawsuits against securities firms—like Goldman Sachs. Angelides may even have a personal vested interest in steering the investigation away from any serious scrutiny of the role of the CRA and other public housing policy in the crisis. In fact, he stands to gain financially from a beefed-up CRA, which is a centerpiece of Obama's new financial regulatory regime.

Public records show that Angelides is owner or partner in several California-based real estate ventures, including Canyon Capital Realty Advisors, which has some $17 billion in assets under management, including urban reinvestment projects. These projects, financed in part by CRA-mandated loans, present at least the appearance of a conflict of interest.

He may also stand to gain politically. Angelides's name has been bandied about as a possible replacement for Treasury secretary Timothy Geithner. When he delivers his final report to the president's desk, Angelides will no doubt make sure Obama, also no fan of Wall Street banks, likes what he reads.

"I've been stunned at the level of betting—the almost casino-like nature on Wall Street," Angelides confided in Press, who succeeded him as head of the California Democratic Party. "I feel like I walked into my local community bank, I inadvertently opened a door, and I saw the floor of the New York-New York Casino."

Responding to Press's listeners who do not think the recently passed Dodd-Frank Wall Street Reform and Consumer Protection Act goes far enough, Angelides cautioned patience, noting that New Deal regulations "took a decade to put into place." His report threatens to lay the foundation for a new New Deal.

Dodd-Frank, the first major piece of legislation in Obama's onslaught of new financial regulations, already dwarfs the centerpiece of Depression-era bank legislation. The Glass-Steagall Act ran 34 pages long, while Dodd-Frank spans 2,319 pages and includes a whopping 16 new federal titles, none of which deal with Fannie and Freddie. There is at least one unintended consequence for the economy on each page. Yet Angelides & Company want more.

Now perhaps you understand why I felt compelled to write this book.

The Angelides Commission has an antimarket, pro-government agenda and cannot be trusted to conduct an honest inquiry into the financial crime of the century. Instead of indicting the guilty culprits, it more than likely will whitewash their crimes, while framing others.

The primary culprits in this crisis are in Washington, and so far they have gotten off scot-free. Angelides gave them blanket immunity. No officials dealing with federal housing *policy* were called to testify during the 14-month inquiry, confirms Peter Wallison, a former Reagan Treasury official and minority voice serving on the Angelides Commission. Nobody from the White House, which revised the Community Reinvestment Act to mandate "flexible underwriting" at CRA-covered banks. And nobody from HUD, which set the aggressive Affordable Housing Goals for Fannie and Freddie that plunged them into the subprime market. It was HUD that also pressured independent mortgage lenders not covered by the CRA—including Countrywide—to sign Memoranda of Agreement with the government to devote more lending to otherwise uncreditworthy minority borrowers. (This has not been widely reported; we will come back to it in greater detail later.)

"Yes, you are correct," commissioner Wallison told me, "housing policy was not part of the narrative for the hearings."

If this is not confirmation of a cover-up of government's role in the crisis, what is? In an "investigation" stretching over 14 months and costing taxpayers $10 million, the congressionally appointed commission did not lay a glove on the real culprits.

While he expected as much, Wallison is still disappointed, convinced as he is that the huge number of subprime mortgages that collapsed the economy were generated by government policy. Discouraged but not defeated, he vows to soldier on. "This is a serious fight," he said in an exclusive interview, "and the stakes are quite high."

Indeed they are. Like the Great Depression, the debate over the causes and cures of the Great Recession is a generational one that will shape the future of not only the American economy but the political landscape. Whoever wins this debate wins Washington and gets to determine the size of government and its mix in the economy.

"The diagnosis determines the prescription," Wallison believes, and right now the prescription is more government.

But before Washington adopts even more laws and regulations to prevent a recurrence, he argues, the American people have a right to know the real causes of the crisis. Unfortunately, Wallison is a lone voice of reason on the panel, and he was drowned out by historic revisionists determined to cover the government's tracks. With its final report, the Democrat-controlled commission plans to make a big political statement on behalf of big government. And the bigger the splash it makes, the likelier the statement will permanently shape the conscience of ordinary Americans.

With the facts aligning against their predetermined, antimarket conclusion, Democrats are desperate for a best seller from Angelides. It is their key to maintaining control of the debate and pushing for more government regulations, including an expanded Community Reinvestment Act. The commission's report will shape final rule-making under the Dodd-Frank Act. The legislation is a broad brush, and regulatory agencies and lobbyists still have to flesh out details. It will take years before the law is fully implemented. As Angelides recently remarked, "The reform debate is just beginning."

To help sell the report, Angelides has retained the major New York publishing house of Little, Brown and Company, whose editorial advisory board happens to include the interim director of Obama's new Consumer Financial Protection Bureau. Angelides even hired former senior *Time* editor Matt Cooper, husband of ex-Clinton aide Mandy Grunwald, to draft the public document, which hit bookstores December 15, 2010.

According to the *Washington Post*, the report "will take readers back to 2003 and 2004 to explore the beginnings of the troubles," even though they began during the Clinton years. Look for it in the fiction section.

The American public deserves better.

*The Great American Bank Robbery* offers a welcome rebuttal not only to the commission's one-sided report, but to the entire false narrative told so far by the mainstream media about how

$14 trillion in household wealth disappeared—a storyline that, according to public opinion polls, has mistakenly convinced an overwhelming majority of Americans that banks are to blame for their lighter wallets. Fully 80 percent of Americans say banks and other financial institutions are responsible for the mortgage meltdown, according to a *Washington Post/ABC News* poll taken in 2009. This book, like no other before it, promises to disabuse the public of such notions.

The $14 trillion in lost household wealth—which translates to an average loss of more than $46,000 for every man, woman, and child—is a hidden diversity tax levied by Washington to subsidize "affordable housing" for "underserved communities." Homeowner equity alone has plummeted by nearly 50 percent from its 2006 peak to $6.6 trillion. This pencils out to an average loss of more than $80,000 for the American homeowner—with much of those losses concentrated in urban areas, which in a cruel joke were hit hardest by Washington's easy credit schemes.

We are not just talking about paper losses. A record 2.5 million families have lost their homes to foreclosure—and more than 10 million more are in the foreclosure process—while more than 8.5 million Americans have lost their jobs.

The subprime scandal has also robbed future generations of wealth, thanks to the record $11 trillion national debt it has helped generate. This looming liability—equal to $36,000 per citizen—is a "grandchild tax," since the debts Washington keeps running up are actually taxes deferred to our children and their children.

Taxpayers already are on the hook for the $700 billion TARP (Troubled Asset Relief Program) bailout of insolvent banks. But that does not include the minimum $400 billion it will cost to bail out Fannie and her brother, Freddie—and that is a conservative estimate. The final price tag could run as high as $1 trillion. With a wave of subprime and other nonprime mortgage foreclosures still to come, taxpayer exposure to the government rescue of these two government-sponsored mortgage giants is virtually unlimited.

"It is the mother of all bailouts," says Edward Pinto, a former chief credit officer at Fannie Mae, who now consults for the mortgage industry. By comparison, the 1990s savings and loan bailout cost $210 billion in inflation-adjusted numbers, $173 billion of which came from taxpayers.

And the administration does not seem to care. It has quietly pledged unlimited backing. On Christmas Eve 2009, it announced that it was lifting the $400 billion cap from what it thinks will be necessary to keep Fannie and Freddie afloat. Yet at the same time, it spared these toxic twins at the heart of the financial crisis from its "sweeping" financial reforms, promising only to continue jawboning about possible fixes into 2011. An overhaul of federal housing policy also has been conveniently deferred. The Democrat-controlled Angelides Commission predictably ignored the issue.

Who has mortgaged your children's financial security? The same Washington social engineers who strong-armed banks into making risky multicultural loans that turned bad and destroyed home and stock equities, robbing ordinary Americans of their nest eggs. And this book promises to identify and indict the guilty muggers—many of whom have returned to the scene of their crime and are planning an even bigger heist.

On the following pages I will show you, in a detailed narrative illustrated by charts and graphs, precisely how they pulled off their last heist; how the shakedown artists colluded with the social engineers at every step of the way—from Chicago to Little Rock to Washington—to formulate the banking regulations and housing policies that socialized mortgages, gutted time-tested underwriting standards, and led to the worst financial calamity since the 1930s.

You no doubt already have heard the media, along with countless other book authors, demonize the bankers and corporate tycoons mentioned earlier as the guilty parties of the "subprime sub-crime," as Jesse Jackson and other race demagogues call it.

While they share blame, now meet the real villains.

# ONE

# PRIME SUSPECTS

History should deal harshly with Bill Clinton.

— Timothy Canova, professor of international economic law at Chapman University School of Law in Orange, California

The first person the commission investigating the genesis of the financial crisis should have called to testify is William Jefferson Clinton. He has a lot of explaining to do.

As "the first black president," Clinton had a strong following among black voters and wanted to secure their loyalty. He hatched a scheme to use banks to close the "mortgage gap" between blacks and whites. In particular, he was not happy with lagging homeownership rates among African-Americans and therefore set a goal to push it for the first time above 50 percent.

Compared to his plan to nationalize the health care system, President Clinton's housing policy seemed a small and rather innocuous plank in his domestic agenda, and few paid it much mind. Many today still do not know about it. But his so-called National Homeownership Strategy was both highly ambitious and cleverly orchestrated. To boost black homeownership, Clinton launched a multifront assault on banks, involving more than "100 specific actions"—none of which required new legislation, and all of which managed to avoid serious public scrutiny.

First, using his executive order powers, he revised federal anti-redlining rules by setting numerical targets for lending in predominantly black Census tracts, while mandating that banks adopt "flexible underwriting standards" to hit those targets. He added several hundred bank examiners to enforce the tougher CRA rules, and they in turn more than doubled CRA examinations of banks. He also toughened CRA grading, making it harder for banks to pass exams. Those who failed had their expansion plans put on hold, a slow death sentence in an era of frenzied bank mergers and acquisitions. And for the first time, bank report cards with the dreaded "CRA rating" were made public, egging on ACORN and other radical inner-city groups, who used the reports to extort banks for billions of dollars in minority loan set-asides and other concessions. (Formerly based in Little Rock, ACORN had a direct line to the Clinton White House and actually helped draft Clinton's tougher fair-lending rules for both banks and Fannie and Freddie, something we will revisit in greater detail in chapter 4. Disturbingly, ACORN'S veteran Washington lobbyist from those days, a bitter socialist, attended Harvard with Obama; and Obama has promised him and his radical new community organizing group a seat at the table to help him "shape" his domestic policy agenda.)

When bankers resisted being saddled with so many additional risky loans, Clinton tapped Fannie Mae and Freddie Mac to take them off their books, while freeing bankers to originate more of the political loans. He directed HUD to hike Fannie's and Freddie's goals for underwriting affordable loans. HUD has the power to enforce their loan programs and required that at least half of all Fannie and Freddie mortgage purchases benefit poor and minority families—a Draconian level that remained in force throughout the 2000s.

When the mortgage giants pushed back, complaining it would be hard to meet the higher targets, Clinton had his HUD regulators encourage them to load up on subprime loans, which charge higher rates and fees to cover the higher costs of servicing riskier borrowers. He also authorized Fannie and Freddie for the first time to purchase securities backed by bundled subprime and other CRA-eligible mortgages to earn credits against the HUD goals. The mortgage giants jumped at the chance, since it allowed them to meet the onerous new goals in wholesale fashion.

For good measure, Clinton, late in his second term, appointed several of his cronies to key board positions, on the inside of Fannie and Freddie, including White House budget chief Franklin Delano Raines, to ensure they continued his affordable-lending crusade well into the next administration.

Ever resourceful, Clinton even enlisted the U.S. Department of Justice in his minority homeownership push. In a flurry of lawsuits, federal prosecutors accused banks and lenders of discriminating against black borrowers, driving banks and independent mortgage lenders alike deeper into urban areas. Prosecutors sued them under the Fair Housing Act and other federal antidiscrimination laws, which covered all lenders, not just depository institutions covered by the CRA.

Meanwhile, the charming new president seduced Federal Reserve chairman Alan Greenspan into issuing a video for bankers in which the central banker decreed the new "10 Commandments" of fair lending—including new "flexible" underwriting guidelines tailored to the "special" credit traits of minorities. As a result, race became the only lending criterion that really mattered.

Clinton justified his entire fair housing crusade on a discredited Boston Fed report that claimed to find structural racism in mortgage lending. The study was based on fundamentally flawed data. Clinton nonetheless hired its author to run economic policy at Treasury.

In the end, his race-based lending mandates created a feeding frenzy for subprime and other risky mortgages that left communities of color worse off than ever.

## BUBBA'S BUBBLE

Before the housing bubble popped, and before minority homeownership rates retraced their gains, Clinton's top regulators boasted that their policies helped create both the primary and secondary markets for subprime loans, as well as the market for subprime securities. They embraced subprime mortgages as offering minorities a "good option" to buy homes and refinance debt. Clinton himself at the time bragged about plundering banks for record hundreds of billions of dollars in loans for minority communities, before falling silent as those loans defaulted (more on that later).

The subprime market indeed grew rapidly in response to Clinton's mandates, and subprime loan standards deteriorated rapidly. Virtually overnight, an embryonic business grew into a trillion-dollar industry. Subprime lending more than doubled during the Clinton years, while the number of subprime lenders mushroomed from a handful to more than 50.

In 2000, the year before his new political loan targets for Fannie and Freddie took effect, the subprime market commanded 2 percent of the broader mortgage market, according to the Federal Reserve. By 2005, after his ambitious targets had been in place for four years, subprime mortgage originations had swelled to 20 percent of all U.S. home mortgage originations—10 times their share in 2000.

Subprime mortgage-backed securities also exploded. Less than half of subprime originations had been securitized in 2000. But by 2007, thanks in large part to the boom in goals-qualifying subprime securities at Fannie and Freddie, virtually all subprime originations were being securitized.

Clinton's new CRA rules, which had regulators zeroing in on the volume of bank lending in urban areas, also were a factor. Clinton wanted numbers, and he got them. The volume of CRA lending exploded between 1993 and 2000, with the number of riskier CRA-eligible home loans originated by CRA lenders and their affiliates ballooning from 462,000 to 1.3 million over that period, according to federal data.

Clinton's policies for the first time threw millions of previously unqualified buyers into the mortgage mix. Between 1995 and 2005, minorities accounted for nearly two-thirds of household growth and contributed a whopping 49 percent of the 12.5 million rise in homeowners over the decade, according to Harvard University's Joint Center for Housing Studies. Their "strong numerical gains," the study noted, coincided with a surge in subprime lending over the same period, with blacks taking out a disproportionately higher share of the subprime loans. As a result, their homeownership rate increased more during the 1990s than in any decade except the 1940s—hitting a record 48 percent by the time Clinton left office.

But the gains would not last, built as they were on shaky credit.

When Clinton enlisted Fannie and Freddie to fund minority homeownership, he triggered a shift to Wall Street–based funding of junk mortgage lending that ultimately proved lethal to the entire financial system. Fannie and Freddie, which pioneered the market for mortgage-backed securities, bundled pools of subprime and other risky mortgages and sold them to investors as securities, or MBS's. Because the government-sponsored mortgage giants were implicitly backed by the federal government, investors perceived their guarantee to have essentially removed the credit risk from the MBS's they issued. So investing in subprime securities backed by Fannie and Freddie was considered as sound as investing in Treasuries, only with higher yields. In fact, their securities are deemed "government securities."

The securitization boom sparked by Fannie and Freddie generally expanded the supply of credit, as mortgage originators had a new source of finance for loan origination. Expanded supply led to lower cost of credit; the lower borrowing costs, in turn, churned even more subprime lending. And the added demand buoyed by securitization drove housing prices even higher.

The dramatic increase in inflation-adjusted housing prices coincided with Clinton's minority homeownership crusade. After decades of moderate gains, real home price growth began to accelerate in the late 1990s. The size of the increase from 1997 to the peak in 2006 is both striking and unprecedented. It dwarfs any previous run-up in home values in American history. And no such bubble occurred in Canada, so what happened here cannot be explained by global trends.

"The subprime and other weak mortgages that were at the heart of the crash in housing and mortgage values enabled large numbers of people to buy homes who previously had not had access to housing credit," Wallison explains. "The infusion of government funds into this market through Fannie Mae, Freddie Mac, and other government housing programs [including the CRA], drove a ten-year housing bubble from 1997 to 2007 that grew to unprecedented size."

Clinton's reckless housing policies fed not only a housing bubble—call it Bubba's Bubble—but a systemic moral hazard, in which lenders and borrowers alike took on more and more risk because they did not have to face the consequences. To wit:

- Lenders had little incentive to carefully screen borrowers for their creditworthiness when they sold subprime and other CRA-eligible loans they originated to Fannie and Freddie. Why should they? They were not holding them in their portfolios, and they did not bear any losses if the borrowers failed to repay.
- Fannie and Freddie did not need to fret about subprime leveraging. Why should they? They operated knowing that taxpayers would bail them out if they ran into trouble.
- Wall Street investors did not need to worry about trading riskier subprime mortgage-backed securities. Why should they? They were backed by the full faith and credit of the U.S. Treasury. Uncle Sam would cover their risk.
- And individual homebuyers and refinancers, along with house flippers and other speculators, did not need to worry about taking on more risk with high-cost

> subprime, interest-only, adjustable-rate, or cash-out equity loans. Why should they? Home values kept appreciating.

Clinton changed the rules for risk. He also changed the rules for lending.

"Adoption of these new and 'innovative' underwriting criteria spread across the banks and eventually to Fannie Mae and Freddie Mac," says Mark Willis, head of community development at JPMorgan Chase, one of the largest CRA-regulated banks.

When Fannie and Freddie relaxed their underwriting rules to satisfy HUD's lending edicts, they in turn influenced credit standards across the entire mortgage industry. Whatever Fannie and Freddie were willing to underwrite on the secondary market, originators were willing to lend on the primary market. And not just CRA-regulated bank originators, but nonbank mortgage originators, as well, who were not even under CRA pressure to bend their underwriting rules (although they *were* under pressure from the Justice Department and HUD to do so). Up and down the mortgage supply chain, thanks to Clinton's housing policies, the long-standing firewall protecting both lenders and consumers from undue risk broke down.

## REVERSAL OF FORTUNE

Clinton's crusade to close the "mortgage gap" has backfired terribly. The gains in black homeownership that Clinton crowed about have collapsed along with the subprime bubble he created. The mortgage gap between blacks and whites is just as wide today as it was when Clinton launched his crusade to close it. In fact, virtually nothing has changed—except that now, blighted urban areas are even more blighted thanks to the wave of subprime foreclosures. Boarded-up, vacant homes are covered in graffiti, and drug dealers have moved into even middle-income neighborhoods in predominantly black cities, such as Baltimore, Cleveland, Detroit, and Obama's hometown of Chicago. The subprime crisis has left almost 30 percent of Detroit's housing stock vacant. The city is pockmarked with roughly 90,000 abandoned or vacant homes and residential lots now. Call it Bubba's Blight.

Widespread foreclosures have drained an estimated $350 billion in wealth from communities of color—more than three times the damage the Gulf States suffered from Hurricane Katrina. While the nation has endured a recession, these communities have suffered a depression. African-Americans—the prime target of Clinton's social experiment—are bearing the brunt of the financial pain. With relatively little in savings, they lose everything when their homes are repossessed. And they will have to wait years for their credit to mend.

And now, thanks to widespread bank closures, there are fewer sources of credit available for first-time minority borrowers. More than 300 banks are expected to go under in the subprime crisis, further contracting credit options for minorities. Currently a total of 775 banks—or one-tenth of all U.S. banks—are on the FDIC's watch list of "problem" institutions. With the coming tsunami of banking regulations generated by the Dodd-Frank Act, the American Bankers Association predicts 1,000 fewer banks by the end of the decade.

It gets worse. Thanks to the subprime-led Great Recession, joblessness for 16-to-24-year-old black men has reached Great Depression proportions, according to the U.S. Department of Labor. At 34 percent, it is more than three times the rate for the general United States population.

Clinton made victims of the very people he deigned to help. His dream of increasing homeownership without increasing mortgage risk turned into their worst nightmare.

So, now let's review the bill of indictment against the 41st president:

COUNT 1: Clinton plunged Fannie and Freddie into the subprime market and turned them into the twin towers of toxic debt they are today. Thanks to his HUD policies, which remained in effect through the mid-2000s, they are now the biggest mortgage risk holders in the biggest mortgage crisis. The minority "affordable" loans he freighted them with ultimately proved costly to everybody.

COUNT 2: Clinton started the subprime crime wave by turning previously inconsequential subprime mortgages into a hefty, trillion-dollar market, and by spreading their risk from Main Street to Wall Street through government-backed securitizations.

COUNT 3: Clinton undercut traditional rules for lending, ordering bankers to throw open their borrowing windows to just about anybody—or else.

COUNT 4: Clinton created an easy credit orgy that fed a historic housing bubble that eventually blew up in the face of anyone connected to a home or home loan.

COUNT 5: Clinton's grand social experiment backfired most severely on the very people he claimed to help—African-Americans, who are now in worse shape than ever.

If Clinton's policies helped create the subprime boom, and there is no shortage of economists who agree they did, then it logically follows that they are equally responsible for the bust.

"History should deal harshly with Bill Clinton," says Timothy Canova, professor of international economic law at the Chapman University School of Law in Orange, California.

But do not tell that to the Angelides Commission, which has let the former president off the hook.

The visible Clinton has done his best to absolve himself of any responsibility in the subprime scandal, and the mainstream media have for the most part helped him. He has offered a number of alibis, while blaming "predatory" lenders, Wall Street "derivatives," the Bush administration, and the Greenspan Fed—anything but his own policies—for the subprime boom and bust.

"This all started because you had too much money, and the only place it could make money was in housing," an unbowed Clinton spun in a 2008 appearance on *The Daily Show with Jon Stewart*. "In 2001, all this money was out there, and it all went into housing and construction, so we had to keep finding funny ways to have more houses, like the subprime mortgages or the derivatives."

With typical Clinton gall, he maintained that if he had remained in power after January 2001, he would have invested all that money in the environment, not housing—even though he had buffaloed banks into investing in high-risk urban housing over the previous eight years. "What if we'd put a lot of this money into solar energy, into wind energy, into a hybrid electric vehicle, into all these things that—making all of our cities as energy-efficient as possible?" Clinton said, continuing his fit of historic revisionism. "We would've created millions of jobs, raised incomes, had the revenues to provide health care to everybody."

## "A RECORD OF ACCOMPLISHMENT"

That, anyway, is what Clinton said in September 2008, as subprime mortgages torpedoed the economy and the markets. Now here is what he said in June 2007, on the eve of the mortgage meltdown, in a speech to a Washington-based welfare-rights organization: "When I was president, we instituted a vigorous enforcement of the Community Reinvestment Act, a little-known law passed when President Carter was in office, that requires banks to loan money. Eight hundred billion dollars in investments were made in those eight years under the Community Reinvestment Act—over 90 percent of all the money that had ever been invested under that law—just because we enforced it."

And how.

But he does not brag about that anymore. And conveniently, evidence of his role in increasing minority borrowing has been scrubbed from his William J. Clinton Foundation Web site. I managed to save copies of the missing pages before they disappeared, while doing research for an *Investor's Business Daily* editorial on the emerging subprime debacle back in 2007.

Under "A Record of Accomplishment," Clinton's Web site at the time had touted as one of his crowning achievements his "increased enforcement of the Community Reinvestment Act in order to pursue fair lending procedures through the elimination of racial discrimination in mortgage and other lending by banks."

Another page that no longer exists describes Clinton's heroic efforts on behalf of black borrowers. During his administration it said, "banks and thrifts subject to CRA made a staggering $800 billion in home mortgage, small business, and community development loans to low- and moderate-income borrowers and communities." As a result, Clinton's foundation added, "the number of home mortgage loans to African-Americans increased by 58 percent."

The Clinton Foundation also boasted that he was the first president to make banks really pay under the CRA law: "Though this law has been on the books since the 1970s, over 90 percent of all loans under the Community Reinvestment Act came during the 8 years of the Clinton-Gore Administration." The superlative failed to mention that Clinton's reforms to the CRA included requiring banks to use "flexible underwriting standards" in approving applicants in "underserved communities." It also failed to mention that his policies corrupted prudent banking practices. Or that they undermined mortgage discipline throughout the industry. Or created an unparalleled moral hazard.

This untold Clinton scandal stayed hidden until the bubble burst. Now the former president is conveniently a critic of the very loans he promoted. He was for them, before he was against them.

Guilty or not, the first *real* black president is picking up where Clinton left off, implementing his own easy credit policies that risk reinflating the housing bubble in the future, as we shall see in a forthcoming chapter.

## CUOMO'S QUOTAS

Clinton's HUD secretary, Andrew Cuomo, should have joined him in the hot seat—if the Angelides Commission had ever put either of them under oath. But it did not. And he, too, managed to escape any tough questioning.

Like Clinton, Cuomo championed the flawed notion that racism was the reason for far fewer black families owning homes than white families. "Discrimination in mortgage lending continues to be a barrier to homeownership," he grumbled in a late 2000 HUD report, citing the same discredited Boston Fed study that Clinton embraced. Despite gains in black homeownership throughout the 1990s, he thought the mortgage gap remained too wide and was obsessed with closing it.

HUD supervises Fannie's and Freddie's achievement of Affordable Housing Goals and compliance with fair housing laws. Displeased with progress on this social front, Cuomo in 2000 intensified HUD's efforts to enforce "affirmative action" lending, as he called it. More simply had to be done. Key, he thought, was enlisting Fannie and Freddie in the crusade. If he could get them to buy more CRA and subprime loans from banks, take them off their books, it would "free up capital" for banks to originate more of these kinds of loans suitable for minorities with poor credit.

"The HUD guidance at the time mentioned looking into the subprime market as a place for potential [minority] targeting to find the housing goals," confirms Alfred Pollard, general counsel for the Federal Housing Finance Agency, now the conservator of Fannie and Freddie. HUD told them, "You may have to look at—to get to these higher levels—subprime, new types of products, whatever it is to try and reach the [minority] community."

Cuomo, with Clinton's blessing, ramped up the Affordable Housing Goals Fannie and Freddie had to meet, explaining in a prepared HUD statement that "it will help reduce the huge homeownership gap dividing whites from minorities and suburbs from cities."

"These new regulations will greatly enhance access to affordable housing for minorities," Cuomo added after setting the unprecedented targets, which remained in force through 2007 when the subprime bubble burst.

Forced to go into a market they normally would have avoided—all to serve the politically targeted populations that HUD wanted them to serve—Fannie and Freddie dutifully waded even deeper into the dangerous subprime game. It was either that or face stiff fines and other penalties administered by HUD, as well as tougher oversight by Congress.

"With the housing goals—these ambitious goals—announced," Pollard adds, "it is clear that the enterprises did increase their purchases in the subprime market."

They also loaded up on securities backed by subprime mortgages, which also count toward HUD's social lending goals, thanks to Clinton's earlier approval.

Fannie and Freddie "began buying subprime securities heavily in 2002," notes former senior HUD official John Weicher. "Their subprime securities doubled between 2002 and 2003, and doubled again in 2004"—from $38 billion to $81 billion to $176 billion, according to the Office of Federal Housing Enterprise Oversight, or OFHEO, Fannie's and Freddie's other (less political) regulator at the time. (See the chart in the appendix.)

By 2004, their market presence was unmistakable. With $176 billion in subprime securities, they together commanded 44 percent of the total market, OFHEO data show. Over the next two years, they purchased another $279 billion in the risky investments—creating a feeding frenzy on Wall Street, which underwrote and traded them with abandon because of the implicit government guarantee they carried. Investors assumed they were backed by Uncle Sam and therefore safe.

As a result, the annual subprime securitization rate—the

percentage of all the originated subprime loans that were securitized—exploded from under 50 percent in 2001 to almost 100 percent by 2007, according to the Securities Industry and Financial Markets Association. It was the first time securitization was applied to an entirely new loan class: risky subprime loans.

And it was a recipe for disaster.

The securitization process allowed subprime-lending risks to be passed from mortgage brokers to lenders, then to securitizers, and finally to market makers on Wall Street, where they ended up as ticking time bombs in major investment fund portfolios across the globe.

## RISING DEFAULT RATES

By 2004, when HUD next revised its goals, Fannie's and Freddie's acquisitions of subprime securities had risen tenfold. Foreclosure rates also were climbing higher. "If you look at first-year defaults, they were low in loans originated in 2002," Weicher said. "They were a little bit higher in loans originated in 2003. They were a little higher than that in loans originated in 2004."

In its own 2004 report, HUD credited the burst in subprime investment "to higher Affordable Housing Goals set by HUD in 2000."

And it all proved poisonous. In 2000, before Cuomo's record goal hike went into effect, Fannie and Freddie held few securities backed by subprime and other nonprime loans from private originators. The year before the mortgage giants collapsed in 2008, those securities made up almost a quarter of their portfolios.

Plunging Fannie and Freddie into the risky subprime market to subsidize housing for those who could not afford it "will rank for

U.S. taxpayers as one of the worst policy disasters in our history," says Wallison, who was one of the first to sound alarms about the two mortgage giants as early as 1999.

By stampeding Fannie and Freddie into the subprime market with an eye toward their domination of it, Cuomo engineered their demise. Yet he has managed to walk away from the disaster unscathed. He was never called to account by the Angelides Commission, never forced to testify under the klieg lights like the bankers he sued as attorney general of New York. The commission, instead, has pooh-poohed HUD's role in the subprime scandal. "That the [HUD] housing goals are consistent with high-risk mortgage activity does not imply that the housing goals caused [Fannie's and Freddie's] high-risk activity," maintains Angelides's hand-picked economist Dwight Jaffee in a 25-page study for the commission. "The housing goals," the Berkeley University professor continued, "were a distinctly secondary priority for [Fannie and Freddie] management compared to profits as a factor motivating their investments in high-risk mortgages."

Really? That is not what Fannie and Freddie executives say. They say HUD pushed them into the risky subprime market to help uncreditworthy minorities. The higher goals "forced us to go into that market to serve the targeted populations that HUD wanted us to serve," said Freddie Mac spokeswoman Sharon McHale.

As the subprime market crashed, Fannie Mae complained in internal communications that the loans HUD pushed it to make were expensive to underwrite and ultimately unprofitable. "We had to absorb significant costs to meet the HUD goals in 2006," then Fannie president and chief executive Daniel Mudd said in a 2007 internal report marked "confidential."

The Fannie official who worked directly under Mudd confirms

that the higher HUD Affordable Housing Goals forced the firm to increase its appetite for risky loans and relax its underwriting rules. "Because the goals were set at higher levels, we had to make underwriting adjustments," says Robert Levin, former Fannie executive vice president and chief business officer, who adds that subprime securities contributed "significantly to the achievement of the housing goals."

The biggest "predatory lender" in the subprime scandal appears to be HUD, by way of its two charges, yet nobody is investigating the agency for financial abuses, least of all Angelides. "The key role played by HUD in this debacle cannot be ignored," former Fannie credit officer Pinto says. Yet ignored it is.

In 1998, Cuomo actually boasted of forcing banks to make risky mortgages to unqualified minority applicants previously rejected due to bad credit. Cuomo viewed such loan denials as racism, regardless of the failure to meet standard underwriting criteria. And he was determined to remedy "discrimination that's hidden behind a smiling face."

"I'm sure there'll be a higher default rate on those mortgages," he said before the C-SPAN cameras covering his announcement of a record $2.1 billion settlement deal with an allegedly racist mortgage lender that garnered little more attention at the time.

But no matter. To him, like his boss in the White House, the only lending criterion that mattered was race; and the darker the loan applicant's skin, the less he felt the rules should apply. This was, after all, about "social justice."

As New York attorney general, Cuomo has prosecuted Bank of America and other banks for allegedly misleading shareholders about the size of losses they incurred in connection with the risky loans he strong-armed them into making. He is now governor-elect of New York and reportedly has ambitions to one day run for president of the United States.

Cuomo's successor, HUD Secretary Mel Martinez, is a coconspirator in the subprime crime, though his fingerprints are not found at the original crime scene. He agreed to nudge Cuomo's record-high Affordable Housing Goals even higher, while refocusing Fannie's and Freddie's minority lending efforts on Hispanic immigrants with unproven credit.

Martinez, a Cuban immigrant, had the blessing of President Bush, who also had a soft spot for first-time Hispanic homebuyers and continued some of Clinton's housing policies in the name of "compassionate conservatism."

"We can't hide from that fact," says Wallison, a Republican.

And this book does not hide from it. In a departure from the commendable, *Architects of Ruin*, a 200-page title on the causes of the global recession by former Bush speechwriter Peter Schweizer, *Great American Bank Robbery* will in forthcoming chapters take Martinez and Bush to task for their roles, secondary as they were, in the subprime scandal.

## RENO'S "WITCH HUNT"

Another prime suspect the Angelides Commission failed to call to testify is Janet Reno. She, too, was spared grilling. But if anybody else deserves to sweat under the klieg lights, it is her.

Clinton's attorney general brought groundless charges of racism against dozens of banks, citing the CRA and other "fair lending" laws. The "witch hunt" she launched against the banking industry has begun anew under her deputy, who now sits in her old chair at the U.S. Department of Justice.

Legal experts say Reno abused her department's "vast enforcement powers" as part of an agenda to carry out socioeconomic reform, not to remedy discrimination. Documents I have obtained reveal the real objective was not racial justice but "economic justice," which is code for "economic equality" (as opposed to opportunity), which is simply socialism by another name.

The first woman attorney general redefined existing discrimination law, setting a dubious standard that is applied today by the department's Civil Rights Division. Previously, the Justice Department did not find lenders guilty of redlining if they denied loans because of "legitimate financial concerns" that were separate from the racial composition of a loan applicant's neighborhood. But under Reno, bankers suddenly were guilty of discrimination even if they did not intentionally exclude certain neighborhoods in their service area, and even if no overt redlining could be proved. If CRA regulators or activists lodged a complaint that a particular bank rejected black loan applicants at a higher rate than white applicants, Reno considered such racial disparities prima facie proof of civil-rights violations—period, end of story. "It is a stretch to label as discriminatory policies which on their face are clearly racially neutral and supported by business necessity," complained former FDIC official Vern McKinley at the time.

It no longer mattered if banks had lending policies and computerized underwriting programs that were race-neutral and fairly and equally applied to all customers. If the outcomes were different—if a lender did not proportionately allocate loans among neighborhoods based on their racial composition—the policy was deemed discriminatory. Reno and her diversity cops termed it "disparate impact." And to equalize outcomes, they demanded "race-conscious affirmative action" in lending—or else.

Those bankers who balked at federal lawyers running their businesses were prosecuted, fined, and branded as racists in the press.

It was not enough that the federal government micromanaged the lending process by setting underwriting rules and de facto quotas for politically desirable outcomes. Reno also dictated advertising, marketing, hiring, and branch location. She cornered banks into making loans even in high-crime areas where no bank owner in his right mind would invest.

Reno's "witch hunt," as it was known within the banking industry and even among many regulators, included press conferences to make public examples of "racist" banks—and it sent a panic throughout the industry. Before long she was herding banks into inner cities, where they dutifully opened new branches and installed new ATMs, hired black loan officers, and advertised in black-owned media to better serve these "underserved communities," a term of art for blighted neighborhoods.

Her legacy is a rash of misplaced branches and unprofitable investments that are still acting as a drag on bank financial statements.

"The lack of profitability at many . . . branches that banks have felt a need to open and the need to subsidize [minority] mortgages have reinforced and perpetuated the impression that serving the [urban] community can never be profitable for banks," laments JP Morgan Chase's Mark Willis.

Reno also herded banks onto American Indian reservations, where they historically had been reluctant to lend because the collateral often was on tribal land, which subjected them to tribal laws and tribal court jurisdiction. They also had to hassle with the United States Bureau of Indian Affairs to gain clear title to properties on trust lands.

Bankers had reasonable reservations about lending on the reservation. But Reno would hear none of it. She warned that rejecting Indian loan applicants was discrimination, even if they could not provide off-reservation collateral or meet traditional credit terms. Even those who made such loans were accused of racism if they charged more in fees and financing to cover the added costs and risks associated with them.

Reno targeted for prosecution a few small banks operating adjacent to reservations who dared to defy her. She fined them and ordered them to revise their definition of a CRA-delineated community to include parts of reservations.

Soon, lending on reservations exploded into the hundreds of millions of dollars, with Native Americans taking out a disproportionate share of subprime loans. Many of them were bought on the secondary market by Fannie and Freddie, as HUD in 2000 revised its definition of "underserved areas" to include more Indian land.

Banks were so cowed by Reno's edicts that they began rubber-stamping just about any applicant who claimed Native American ancestry. Word spread that it was easier to qualify for a home loan if you could claim you were at least 1 percent American Indian. The easy credit bonanza spread to applicants not even living on reservations.

But there was just one problem: the lion's share of these new borrowers failed to repay their mortgages on time, and eventually, at all. Underwriters hardly were surprised. Native Americans typically default on about 6 percent of their loans—second only to African-Americans. But the nation's top cop and her diversity police ordered banks to make the risky loans anyway—effectively at the barrel of a gun.

## BENDING LENDING RULES

Reno's aggressive anti-redlining suits and related settlements had lasting repercussions on the banking industry, including degraded lending standards and greater exposure to unsafe loans.

After Reno made examples of supposedly "racist" banks in a frenzy of prosecutions—including the very public persecution of Chevy Chase Federal Savings Bank of the Washington suburbs, which was splashed across the pages of the *Washington Post*—the banking industry's chief lobbyist, the American Bankers Association, retained a prominent Washington law firm to warn members about the Justice Department's "aggressive" enforcement.

The ABA then put together a "fair-lending toolbox" for all its members—representing more than 95 percent of the industry—that contained suggestions for "flexible" inner-city underwriting practices to help protect them from Reno and her diversity cops. Designed to inoculate bankers from antidiscrimination prosecution, this "toolbox" included new underwriting guidelines recommended by the Boston Fed economist who joined Clinton's economic team. Her staff's widely distributed guidebook, *Closing the Gap: A Guide to Equal Opportunity Lending*, strongly suggested bankers and mortgage lenders dump traditional underwriting standards that fail to qualify "minority customers," and to take "special care" to ensure lending "standards are appropriate to the economic culture of urban, lower-income, and nontraditional consumers."

The new guidelines were officially endorsed and promulgated by Greenspan, who went along with Clinton's multicultural schemes. The central banker deserves blame for the subprime crisis chiefly for giving his stamp of approval to race-based lending and the trashing of time-tested underwriting principles, not for, as conventional wisdom would have it, lowering interest rates on overnight bank loans (which were not tied to long-term mortgage rates).

The underwriting guidebook also cautioned lenders that a "lack of credit history should not be seen as a negative factor" when approving minority applicants. It further advised loan underwriters to consider as "valid income sources" child support payments, unemployment benefits, welfare checks, even food stamps. The message to lenders was clear: Think "flexibly." Bend the rules. Do whatever it takes to put more minorities into home loans.

By the end of the decade, the entire mortgage industry had adopted the government-mandated "flexible" underwriting standards for all its customers—no income, no job, no assets, no problem. "Flexibility" became the industry norm going into the next decade. Recall that the same term was codified in Clinton's historic changes to the CRA regulations. His revised regulations, which had the force of law, effectively homogenized industry underwriting standards.

Today's wave of mortgage defaults is "a direct result of an intentional loosening of underwriting standards done in the name of ending discrimination, despite warnings that it could lead to widescale defaults," says University of Texas economist Stanley Liebowitz.

The really tragic thing in all this is that there never really was any structural lending racism to correct, as I document in a forthcoming chapter. The reforms were predicated on a false assumption that minorities automatically get bum deals from predominantly white bankers. In fact, federal data reveal that Asians get the best deals on loans—even better than whites. Why? Because they generally have the best credit among all racial groups, including whites. Blacks generally are offered higher priced loans or are denied them outright simply because they tend to have the worst credit—even at the highest income levels. The Clinton administration essentially restructured standards and practices of the entire mortgage industry to stamp out an imaginary problem.

Yet the Justice Department is at it again. Under the nation's first black attorney general, it is warning lenders, "It is illegal to discriminate in any credit transaction . . . because income [reported by a minority loan applicant] is from public assistance"—whether that assistance comes in the form of unemployment benefits, welfare checks, or even food stamps.

Reno's "witch hunt" against allegedly discriminatory lenders threw such a scare into the mortgage industry that even unregulated mortgage companies—most notably, Countrywide Financial, the nation's largest subprime lender—signed formal agreements with HUD to use "flexible underwriting standards" to aggressively serve "minority and urban communities."

Even the Mortgage Bankers Association, the top lobbyist for mortgage lenders, signed a fair-lending "master agreement" with HUD, which had threatened to expand regulations to cover mortgage lenders. The "voluntary compliance" was an unprecedented development in the industry, and one that carried over into the next decade.

As a result, independent mortgage companies not regulated by the CRA took "the lead in focusing on lending activity in the riskier segments of the mortgage market," according to a report by the Federal Reserve Bank of Dallas.

So? What's past is past, right? Hardly. Both Cuomo's and Reno's deputies are working in Obama's Cabinet. The accomplices have returned to the scene of the crime. And they are planning another heist.

# TWO

# RETURNING TO THE SCENE OF THE CRIME

"We will require lenders to invest in the community that they've harmed."

— Thomas E. Perez, chief of the Civil Rights Division of the U.S. Department of Justice

One radical retread from the Clinton years who landed a key housing-policy position in the Obama administration is former top Cuomo aide William Apgar—the very architect of HUD's drastic affordable housing targets that plunged Fannie and Freddie into the dangerous subprime market from 2001 to 2004 and beyond. He is now senior adviser to Obama's HUD secretary for mortgage finance, after sitting out the Bush years at Harvard University.

In his previous role at the Clinton HUD, Apgar was as obsessed as his boss with eradicating what he saw as "insidious" banking and housing discrimination. He accused Fannie and Freddie of discrimination in lending, particularly when it came to black applicants, who are more likely to be rejected for loans (but also more likely to default on them than any other minority group).

"We believe that there are a lot of loans to black Americans that could be safely purchased by Fannie Mae and Freddie Mac if these companies were more flexible [in their lending standards]," Apgar told the *Washington Post* in 2000.

More worrisome, HUD has attracted other repeat offenders taking up the banner of "affordable housing."

John Trasviña, another former Clinton appointee, worked under Reno as the highest-ranking Latino official at the Justice Department. He returns to the federal government as assistant secretary of fair housing at Obama's HUD, picking up where Clinton appointee Roberta Achtenberg, a radical housing-rights activist, left off at the agency.

Trasviña's passion for ending what he calls "the scourge" of lending discrimination is as boundless as Achtenberg's was when she was cracking down on banks. In 2009, in his first year on the job, Trasviña squeezed banks for more than $2 million in compensation or assistance to victims of alleged racism, while ordering underwriting "policy changes that opened lending opportunities to thousands" more minority borrowers. He has also ordered a review of underwriting guidelines at Fannie and Freddie, which his office directly regulates, to determine if they have become too conservative in verifying the income of underserved loan applicants.

Like Achtenberg, Trasviña came to Washington from San

Francisco, where he headed two far left groups: the Discrimination Research Center and, most recently, the Mexican American Legal Defense and Education Fund, or MALDEF, whose Mexican co-founder is on record making racist statements against whites and Europeans.

## RENO'S LEGACY LIVES ON

Then there is Eric Holder, who as Clinton's deputy attorney general helped Reno carry out her crusade against allegedly racist banks. He was her top henchman in the landmark case against Chevy Chase Federal Savings Bank in Washington. Holder accused its management of racism and announced a federal order to force it to "hire more African-Americans," open more branches in black neighborhoods, and make at least 1,000 cheap loans to blacks—even though Chevy Chase showed no intent to discriminate against them.

Now acting as the nation's first African-American attorney general, Holder has promised Obama he will "reinvigorate" civil-rights enforcement at the department, making prosecution of "racist" lenders a top priority.

Calling enforcement of housing discrimination laws "the unfinished business of the civil rights movement," Obama has unleashed Holder to rekindle the 1990s fair-housing crusade against banks. The president is convinced racism is behind the "stubborn gap" between black and white homeownership, and has vowed to close it. "Even middle-class blacks are less likely to own their own homes," he complains. He has warned that if "the white person is consistently preferred" over the black person in home loan processing, "then the government, through its prosecutors and through its courts, should step in and make things right."

Holder has pledged, in return, to enhance the enforcement of fair housing, going after lenders wherever statistics show that minorities fare disproportionately worse in the lending-approval process. To that end, the attorney general has beefed up the budget and staff of the department's powerful Civil Rights Division, adding millions of dollars more in funding along with more than 100 additional prosecutors and staff, mainly African-American attorneys. He has quadrupled the number of mortgage fraud cases to more than 2,800 from five years ago, and has taken some 50 FBI agents off the terror-fighting beat and other duties to help investigate "predatory lenders."

His newly muscular division is led by Thomas E. Perez, another former high-ranking Clinton official and Reno protégé.

In the 1990s, Perez served as a federal prosecutor in the division, before Reno promoted him to deputy division chief. In his larger role today, he has pledged to ramp up federal prosecution of alleged lending discrimination to rival activity during the Clinton administration—which brought 676 cases through the division's housing section, compared with 324 cases during the two terms of President Bush. And judging from the first round of cases, he is applying the same standard of proof as Reno. Like his mentor, he views "disparate impact" as prima facie evidence of discrimination even in cases where there is no intent to discriminate but merely a difference in loan application outcomes. "Perez is going to depend on disparate impact theory, where the intent does not have to be proven," says Andrew Sandler, a Washington lawyer specializing in fair-lending compliance.

## REPARATIONS BY ANOTHER NAME

Take the 2009 case against First United Security Bank, a small Southern institution with branches around Birmingham, Alabama.

Even though the Civil Rights Division presented no factual finding of lending bias, it ordered the tiny bank to, among other things, set aside an initial half million dollars for a "special financing program" for African-Americans with bad credit, unverified income, no down payment, and who were otherwise unqualified for financing. The program must offer them terms more attractive than those offered to even the bank's best customers, according to the 25-page federal decree.

The $500,000 fund is separate from the settlement fund set up to compensate individual victims of alleged racist lending. It is designed, rather, as reparations for the local black community, and it is just a down payment. The division also required First United to meet each year with "community organizations and fair housing groups" to assess the ongoing "credit needs" of such borrowers—even though bank management, on its own initiative, had expanded its CRA assessment area the previous year to include more African-American census tracts. More shocking, Perez is steering settlement funds to such advocacy groups, even though they are neither victims of alleged discrimination nor parties to the cases filed.

In a March 2010 consent order, two AIG subsidiaries—AIG Federal Savings Bank of Delaware and Wilmington Finance Inc. of Pennsylvania—agreed, among other things, to pay $1 million to "qualified organizations" that help "African-American borrowers." The unusual deal is part of the $6.1 million fine slapped on the banks—the biggest fair-lending punishment in Justice Department history—for allegedly discriminating against blacks by charging them more for home loans, even though both banks denied any wrongdoing and prosecutors presented no factual finding of discriminatory behavior. The money will go to activist groups *approved by Perez's office* that have no direct connection to the case and its claims of discrimination. Favored groups include community organizers as militant as ACORN. More on them later.

In effect, the federal government is ordering banks to support nonprofit groups that exist to pressure banks into making unprofitable loans. Industry analysts argue such action chills the business climate and will only end up hurting the very people the administration is trying to help.

Perez brushes aside such concerns. "We are doing business in new, different, and better ways," he asserts. That includes holding the financial industry accountable for "past" discrimination, he says, and finding "ways to repair some of the damage done to communities."

His job, he says, is to "transform the division" into a catalyst for economic, not just racial, justice. "That is the charge I have received from the president and Attorney General Holder, who describes himself as an impatient attorney general." He adds that the Obama administration has made fair lending "a top priority" and has created "the necessary infrastructure to support and expand our fair lending work," while committing "the resources necessary to ensure economic fairness for all Americans."

## BANKERS AS KLANSMEN

Indeed, thanks to one of the largest budget increases in the division's history, Perez is adding 102 new prosecutors and assistants to a force that already boasts 715. The nearly 15 percent boost in staffing includes the creation of a brand-new position—"Special Counsel for Fair Lending"—which will oversee a newly created fair-lending enforcement unit with its own dedicated staff of attorneys, economists, and investigators. Department insiders say minorities are being heavily recruited to fill the new slots. The unit "will address discrimination in all areas of lending," not just home loans, Perez says—including small business loans, unsecured consumer loans, auto loans, and credit cards.

And it is already flexing its muscle. As of the summer of 2010, the new fair-lending squad was working on 50 referrals and 18 active investigations. Expect more cases to follow: Perez is building a "pipeline" to speed the flow of referrals to his unit from the Department of Treasury and other federal agencies enforcing bank compliance with the Community Reinvestment Act.

He also is working in "close collaboration" with Apgar and Trasviña at HUD, which is actively soliciting lending-bias complaints from community organizers, who make it their business to find victims. In fact, the agency is even paying these groups to go into banks posing as minority borrowers, whereupon they "test" loan officers to see if they treat minorities differently. Additional complaints will be funneled through the newly formed Consumer Financial Protection Bureau, a creation of the financial reform law.

The goateed Perez is a longtime social activist who believes—like his late boss, senator Ted Kennedy, and his new boss, Obama—that civil rights "remain the unfinished business of America." The 1960s struggle, he maintains, was not just about eliminating segregation but achieving "economic justice" for African-Americans and other minorities—and that requires "real, systemic social and institutional change."

Perez, 48, sees the financial sector as the last refuge of hoary white racists, and the last major battleground in the civil-rights war.

In a January 2010 speech to Rainbow-PUSH Coalition's annual Wall Street conference, he compared bankers to Klansmen—only, bankers discriminate "with a smile" and "fine print." Though more subtle, this kind of racism, he says, is "every bit as destructive as the cross burned in a neighborhood."

In cracking down on bankers, he intends to use his power "holistically"—not just to compensate individual victims of discrimination, but to "reverse the damage" done to their whole communities. "When we bring a lawsuit against a lender whose conduct has caused harm to a community—whether it is a single neighborhood or a dozen cities," he says, "we must decide, how do we make people and communities whole?"

This is where Perez plans to get "creative." He intends to use all the fair-lending tools in his "law enforcement arsenal" to leverage private-sector resources. "We will require lenders to invest in the community that they've harmed," he vows.

## OLD CLINTON GANG

Legal analysts say his interpretation of the division's mission is even more radical than Reno's. For the first time, the powerful Civil Rights Division will judge violators for the *secondary impact* their actions have on minority neighborhoods. And his prosecutors will order reparations—"to repair the damage"—accordingly.

When Perez talks about "transforming" the division, he essentially means turning it into a government-funded version of the NAACP or MALDEF, the Latino legal defense fund. In fact, Obama originally appointed MALDEF's top lawyer to head the division but had to withdraw his first choice after I exposed his radical past in *Investor's Business Daily*. (The *New York Times* scolded *IBD* for making Obama flinch. "In a little-noticed act of political faintheartedness, the Obama administration has pulled back from nominating Thomas Saenz," the *Times* bellyached in a March 2009 editorial, after "*Investor's Business Daily* slimed Mr. Saenz by calling him 'an open-borders extremist.")

Normally banks protect themselves from risk. Now they are scrambling to protect themselves from a race-obsessed Justice Department hell-bent on prosecuting them for protecting themselves, as any business would, from undue risk. Many already have created internal programs to monitor their fair-lending activity to ensure it meets the new Obama standards, which ultimately means lowering their own standards and taking on more risk.

Meanwhile, over at the White House, we find yet another recidivist from the Clinton operation.

Formerly a top Clinton White House aide, Rahm Emanuel ran the White House as Obama's chief of staff for the first two years, shepherding through financial reform and other regulations. Like his boss, Emanuel got his start in Chicago as a community organizer working for an anti-redlining group founded by Marxist radical Saul Alinksy, a subject we shall return to shortly.

In his final year in office, Clinton named Emanuel to the board of Freddie Mac, along with Harold Ickes and Dwight Robinson, other high-level Clinton officials, where they encouraged the mortgage giant to continue loosening lending standards and buying risky subprime loans. Meanwhile, Clinton stacked the board of Fannie Mae with trusted former advisers—including Jack Quinn, Eli Segal, Jamie Gorelick, and Raines (now an informal housing adviser to Obama)—ensuring that the affordable-housing fix was in at that government-sponsored mortgage giant, as well. (Because of their federal charters, the boards of Fannie and Freddie were hybrids of directors appointed by the president and those elected by shareholders.)

After his tenure at Freddie, where he pocketed $320,000, Emanuel made millions more working for an investment banker in Chicago that brokered high-cost subprime loans to minorities.

The old Clinton gang is back to do more damage to the economy and your wallet. Obama has rehired the same hold-up men—only he is planning an even bigger heist than Clinton.

# THREE

# OBAMA'S FINGERPRINTS

With a former organizer in the White House and a national climate favorable to advancing progressive policy changes, it is truly a moment that calls for . . . advancing a national racial and economic justice platform on housing and banking issues . . . Now is an opportune time to press for greater public control of financial institutions.

— National People's Action, a radical Chicago housing-rights group tied to President Obama

Obama's own fingerprints are on the subprime scandal. His role dates back to his days as a community organizer in South

Side Chicago. His mentor there, 1960s civil-rights activist John McKnight, distrusted banks, convinced as he was that they intentionally discriminate against black borrowers. The fair housing zealot coined the term "redlining," laying the intellectual groundwork for passage of the Community Reinvestment Act. In fact, he is known as the father of the CRA and the anti-redlining movement that paved the way for its enactment into law in 1977.

A follower of socialist street agitator Saul Alinsky, McKnight was also one of the pioneers of community organizing in Chicago. Like Alinsky, McKnight presupposes that the problems afflicting the ghetto come from outside the ghetto—namely, an oppressive white power structure that "has erected the most elaborate system of race and class segregation the nation, and perhaps the world, has ever seen." Like many in the Obama administration, he believes housing is a right, and that banks should function like public utilities, serving the community instead of shareholders.

McKnight later became a professor at Northwestern University, where he penned Obama's letter of recommendation to Harvard Law School. He had been working closely with Obama as an Alinsky organizer at the time. He was his adviser. In fact, he placed him in his first organizing job after Obama graduated from Columbia University.

He recalls interviewing Obama along with a group of twenty or so young leftists who had applied for organizing jobs "to change the world." "The last person there to introduce himself was a tall, skinny guy with big ears and a funny name—Barack Obama," McKnight remembers. "So Barack was one of our first people trained in neighborhood organizing, and they were organized in 1983 and 1984.

"Toward the end of those two years," the white-goateed McKnight continued, in his strange, lilting cadence, "he came to me and said, 'You know, I want to go into public life. I think I can see what can be done at the neighborhood level, but it's not enough change for me. I want to see what would happen in public life, [but] I think I have to go to law school to do that.'"

So Obama asked McKnight for a reference, remarking that he was the only professor he knew who would write him a letter. "I think he didn't do too well in college," McKnight says. "So I wrote him a letter." And the rest is history.

McKnight is now director and treasurer of a community organizing group—the National People's Action—that has received less press attention than ACORN but is arguably more powerful now with Obama in the Oval Office.

NPA has a nasty reputation as a street fighter. While Clinton and his regulators attacked bankers in their boardrooms, Chicago-based NPA dispatched busloads of goons to their doorsteps, where they trashed their yards and frightened their children. "Housing is our right," they shouted, "and we gonna take it!" The reign of terror lasted over a decade, and is picking back up again, as bankers are demonized anew—this time for doing too well what they were extorted into doing then.

And while ACORN is folding its national operations due to financial and legal woes, the battle-hardened NPA is revving up its attack machine and picking up ACORN's slack. "With a former organizer in the White House and a national climate favorable to advancing progressive policy changes, it is truly a moment that calls for a new level of vision, strategy, and collaboration amongst organizing and advocacy groups," NPA told members in a 2009 platform statement.

"The NPA network will take the lead on advancing a national racial- and economic-justice platform on housing and banking issues," it continues. "Now is an opportune time to press for greater public control of financial institutions."

Opportune, indeed, as NPA enjoys West Wing access to press its case. Obama invited NPA chairman Eugene Barnes to attend the Washington ceremony at which the president signed the financial reform bill his group had a hand in shaping. "The work we're doing has not been in vain," Barnes told the local black press upon returning to Chicago.

The following month, Barnes got a seat at the administration's hearings in Chicago to discuss expanding CRA's reach. At least five other NPA officials joined him. (Notorious ACORN affiliate SEIU, or Service Employees International Union, was also in attendance.)

## "THE TARGET SHOULD BE THE BANKS"

Alinsky identified banks as one of the "power sectors" topping the industrial food chain, and therefore a top "target" for street agitators—which explains why his most famous acolyte, Obama, is at "constant war" with banks, as Wells Fargo recently complained.

"The target, therefore, should be the banks," Alinsky wrote in *Rules for Radicals*, the Bible of the Left. This was drilled into Obama by his Alinsky trainer, Jerry Kellman, McKnight's partner and the person who actually hired Obama. "The real enemy," Kellman told Obama, are "the investment bankers."

"Don't fight [reforms]," Obama recently told his targets on Wall Street. "Join us on them. In the long run it will be good for [you]."

Wall Street, of course, is not buying it. The Financial Services Roundtable, an industry group representing large Wall Street institutions, argues that the president's banking reforms threaten to "take the industry and the economy back to the 1930s."

Obama was trained in Alinsky agitation tactics, running off for weeks at a time during breaks at Harvard to attend Alinsky workshops in Los Angeles and Chicago. After Harvard, he returned to South Side Chicago to train ACORN's and NPA's leaders in those tactics. They, in turn, deployed busloads of thugs to terrorize allegedly racist bankers into making easy loans and subsidies in a multibillion-dollar shakedown that sped the collapse of the banking and housing industries. In the 1990s, Obama also represented alleged victims of racist lending rounded up by ACORN and NPA in class-action lawsuits against Citibank and other financial institutions.

The people connected with the same man who penned the *Rules for Radicals* wrote the rules for "fair lending" and are helping to write them again to make credit for the uncreditworthy even easier.

Obama said that while the ugly history of the subprime crisis cannot be changed, "we have an absolute responsibility to learn from it, and take steps to prevent a repeat of the crisis from which we are still recovering."

So far the steps he is taking would only repeat a crisis. Consider the following:

- Hidden inside the mammoth new financial reform law is a scheme to socialize small business loans for minorities, setting the stage for another lending disaster.
- The new law also sets up the first ever Federal Insurance Office to monitor, under threat of subpoena, insurance underwriters to make sure they are offering minorities "affordable" premiums, potentially subjecting the insurance industry to the same race-based standards that sank the banking industry.

- The new regulatory regime does not "discourage risky lending" with tough new mortgage standards, as the media have reported; in fact, it does nothing to establish minimum underwriting guidelines, failing to specify credit scores or down payments.
- Far from mitigating risk through tighter lending criteria, the Dodd-Frank Act demands the "underserved" continue to have access to "affordable mortgage credit," even waiving the income verification requirement for applicants refinancing federal loans.
- The Obama administration is pressuring loan officers to consider as valid sources of income unemployment benefits, welfare checks, or food stamps—repeating the cycle of lower underwriting standards that led to the housing crisis.
- In addition to home loans for minorities, CRA lobbyists are urging the administration to shake down banks for vendor contracts, retirement funds, stock holdings, and jobs for minorities—making inner-city "wealth-building" the next CRA frontier.
- Their ultimate goal is to bring all of corporate America, not just banks, under the purview of the CRA. In fact . . .
- CRA activists are also lobbying the administration to subject any industry benefiting "in any way" from federal policies to racial litmus tests, including measures on hiring, contracting, and even corporate philanthropy.
- The administration, meanwhile, is laying the groundwork for overhauling the bedrock standard of

the banking industry—the FICO credit scoring system used to determine financial risk—to make it more minority friendly.

- Among other changes, it seeks to "enhance the credit score" of immigrant borrowers—including those living in the United States illegally—by counting their remittance payments to Mexico.
- Meanwhile, the activist Obama Justice Department is ordering lenders to scrub clean the bad credit histories of minorities who have defaulted on subprime loans.

## SON OF CRA

Over at the Department of Treasury, a coven of new regulators—overseen by Obama's regulations czar Cass Sunstein, who wants government to guarantee a "Second Bill of Rights," including a universal right to a "decent home"—are brewing up a major expansion of the CRA to cover, for starters, all lenders, including credit unions and independent mortgage companies and their brokers.

"The appropriate response to the crisis is not to weaken the CRA," argues Treasury in its proposal for bank regulatory reform. "It is rather to promote robust application of the CRA," so that banks continue to meet the credit needs of underserved communities. Never mind that the CRA, as Chicago economist Brian Wesbury points out, echoing other economists, "helped create the subprime mortgage mess in the first place."

That is not enough for ACORN clones. They demand wholesale changes, including the addition of a specific discrimination litmus test that banks would have to pass. They are also lobbying to add insurance companies and securities firms under CRA's umbrella and are even eyeballing your 401(k)s—the ultimate target of redistributionists—to serve "broader community needs," such as urban renewal. They want CRA regulators to apply a separate "community development" test to pressure banks to "invest" in "community health clinics" and "green affordable housing construction," among other pet projects of the Left.

Treasury thinks the banking industry should help pay for the broader, more "vigorous" CRA enforcement it has in store for it, and has proposed a special tax on banks and mortgage lenders to defray costs.

Like Clinton, Obama plans to revise the CRA through executive order. He already has ordered a "comprehensive review" of the CRA regulation—the first since 1995. The four federal agencies dealing with the CRA have begun gathering input from banks and community activists and are already proposing rules changes, including pushing banks to fund "neighborhood stabilization" projects launched by inner-city organizers.

If Clinton added teeth to banking regulations, Obama is adding fangs and claws.

"The idea of imposing new regulations on the entire financial system—and thus slowing or stopping economic growth—is appalling," Wallison, the crisis inquiry panelist, told me in an exclusive interview. "It's particularly galling that the people who are using the crisis to extend regulation are the same ones who sponsored the government policies that created the crisis."

A rearmed CRA is not the only thing bankers have to fear. CRA regulators will be assisted in their fair lending mission by the White House's baby: the Consumer Financial Protection Bureau, a huge new federal bureaucracy that will, among other things, police lenders' underwriting for "traditionally underserved consumers," and punish companies who do not do enough of it.

The consumer watchdog agency will wield a big stick in the form of an Office of Fair Lending and Equal Opportunity, whose role will be enforcing "nondiscriminatory access to credit." It will be staffed with bank examiners, attorneys, compliance specialists, economists, and statisticians, who will "target areas of greatest risk for discrimination"—including lending to minority small businesses. These new diversity cops will have the power to subpoena bank documents and witnesses, as well as issue temporary orders requiring banks to cease and desist any practice deemed discriminatory. They will work with HUD's and Justice's own diversity police to enforce fair lending, which means banks will come under enormous political pressure to bend underwriting rules for protected classes with iffy credit.

This massive new agency has broad authority to tailor protections against discrimination in not just lending but across the entire financial spectrum.

"Providing this much power to one agency is truly frightening," says financial analyst Andrew Busch of BMO Capital Markets in Chicago, "as they will get to set the rules and pick the winners [and] losers for the financial sector."

If that weren't enough, the bureau will also oversee the placement of a diversity czar in each federal financial agency, including the Federal Reserve and its 12 regional banks.

Establishing a so-called Office of Minority and Women Inclusion within each agency is the brainchild of Democrat representative Maxine Waters, a Congressional Black Caucus leader and financial reform bill conferee now under investigation for steering federal bailout money to a troubled black-owned bank in which she and her husband held a large financial stake. Waters had direct input into CRA changes in the 1990s and is involved in the new round of "improvements."

According to her amendment to the Dodd-Frank Act, "Each agency shall take affirmative steps to seek diversity in the workplace of the agency, at all levels of the agency," including:

- recruiting at "historically black colleges and Hispanic-serving institutions";
- recruiting in urban communities;
- placing ads in African-American and Spanish newspapers; and
- "partnering with organizations that are focused on developing opportunities for minorities."

## WHAT'S PAST IS PROLOGUE

Clinton history is repeating itself and influencing Obama bank policy. It is 1995 all over again, only worse. Clinton's old gang is not only serving directly in the Obama administration but advising it on key financial issues in the middle of a crisis of its doing.

"The CRA serves its purpose, and I'm very, very encouraged that bank regulators are working extremely hard right now to make it work better," Ellen Seidman, who enforced the CRA as one of Clinton's top bank regulators, said during a 2010 Treasury conference. However, she advised Treasury secretary Tim Geithner that banks will be reluctant to make the "riskier" (her word) CRA loans if they do not have Fannie and Freddie or some successor entity to dump them on. "The secondary market needs to be there for those loans or they won't get made," Seidman said, arguing for protecting Fannie's and Freddie's role in housing markets even as their losses mount.

HUD Secretary Shaun Donovan, also attending the conference, agrees. In previous testimony he has asserted that Fannie and Freddie over recent decades have facilitated "an important democratization of credit," which is doublespeak for reallocation of credit. "This provided many of those families that had previously been shut out and unable to make investments in homeownership with an opportunity to access this option for the first time," he said. "And we subsequently witnessed a dramatic growth in ownership among underserved groups."

Yes, and now we are witnessing a dramatic decline. Never mind that. Donovan asserted that "ensuring that homeownership opportunities are available to members of these communities should remain a priority."

Another former Clinton appointee, National Community Reinvestment Coalition president John Taylor, has submitted his wish list, as well, which includes expanding CRA regulations to cover nonbank institutions. "Non-CRA covered credit unions and insurance companies," Taylor explained in a recent Washington hearing on CRA "modernization," "have not served minority and working communities in a satisfactory manner."

In the meantime, he argued, banks should have to pass "more rigorous" CRA testing of their lending "to minorities and communities of color," and be punished with harsh penalties, including stiff fines, for noncompliance.

It was Taylor, moreover, who got a provision inserted into the financial reform bill to mandate collection of data on loans to minority small businesses to enhance CRA enforcement of "fair lending" to such minorities.

All this dovetails with Obama's own wish list. In fact, Taylor helped draft his original plan and joined Obama for the signing ceremony of the financial reform bill.

Taylor says he and his group are selflessly promoting "economic justice." But, as you shall see later, this Washington lobbyist personally profits from such social policies, pocketing hundreds of thousands of dollars in compensation and stock payoffs.

Then there is Eugene Ludwig, a Rhodes scholar pal of Clinton who led his CRA reform as Comptroller of the Currency. He proposes going even further. Ludwig wants the administration to apply the CRA to hedge funds and private equity funds to force them to "invest" in inner-city development projects. He also wants Wall Street firms to offer "pro bono" financial services to minorities. "With these changes, the CRA could become an even more powerful engine for revitalizing low- and moderate-income neighborhoods," Ludwig argues, "coming to the fore just when the government's ability to use tax revenues to pay for infrastructure improvement and to invest in urban development is greatly diminished."

In other words, he wants banks to pick up the slack in social spending. For starters, he wants the private sector to directly subsidize the inner-city redevelopment needed in the wake of the subprime disaster that Ludwig's own regulations helped cause.

That is not all. Ludwig is lobbying for an additional federal statute mandating that all United States corporations publicly report steps they have taken to target minority markets and modify their products and services accordingly. He wants the government to keep tabs on them in a database tracking "corporate social responsibility."

These are the radicals rewriting the rules for business today. And their ultimate goal is to reallocate credit on a massive scale by subjecting all of corporate America to a CRA racial litmus test.

Astoundingly, the banking industry lobby is not putting up much of a fight, even though banks are now in virtual full compliance with anti-redlining rules and can confidently argue that they do not need to be subjected to more. Nearly 98 percent of banks and thrifts receive composite CRA ratings of satisfactory or better, according to federal data. Yet they have agreed in principle to CRA's "modernization," while only urging regulators to "proceed with caution" amid the fragile recovery.

By pushing lenders even harder to make unsafe loans—and in effect subsidize risk—the administration risks undoing any good the CRA might have done in opening up underserved markets.

"Some banks have felt forced to open branches in [poor and minority] communities that are already being served," notes Mark Willis, whom we introduced earlier. Indeed, he adds, "Some of these new branches not only have turned out to be unprofitable, but their addition has even undermined the economics of the other pre-existing branches."

In other words, CRA-mandated markets have reached a saturation point, with banks stepping over each other to serve them, competing even with minority-owned banks for business—whatever it takes to get a passing grade from regulators and get them (and NPA's thugs) off their backs. Compelling them to make even more unprofitable loans in these markets, which is bound to happen, would merely sow the seeds of the next crisis. And like the current one, it would wind up hitting communities of color hardest.

Black, white, or purple, anybody who is creditworthy should have access to credit. But extending credit based primarily on skin color rather than on an individual's ability to repay is a recipe for the kind of financial disaster we are all still experiencing, not to mention racism of a different kind.

The fingerprints of radical redistributionists are all over this economic crime, and now they want to roll banks again, this time in the name of "reform."

"Wall Street owes a debt to Main Street," CRA lobbyist Taylor says, "and it's time they paid up."

Only, the evidence is overwhelming that Beltway social engineers, not Wall Street financial engineers, created the market for high-risk subprime mortgages in order to promote "affirmative-action" lending, as they themselves have referred to it.

As you will see in the following narrative, which provides new details and a picture fuller than any revealed previously, the conspiracy began with Clinton, who, in effect, held a gun to lenders' heads as radical organizations like ACORN and NPA picked their pockets, and civil-rights lawyers like Barack Obama trained their leaders and represented their inner-city clients in court.

This is the fiscal forensics that the Angelides Commission failed to do. Now let's follow the trail of evidence.

# FOUR

# THE HEIST

Why did Jesse James rob banks? Because that's where the money was.

— Jesse Jackson, addressing hundreds of ACORN delegates shortly before the 1992 Democratic National Convention in New York

When I was president, we instituted a vigorous enforcement of the Community Reinvestment Act, a little-known law that requires banks to loan money.

— Bill Clinton, 2007

In the heat of the 1992 presidential race, Alicia Munnell, director of research at the Federal Reserve Bank of Boston, teased the press about the release of a "comprehensive study" of mortgage lending that promised to determine, definitively, whether area banks discriminate against blacks and other minorities. "It will be socially important," vowed the Wellesley College graduate and friend of Hillary, confidently adding, "It will definitely be a sound piece of research."

One month before the election, the Boston Fed released the findings of its bombshell study on bank redlining, which showed that 17 percent of black loan applicants at 70 FDIC-supervised banks were rejected for mortgages, while just 11 percent of white customers were turned down. The report blamed the gap squarely on racism.

"This is discrimination," Munnell declared.

The study, however, did not take into account a host of other relevant data factoring into denials, including applicants' net worth, debt burden, employment records, or credit histories. Other variables, such as the size of down payments and the amounts of the loans sought to the value of the property being bought, also were left out of the analysis.

"Maybe you can explain away these discrepancies [with additional data]," Munnell said, addressing concerns at the time. "My personal opinion is you probably cannot."

The disparity in loan approvals simply confirmed her hunch that predominantly white lenders loan to their own and exclude applicants who do not look like them. "There's a natural tendency to be nicer to the man or woman who went to the same school you did or the same church you did or lives in the same neighborhood as you," she suggested.

Munnell's motives were not purely scientific. She initiated her study in response to complaints from "community activists," with whom she clearly sympathized, that mortgages were not being made in minority communities, and that banks were not taking the Community Reinvestment Act seriously. In fact, her study was adapted from an earlier one conducted by one of her researchers, Connie Dunham, an Urban Institute activist, that proposed broadening the CRA's reach.

One anti-redlining activist who had Munnell's ear was Bruce Marks, who had been leading the charge against local banks as director of the Boston-based Union Neighborhood Assistance Corporation (now known as the Neighborhood Assistance Corporation of America, or NACA). "We've got the most racist bankers in the country," he maintained. Another was John Taylor, a longtime housing-rights activist who had led CRA efforts in the Boston area as head of the newly formed National Community Reinvestment Coalition.

They, in turn, held Munnell's report up as the smoking gun proving that banks blackball applicants based on skin color. Taylor called it "an important watershed event." Marks used it to paint all bankers as out-and-out "racists." They both argued that the data demanded a crackdown by bank regulators, along with an overhaul of the CRA.

"The Fed said the banks are guilty," Marks said. "Now what's the punishment? Do the bankers go to jail or are they forced to compensate affected communities with millions of dollars they should have been lending to begin with?"

In Washington, the top lobbyist for ACORN, which represents mainly black home buyers, said the report presented "overwhelming evidence that discrimination is alive and well in our banking system." Now, demanded ACORN legislative director Deepak Bhargava, "what is the government going to do about it?"

The national media, meanwhile, hailed the Boston Fed study as "landmark" and "groundbreaking."

But it took private analysts, as well as at least one FDIC economist, little time to determine that the study was terminally flawed. In addition to finding embarrassing mistakes in the data, they concluded that more relevant measures of a borrower's credit history—such as past delinquencies and whether the borrower met lenders' credit standards—explained the gap in lending between whites and blacks, who on average had poorer credit and higher defaults.

## PHANTOM RACISM

And far from practicing racism, the majority of the banks reviewed by the Boston Fed eagerly loaned to blacks in spite of their checkered credit reports. "In fact," noted Emory University finance professor George Benston, 49 of the 70 FDIC-supervised banks in the survey "did not reject any minority applicants." He also pointed out that two of the remaining 21 banks were responsible for half of the total denials of black applicants. And one of those banks was *minority owned*, while the other had extensive minority outreach programs. All 70, moreover, had passed anti-redlining examinations by CRA regulators.

Since there was no conclusive evidence of "discrimination in the mortgage market," as Munnell put it, it would seem there was no cause to intervene in the mortgage market, as many, including a host of outraged politicians, demanded.

But that is not what happened.

In April 1993, six months after the release of Munnell's report, the Federal Reserve issued new underwriting guidelines for bankers "to combat possible discrimination in lending." The 27-page booklet, "Closing the Gap: A Guide to Equal Opportunity Lending," laid out 10 strategies for banks to improve minority lending, including adopting "flexibility in applying underwriting standards." In evaluating such customers, it strongly recommended the mortgage industry stretch, even junk, time-tested qualifying rules by:

- giving "special consideration" to minorities with high household debt;
- accepting gifts in lieu of down payments from "nonprofit organizations," such as NACA and ACORN;
- considering "extenuating circumstances," such as "unforeseen expenses," in bad credit cases; and,
- accepting temporary "welfare payments and unemployment benefits" as "valid income sources," noting that Fannie Mae and Freddie Mac had agreed to accept them as well.

The widely distributed federal manual also advised lenders that job turnover should not be a "focus" of concern and "lack of credit history should not be seen as a negative factor." This is the very definition of the risky "NINJA"—no income, no job, no assets—loans that federal officials now blame lenders for carrying on their books.

Shockingly, the government was encouraging lenders to rubber-stamp applicants with a history of failing to hold a steady job and pay their bills on time. And it was just getting started, as we shall see further on.

The feds argued that traditional credit rules for judging the creditworthiness of loan applicants were too "arbitrary" and "unreasonable" (politically correct shorthand for "discriminatory"), and ought to be tailored to the "special" credit needs of minorities. "Even the most determined lending institution will have difficulty cultivating business from minority customers if its underwriting standards contain arbitrary or unreasonable measures of creditworthiness," advised the manual, which gathered input from Marks, Taylor, Bhargava, and other community activists clamoring for easier credit rules, including counting welfare, even food stamps, as verifiable income. "Special care should be taken to ensure that standards are appropriate to the economic culture of urban, lower-income, and nontraditional consumers."

The guidebook listed penalties for noncompliance with federal fair-lending laws, including up to $500,000 in punitive judgments. The warning to lenders was clear: play or pay.

To spread the word, Federal Reserve Board governor Lawrence Lindsey recommended the softer lending guidelines as "important reading for all individuals in the financial services industry." "Banks have a responsibility not only to end the practice of discrimination," he told a gathering of the Mortgage Bankers Association of America, "but end the appearance that discrimination is occurring as well."

More than 50,000 copies of the new federal guidelines were put into circulation. In addition, the Fed offered training workshops for its member banks.

Then, in an extraordinary move, the Federal Reserve Board held a press conference in Washington to release a video adapted from the booklet. It featured an introduction by Federal Reserve chairman Alan Greenspan, who warned lenders: "We all know a lot of work needs to be done to eliminate discrimination from the marketplace."

Now, with Greenspan's stamp of approval on the fair-lending guidelines, no one in the mortgage industry could take them lightly.

## GREENSPAN'S IMPRIMATUR

"When they are put forward with the imprimatur of chairman Greenspan, they go above and beyond recommendations," said Kenneth Guenther, then executive director of the Independent Bankers Association of America. He added that the guidelines instantly became the new "10 commandments" of mortgage underwriting.

The 23-minute video, *Closing the Gap: A Guide to Equal Opportunity Lending*, called on banks to adjust lending standards to help otherwise uncreditworthy minorities applying for credit. "Policies regarding applicants with problem credit history should be reviewed," it advised. It also cautioned lenders against viewing lack of credit history as a shortcoming, because "some cultures encourage cash payments."

Basically, the central bank was telling underwriters to ignore everything *but* race.

And they listened. The American Bankers Association broadcast the video on its satellite communications network. The Fed's toll-free number was deluged with orders for it. In addition, the Federal Reserve provided copies of the tape to the presidents of all state banks it supervises.

With every major financial lobbying group advising members to go along with the slacker standards, the seeds of the mortgage crisis were planted, far and wide. To question the new rules was to run the risk of being branded a racist. Shunning them might invite a regulatory crackdown.

This is precisely what Lindsey warned would happen in his 1994 address to mortgage bankers. He said if lenders failed to assuage critics, including community organizers like ACORN agitating on behalf of minority customers, "greater regulation remains a likely prospect."

In fact, a regulatory juggernaut already was heading their way.

That same year, President Clinton launched his National Homeownership Strategy to ambitiously push the black homeownership rate well above 50 percent. Citing the Boston Fed study as evidence, he assumed racism was behind the "mortgage gap" and pulled out all the stops to try to close it.

By then, it was clear from critical reviews of the study that Munnell, despite her Harvard PhD in economics, misinterpreted the data and failed to include key variables that would have altered her findings. Fellow economists even knocked Munnell in the press as a political hack advocating radical economic theories and using overly simplistic economic models that produced misleading results.

But Clinton was not interested in such inconvenient facts. He not only embraced the discredited report, but hired its authors. Munnell became his assistant secretary of treasury for economic policy. Her assistant, Dunham, also landed an economist job at Treasury.

To help achieve his homeownership goal, Clinton ordered Janet Reno to lead an anti-redlining crusade against the banking industry. She in turn deployed a battalion of United States attorneys to prosecute banks, suing them for so much as not smiling at black customers. "No loan is exempt, no bank is immune," warned the six-foot-one attorney general. "For those who thumb their nose at us, I promise vigorous enforcement."

Reno advised banks to rethink their credit standards. "We don't want banks to make bad loans," she said, "but we want them to make fair loans," adding, "Don't make the mistake of assuming that because an area is mostly African-American, it must be economically riskier. That's just not so." She then warned that her department planned to prosecute any bank, regardless of size, that failed to aggressively market loans in black neighborhoods.

Inner-city housing activists were energized by what they described as the attorney general's declaration of "war" on bankers. "We're going through the civil-rights era in the banking industry," ACORN's Bhargava rejoiced.

## *OBAMA V. CITIBANK*

Reno also made it known that she would side with private lawsuits claiming racial bias in lending. One such case was filed by Barack Obama, who at the time was working in Chicago as a young civil-rights lawyer specializing in fair housing at Davis Miner Barnhill & Galland PC. In 1994, he tried to bring a class-action suit against Citibank on behalf of Chicago-area blacks who claimed they were rejected for home loans simply because of the color of their skin. Obama demanded that Citibank turn over loan files from the entire Chicago metro area to prove that the bank regularly engaged in a pattern of discrimination, or "redlining." He was not awarded the files, and Citibank eventually settled the claims out of court.

(According to the docket papers I have reviewed, the plaintiffs' claims lacked merit. Factors other than race figured in the bank's decision to turn them down for loans. One of Obama's clients had "inadequate collateral" and "an incomplete application," while another had "delinquent credit obligations and other adverse credit history." Obama argued that such facts miss the point: that Citibank's neutral underwriting criteria as a *whole* may have adversely impacted his clients as a class of people. Despite the weak case, Citibank, which two years earlier had been accused of discrimination by ACORN in a rowdy protest at its New York headquarters, agreed to make more loans to marginally qualified African-American applicants.)

After Reno sued a popular bank in the Washington suburbs based on a wildly expanded definition of discrimination—one that for the first time included failure to market bank services in minority neighborhoods—no banker, no matter what they did, felt safe from charges of racism, and they flocked to industry lawyers for advice. Legal seminars for concerned lenders drew overflow crowds. The American Bankers Association hired a prominent Washington law firm to prepare a legal analysis of Reno's anti-redlining crusade. In its 1995 briefing to the ABA, Skadden Arps quickly determined that there was no legal basis to support her novel arguments and advised bankers that she was exercising an "aggressive" agenda to "reform banking industry practices." The 106-page briefing, a copy of which I have obtained, concluded: "In sum, DOJ [Department of Justice] has been using its vast enforcement powers to seek to extend the law by alleging in its complaints that legitimate, race-neutral lender business practices that are inconsistent with DOJ's policy views either constitute, or provide circumstantial evidence of, intentional race discrimination."

ABA decided to arm its members with a fair-lending "toolbox" to protect them from similar prosecution. The toolbox included the new federal guidelines for "flexible" underwriting.

"The Clinton administration is cutting no corners in its efforts to root out lending discrimination—in fact, they're laying out new groundwork," warned then ABA president Daniel Smith. "It's crucial for every bank to reevaluate its policies and procedures in light of these changes." Translation: adjust your credit standards and volume of lending in urban areas to conform to the Justice Department's stricter definition of fair lending.

Clinton also set a goal to double the number of fair-housing enforcement actions brought by HUD. So while Reno's "witch hunt," as the banking industry dubbed it, spooked Washington-area Chevy Chase Federal Savings and other banks into signing Justice Department orders to set aside large numerical quotas of loans for minorities, HUD launched its own fair-lending investigations to compel additional minority lending.

And lenders had one more agency to fear. "Our concern is that HUD appears to be taking on a major regulatory-type role over banks," complained Ed Yingling, ABA's chief lobbyist at the time. "This seems to be yet another agency we have to deal with when obviously the banking agencies and Justice Department are going after this very vigorously."

## TIGHTENING SCREWS ON LENDERS

Led by assistant HUD secretary Roberta Achtenberg, a former civil-rights activist who worked closely with Bhargava at ACORN, HUD's own crusade targeted mortgage bankers *not covered* by the CRA. These lenders, in turn, signed what in effect were consent decrees with HUD, in which they pledged to make risky low-income minority loans they would not have otherwise made. Because HUD oversees Fannie and Freddie, it has major leverage over mortgage bankers. If the agency denied them the right to sell their mortgages to these secondary market leaders, it could force bankers out of business.

First to ink a "voluntary" deal was Countrywide Financial Corporation, which went on to become the nation's largest subprime lender. But the deal was more like a shotgun marriage, since the lender was under preliminary HUD investigation for alleged discrimination. After Countrywide signed the HUD pledge in 1994, it undertook a companywide cultural diversity program and quickly liberalized its underwriting policies. Within four years it had doubled the share of home loans it made to minorities. As time wore on, it made more loans to minorities than any other lender. Two years after signing its "Declaration of Fair Lending Principles and Practices" with HUD, Countrywide established a subprime unit to deal with the higher volume of urban loans, hitching its fortunes even closer to black and Hispanic neighborhoods.

"We are working with some very big mortgage lenders," Achtenberg boasted in 1994. "We have some 400 expressions of interest [from lenders willing to sign individually tailored fair-lending agreements with HUD as insurance against investigation and secondary market blackballing]." Even the Mortgage Bankers Association of America signed one, shocking the financial world at the time. Among other things, MBA promised to work with its 2,900 member companies to:

- "develop underwriting standards that broaden credit opportunities for traditionally underserved groups";
- "encourage . . . stronger relationships between . . . mortgage brokers . . . and groups active in minority neighborhoods"; and
- "target advertising and marketing efforts to reach potential low-income and minority customers."

Meanwhile, Clinton's top banking regulator hired hundreds of new bank examiners to comb through loan files and lending data to identify racist banks (see the chart of yearly bank examiner totals in the appendix). And his office referred a number of alleged race-bias cases to Reno (almost all of which proved meritless). Explaining the crackdown, comptroller Eugene Ludwig asserted, "We have to use every means at our disposal to end discrimination and to end it as quickly as possible." He vowed to eliminate bias from the financial system, "root and branch."

But Clinton did not stop there. He also turned to Ludwig to codify as part of the CRA the "flexible" lending guidelines recommended by the Federal Reserve. Ludwig began rewriting—with direct input from Bhargava and NCRC's Taylor—CRA regulations to make it harder for banks to get satisfactory ratings unless they stretched their underwriting rules. Bhargava asked for "aggressive enforcement of the CRA" and got it, calling Ludwig "great" for his commitment to the cause. The new regulations, implemented by executive order in 1995, imposed performance tests mandating banks dramatically increase their loans to risky borrowers in the inner city—or face penalties including rejection of expansion plans.

"With CRA," Bhargava said, "the rubber meets the road where the loans meet the 'hoods."

## DEFYING THE RULES OF BANKING

Bank examiners for the first time were ordered to use federal home-loan data broken down by neighborhood and income group to rate banks on their performance lending in "underserved communities." "No more As for effort," as one analyst put it. Now only results would count. And they would be counted more often, as Clinton nearly doubled the average number of CRA examinations to 4,750 a year, according to the Federal Financial Institutions Examination Council.

Washington's message to banks was clear: Be more "flexible"—or you will be sorry. And banks obeyed almost in unison, marking what would prove to be a tragic turning point in financial history.

"When government regulators bark, banks jump," says University of Texas economist Stan Liebowitz. "Banks began to loosen lending standards. And loosen and loosen and loosen."

And they relaxed them not just for minorities, but for all their customers.

"Of course, the new federal standards couldn't just apply to minorities," says Manhattan Institute senior fellow Steve Malanga. "If they could pay back loans under these terms, then so could the majority of loan applicants." And bank regulators who set the lower bar could hardly disapprove. "Quickly," added Malanga, "these became the new standards in the industry."

With normal safeguards tossed, money soon became ridiculously easy to obtain. The new CRA-institutionalized rules led banks to underwrite loans for even deadbeat borrowers. As time wore on, virtually anybody could qualify for a loan.

"The most important fact associated with the CRA is the effort to reduce underwriting standards so that more low-income people could purchase homes," notes Financial Crisis Inquiry commissioner Peter Wallison, an early critic of the CRA. "Once these standards were relaxed . . . they spread rapidly to the prime market and to subprime markets where loans were made by lenders other than insured banks" subject to the CRA.

In the decade leading up to the 2007 crisis, most, if not all, the products offered to subprime borrowers were offered to prime borrowers. In fact, according to the Milkin Institute, prime borrowers obtained 31 of the 32 types of "flexible" and "innovative" mortgage products obtained by subprime borrowers.

"Standards were loosened across the board," Liebowitz says,

"so that even a prime loan applicant could avoid making virtually any down payment."

Clinton, meanwhile, made sure Fannie and Freddie did their part in his race-based lending project by slapping them with "affordable housing" targets. He had the agency that oversees the government-subsidized mortgage giants make sure that his political goals were met. In 1995, HUD required that 42 percent of the mortgages they purchase serve lower-income families. Five years later it sharply increased the affirmative housing ratio to an alarming 50 percent, which carried over well into the Bush administration, a subject we shall revisit later.

Thanks to the new pressure from HUD—which set up a banking department exclusively to enforce "fair lending"—the two mortgage giants eventually bought $1.8 trillion in subprime and other questionable loans from neighborhood lenders. Banks and mortgage companies used the steady flow of cash from Freddie and Fannie to originate more of the risky mortgages, keeping the subprime bubble inflated. Fannie's top client became subprime behemoth Countrywide, which, not surprisingly was the first lender to fail when the bubble burst.

But Clinton's most significant contribution to the subprime bubble was his fateful decision, also made in 1995, to authorize Fannie and Freddie to earn affordable-housing credit for buying subprime mortgage-backed securities. With that move, he pushed the mortgage giants into uncharted and risky territory. He also started a frenzy of subprime securitization that spread the risk to Wall Street.

## WASHINGTON INTERSECTS WALL STREET

Subprime securities were generally viewed as the junk bonds of the mortgage world, since the loans backing them historically foreclose at ten times the rate of prime mortgages. But that changed when Clinton drafted Fannie and Freddie to issue and guarantee them. More and more investment banks, as a result, securitized subprime and other CRA-eligible loans, and aggressively hawked them as "guaranteed" by Fannie and Freddie. Wall Street's pitch was that these mortgage-backed securities were as safe as Treasuries, but with a higher yield.

In 1997, Bear Stearns, a major underwriter of mortgage-backed securities, pioneered the first public securitization of such mortgages, a $416 million offering guaranteed by Freddie. The "affordable mortgages" backing the securities were underwritten using "flexible" criteria, according to the press release announcing the deal; but because they were guaranteed by Freddie, they had "an implied 'AAA' rating." Over the next year, the Wall Street giant issued other pools of the risky loans worth $1.9 billion and backed by Freddie or Fannie. Lehman Brothers and other investment banks followed suit. They, in turn, sliced the implicitly guaranteed and supposedly safe securities up into collateralized debt obligations, or CDOs, which by the mid-2000s had flooded U.S. and world markets mainly in Europe and Asia. The exotic securities generated huge fees on Wall Street.

Meanwhile, major banks seeking CRA investment credit also bundled or bought the securities. Almost overnight, subprime securitization became big business. In 1994, 31 percent of subprime loans were securitized. By 2006, the share had more than doubled to 81 percent. And to get a piece of the action, document requirements were loosened from Main Street to Wall Street.

In a 1998 pitch for more CRA securitization business, for example, Bear Stearns followed the script laid out by the Boston Fed. No, "CRA loans do not fit neatly into the standard credit score framework," given their low credit scores, but "forget about scores," the leading CRA underwriter argued in a promotional article published in Mortgage Bankers Association of America's organ. "Do we automatically exclude or severely discount these loans? Absolutely not," it added. "One has to look at the underlying credit variables" unique to first-time minority homebuyers. As for credit defects: "Counseling is often available for those who are delinquent with their payments."

By underwriting such loans, Bear signed its own death warrant. So did Lehman. It is no coincidence that the first to fall on Wall Street were the first to fall for Washington's social investing scheme.

But the more subprime securities investors bought, the more money Fannie and Freddie could throw back at neighborhood lenders on Main Street, feeding a frenzy of subprime lending concentrated in urban areas already at risk of widespread foreclosures.

## BUBBA'S BUBBLE . . . AND BLIGHT

When Clinton took office, 42 percent of African-Americans owned their own homes. By the time he left the White House, a record 48 percent did—a quantum leap historically, and nearly three times the pace for white homeownership. The overall minority homeownership rate increased more in the 1990s than in any decade in the last century except the 1940s, when minorities joined in the postwar housing boom.

The media attributed the growth to the "first real enforcement of the Community Reinvestment Act." Indeed, the black homeownership rate first spiked in 1995 when the CRA revisions went into effect (see the chart in the appendix). Between 1993 and

1998, home loans to poor black borrowers shot up an unprecedented 122 percent—four times greater than for similar white borrowers, according to a little-noticed Clinton Treasury report published in 2000.

Astoundingly, half the growth in U.S. homeownership from 1995 to 2005 came from minorities. The national homeownership rate turned sharply higher in the mid-1990s for the first time in years, hitting 68 percent by the time Clinton left office. The four-point gain was a sea change. Homeownership had been relatively flat for decades, even in the go-go 1980s, but suddenly it was shattering records.

First-time homebuyers who otherwise would not have qualified for mortgages suddenly flooded the market. Higher home prices soon followed the home-buying frenzy. A seminal study of historic home prices by Yale University economist Robert J. Shiller shows the housing bubble that recently burst began in 1997 (see the chart in the appendix). Before Clinton put teeth in CRA regulations, housing prices had generally tracked inflation. But in the mid-1990s they broke trend, climbing at a 7 percent annual clip, thanks in large part to the artificial demand for housing created by Clinton's easy credit policies.

A groundbreaking study shows his CRA revisions played a key role in the boom. In the 1990s, more than half of subprime refinances were in predominantly African-American census tracts, indicating that banks were targeting minority neighborhoods to show CRA regulators they were serving such communities. The National Bureau of Economic Research found that a tectonic shift in the supply of credit had taken place during the 1990s in zip codes covering depressed areas. People in the ghetto previously denied credit prior to Clinton's housing policies were suddenly approved for home loans after his policies took effect—even though their credit and employment situations *worsened.*

The NBER study blames the massive credit shift on undue government pressure to bend lending rules in order to expand housing to minorities, throwing more risky borrowers into the market. The sudden entry of new customers in the mortgage market "led to both greater house price appreciation and the subsequent sharp increase in defaults," the study found. And defaults were concentrated in poor, predominantly minority zip codes, which means Clinton's housing policies left residents living in them even worse off. In effect, they turned urban zip codes into breeding grounds for defaults. This "would not have occurred in the absence of the expansion in mortgage credit availability," the NBER report concluded. The defaults have led to an epidemic of foreclosures, reversing gains in minority homeownership and inviting more blight and crime to minority neighborhoods.

## BREEDING GROUND FOR DEFAULTS

According to Chicago economist Brian Wesbury, "The CRA forced many lenders to finance homeowners who had a tenuous ability to repay, and," he says, "we had a recipe for excess risk-taking in housing and painful increases in commodity prices."

As Clinton's regulators cracked the whip, the share of banks flunking the CRA exam rose, while those passing it with high marks shrank dramatically. Prior to the 1995 reforms, 24 percent of banks covered by the CRA received an "outstanding" rating. By 1998, the share had dropped to 19 percent; and by 2002, less than 10 percent of banks earned that top score, according to government data (see the chart in the appendix).

Banks scrambled to originate urban loans that would impress CRA regulators. Washington Mutual eventually received the CRA Community Impact Award for its "flexible menu of loan products that can be personalized to meet the unique financial needs of customers . . . [in] under-served communities." That, of course, was before such risky loans forced it into receivership. Like Countrywide, Washington Mutual became one of the first casualties of the subprime crisis.

As "the pressure from the CRA continued," says Mark Willis, CRA compliance officer for JPMorgan Chase, "banks may have lowered credit standards."

The new CRA rules also pushed banks into the subprime securities market. Banks without subprime lending units found it hard to originate such loans to meet the tougher CRA mandates. So they turned to buying subprime loans already originated, something Clinton gave them credit for in an effort to develop a secondary market for such risky loans.

The policy "encouraged the trading of loans that had already been made," Willis says. "A new business was born."

More like a racket. Banks knew they had to make enough loans to the government's preferred clients before they could make any major changes in their business operations. Expansion plans were (and still are) contingent on regulatory approval, which hinge on strong CRA ratings and the blessing of community activists, who were empowered by the CRA changes.

It was a powerful coercion. Delays in billion-dollar mergers were expensive. Bankers would rather negotiate than fight charges of racism, protests, and boycotts—and activists knew it. Witness this stunning preemptive threat by Jesse Jackson, CEO of the racism industry, in 1999, against any banker who might support a proposal by Phil Gramm, then head of the Senate Banking Committee, to reform the CRA (Jackson made it clear they would not even think about it if they knew what was good for them and any merger offers they were weighing): "I want to see Mr. Gramm line up the major bankers who will stand with him against CRA. Who is he representing?" Jackson bellowed at a press conference held jointly with NCRC's Taylor at the National Press Club in Washington. "Let him name ten major bankers who are against CRA. Let him name ten major bankers who want mergers and consolidation. Let him name ten major bankers who will stand with him. Let's take the covers off."

## EARLY WARNINGS

By 1998, underwriting standards were under assault from every branch of the federal government remotely dealing with housing policy. Though the economy was booming, the trend alarmed some economists.

"After the warm and fuzzy glow of 'flexible underwriting standards' has worn off," Liebowitz warned in an academic paper that year, "we may discover that they are nothing more than standards that lead to bad loans."

Other analysts saw a major financial crisis brewing on the horizon from the excessive social risk the government had injected into the system.

In 1999, Cynthia Latta, then an economist with DRI/McGraw-Hill in Boston, warned that mortgage lenders had come under tremendous political pressure to lower their lending standards to tap into minority markets, despite studies showing that they are more likely to default than whites even when economic times are good. The fallout from politically mandated lending, she predicted, may be soaring levels of defaults and bankruptcies in the next recession.

"If the economy turns down and the unemployment rate starts to rise," Latta explained, "minorities are going to be some of the first to be laid off, and they won't be able to continue paying their mortgages." And when it happens, she said, blame Washington. "The banks are under a great deal of pressure to lend in these communities," Latta told the *Washington Times*. "It is very political."

Ominously, she added, "We have created a tremendous amount of risk."

The subprime scandal has many starting points, but the years 1995 and 2000 are key. In order to meet higher affordable housing requirements set by HUD in 2000, Fannie and Freddie dramatically reduced their underwriting standards and stockpiled subprime loans and securities. Under withering pressure from their mission regulator, including threats of investigation, the federally charted mortgage giants even modified their automated underwriting systems to accept loans with characteristics they had previously rejected.

"The effort to reduce [their] mortgage standards was led by the Department of Housing and Urban Development," Wallison asserts.

HUD Secretary Andrew Cuomo mandated that, starting in 2001 and running through at least 2004, fully 50 percent of their portfolios had to consist of affordable loans to low-income and minority borrowers. It marked a new high, and a 19 percent increase over the last goal set five years earlier. He even set a volume target of $2.4 trillion dollars over 10 years. "The higher . . . goals will disproportionately benefit minorities and city residents," he explained, "helping to close the homeownership gap."

To hit these sharply elevated goals, which even HUD insiders had described as too drastic, the race-obsessed Cuomo advised Fannie and Freddie to invest *specifically* in subprime loans. He announced in a HUD report that their "expanded presence in the subprime market could be of significant benefit to lower-income families, minorities, and families living in underserved areas."

## CUOMO'S PLAN

"We have not been a major presence in the subprime market, but you can bet that under these goals we will be," Fannie's new chairman, Franklin Raines, a Clinton appointee, said at the time. He offered that half of all mortgages in the subprime market were candidates for purchase, and promised, "We can bring lower cost credit to thousands and thousands of African-American families." At least Raines, an African-American who thought home ownership was "unevenly distributed in society," was on board with Cuomo's ambitious plan.

HUD noted that its research showed that African-Americans comprised 5 percent of market borrowers, but 19 percent of subprime mortgage borrowers. This suggested subprime loans were key to reaching out to blacks and putting them in homes. If Fannie and Freddie tapped into the subprime market, it would tap into the African-American market. Here they would find their "goals-qualifying" mortgages, HUD encouraged, even though subprime loans were performing poorly even back then.

Cuomo envisioned the government-sponsored mortgage giants playing "a significant role in the subprime market"—so significant, in fact, that it would erase the stigma, if not the risk, of subprime lending industry-wide. If everybody felt "more comfortable with subprime lending," Cuomo revealed in HUD's final report of rules governing Fannie and Freddie, the line between subprime and prime lending would eventually blur to the point where, counter-intuitively, lending to "credit-impaired borrowers will increasingly make good business sense."

Cuomo also wanted them to buy more CRA-eligible loans, which included low-documentation Alt-A, or "liar loans," as well as subprimes. "Purchasing these loans could be an important strategy for reaching the housing goals," his 186-page report, entered into the *Federal Register*, continued, "and provide needed liquidity for a market that is serving the needs of low-income and minority homeowners."

Cuomo insisted that providing easier credit to minorities was critical because "discrimination in mortgage lending continues to be a barrier to homeownership." As proof, he cited "a major study by researchers at the Federal Reserve Bank of Boston [that] found that mortgage denial rates remained substantially higher for minorities." That's right: his Draconian goals were predicated on Munnell's flawed study.

There was just one problem. Fannie's and Freddie's underwriting guidelines were too "rigid" to allow such a risky plunge. Though they had both taken mincing steps toward subprime lending, they resisted jumping into that market because of the higher risks. Fannie's and Freddie's "guidelines remain somewhat inflexible," Cuomo complained in the report.

Their chief regulator insisted that they be more permissive, lowering their down payment requirements, raising their debt-to-income ratios, and allowing for poorer credit histories to accommodate "minority borrowers who have lower incomes and wealth." Only then could they earn enough "goal credits" to meet Cuomo's higher targets and get his regulators off their backs.

If Fannie and Freddie, who together control the national market for home loans, relaxed their qualifying standards, Cuomo hoped in his report, it would have a "profound influence on the rate at which mortgage funds flow to underserved neighborhoods." Even lenders who do not sell many of their mortgages to the dual mortgage pillars would adopt their lower credit standards, because Fannie's and Freddie's "underwriting guidelines are followed by virtually all originators of prime mortgages." In fact, Cuomo wished that the credit guidelines separating subprime loans from prime loans would "deteriorate" to the point where Fannie's and Freddie's purchases of subprimes would "look more like an increase in the prime market."

The HUD secretary's message was unmistakable: *Forget time-tested rules for determining risk. Prudent lending may be good business, but it doesn't get us where we need to be socially. Bend a little.*

Under such pressure, Fannie and Freddie put aside any misgivings. What choice did they have? The federally subsidized firms had to meet HUD's affordable-housing mandates as part of their federal charter. Failure to meet the goals would result in stiff fines imposed by HUD.

## FANNIE, FREDDIE LEARN TO BE MORE "FLEXIBLE"

Soon, Fannie and Freddie developed lines of "flexible" mortgages requiring no money down and weaker credit, and the nation's largest subprime lender, Countrywide, developed into Fannie's largest customer, enjoying its best pricing. By 2007, the subprime dealer accounted for a stunning 29 percent of Fannie's business. Under Raines's leadership, Fannie gave Countrywide privileged status as a reward for adopting "the most flexible underwriting criteria."

Countrywide chief Angelo Mozilo credited these "flexible underwriting techniques" with "fuel[ing] a record period of growth" in housing. These credit contortionists ruled the day.

Starting in 1997, Fannie began offering mortgages with just 3 percent down, well below the standard down payment of 20 percent. But in 2001, it underwrote mortgages with no down payments at all. Freddie also relaxed down payment requirements.

From 2000 to 2004, HUD data show that the share of home loans Fannie purchased with down payments of 5 percent or less jumped from 4 to 14 percent, while Freddie's increased from 6.1 to 6.4 percent. By 2007, their share of loans with this risk characteristic had grown to 26 percent and 19 percent, respectively (see the chart in the appendix). The share of "goal rich" loans they carried in their mortgage portfolios with low credit scores and high default risk also surged.

Obeying HUD's new underwriting standards, an alarming 61 percent of the loans Freddie purchased were made to home buyers with lousy credit scores of below 620 (660 is considered subprime), according to its 2007 financial report. Fannie, for its part, bought a whopping 58 percent of its loans from this extremely risky category during that same period.

They "relaxed their underwriting standards generally in the early [2000s]," says former senior HUD official John Weicher. "They began making significantly riskier loans to homebuyers beginning in 2002 [and] took still more risk in 2003."

Cuomo's goals, which were de facto laws, had their desired outcome of degrading standards across the industry, and rubber-stamping more African-American loans. In 1998, 57 percent of black mortgage applicants were denied; by 2004, the share had plunged to 27 percent.

That year, Raines, Cuomo's ally at Fannie, told lenders gathered at the Mortgage Bankers Association of America's annual convention in San Francisco, "We have to push products and opportunities to people who have lesser credit quality." These types of statements, said former Fannie chief credit officer Edward Pinto, "alerted the originator community that if they could make subprime and Alt-A loans, there was ready market for them, and this stimulated an orgy of junk mortgage development."

By 2008, after making additional alterations to their underwriting guidelines, Fannie and Freddie held or guaranteed almost half the 27 million subprime and other nonprime loans outstanding—"and these loans are the source of the financial crisis we now confront," Pinto confirmed.

"Fannie and Freddie abandoned income qualification entirely, eliminated down payments, and catered to borrowers with damaged credit," he said, calling it an "unprecedented abandonment of underwriting principles" that fundamentally altered the terms by which mortgage credit was offered in the United States from the 1960s through the 1980s. They had achieved Cuomo's vision of standardizing guidelines down.

And their "flexibility" in approving risky loans coincided with the ever-increasing affordable housing goals set by their regulator.

"With the encouragement of HUD," Pinto said, "a relentless assault was made upon the three underpinnings of underwriting: capacity (measured by a borrower's overall income), collateral (measured by loan-to-appraisal ratio), and credit (measured by FICO scores)." And starting in 2002, after Cuomo's drastic new three-year targets went into effect, they plunged deeper into the risky securities market, underwriting billions of dollars in subprime and Alt-A paper. "They increased their risk through 2004," said Weicher, former federal housing commissioner at HUD. "And their appetite for risk remained about the same after 2004."

By 2004, when HUD next revised its Affordable Housing Goals, Fannie's and Freddie's purchases of subprime securities had jumped tenfold. Gobbling up $176 billion in subprime securities that year alone, the home loan twins together commanded almost half of the total market for such securities, HUD data show (see the chart in the appendix). Starting in 2002, default rates on these risky loans rose higher each year, reaching crisis proportions by 2006.

Today, subprimes make up most of the toxic debt taxpayers are now having to help Fannie and Freddie and private banks clean off their balance sheets in the wake of record defaults by mostly unqualified borrowers.

In effect, HUD in 2000 had set a ticking time bomb.

When Clinton officially unveiled his affordable housing campaign during a June 1995 White House ceremony—which included ACORN officials as guests of honor—he promised it would not burden taxpayers. "Our homeownership strategy will not cost the taxpayers one extra cent," he clucked. "It will not require legislation. It will not add more federal programs or grow federal bureaucracy."

Few ironies have been as tragic.

## *FOR* SUBPRIMES BEFORE THEY WERE *AGAINST* THEM

Clinton and his regulators at the time boasted that their tougher anti-redlining rules fueled the subprime boom, which they credited with benefiting minority homeowners. The facts bear them out:

- In 1993, when Clinton took office, subprime credit was a sliver of the overall credit market. By the time he left office in 2001, subprime credit accounted for approximately 25 percent of home equity credit outstanding, according to the American Financial Services Association.

- Federal data show that the number of subprime mortgages originated by lenders soared from 104,000 in 1993 to 210,000 in 1995 to a whopping 997,000 by 1998.
- Subprime mortgage activity grew an average of 25 percent a year from 1994 to 2003, outpacing the rate of growth for prime mortgages.

Dangerous as the trend was toward riskier and riskier home financing, Clinton administration officials could not have been happier. At the time, long before the subprime market soured, they took credit for creating it, even boasting of leveraging the secondary market and ginning up demand on Wall Street for subprime securities.

In 1999, Ellen Seidman, one of Clinton's top CRA regulators, freely admitted that the subprime market emerged as a result of the administration's amendments to the CRA in 1995. And she expressed her faith in subprime loans. Their surge showed that the administration's strategy was working, since subprimes provide a major source of credit for people hard-pressed to qualify for mortgages. "Growth in the sub-prime credit market indicates that credit needs in many low- and moderate-income areas are being met," Seidman blithely proclaimed.

She also cheered the relaxation of credit standards. Spurred by the threat of CRA challenges, she confirmed, banks loosened "their underwriting practices, making lending standards more flexible." (Seidman, who has suggested that the government set underwriting standards for the private sector, thinks bankers "overestimate the risks involved in serving [urban] communities." She argues that they should bend rules to make more loans there, covering any losses from "difficult" borrowers with "savings realized in processing applicants with good credit.")

Seidman, then head of the Office of Thrift Supervision, even stated with pride that the administration's policies stimulated Wall Street demand for securities backed by subprime and other CRA-eligible mortgages. "The 1995 revisions to the CRA . . . spawned a new market for investment in affordable housing and economic development securities," she crowed in a little-noticed article published in *Mortgage Banking* magazine. "Fannie Mae, Freddie Mac, investment bankers and mortgage companies are offering targeted, mortgage-backed securities."

"Without CRA as an impetus," Seidman added, "this market would likely not have developed."

And because it did, mortgage bankers not regulated by the CRA had devoted a growing share of their lending to subprime borrowers, she pointed out. "Even though mortgage companies are not subject to CRA," Seidman continued to gush, "mortgage bankers have responded to the improved secondary market opportunities CRA has fostered."

Of course, she trumpeted these dubious accomplishments while noting that "homeownership is at an all-time high." It was all good, until it all went so badly.

## RENO GLOATS

As Cuomo made his exit in January 2001, his agency issued a final, self-congratulatory—and very revealing—public brief, which stated the following:

> Lower-income and minority families have made major gains in access to the mortgage market in the 1990s. A variety of reasons have accounted for these gains, including improved housing affordability, enhanced enforcement of the Community Reinvestment Act, more flexible mortgage underwriting, and stepped-up enforcement of the Fair Housing Act. But most industry observers believe that one factor behind these gains has been the improved performance of Fannie Mae and Freddie Mac under HUD's affordable lending goals. HUD's recent increases in the goals for 2001–03 will encourage [them] to further step up their support for affordable lending.

This sums up the complete Clinton administration recipe for financial disaster. Unwittingly, Cuomo left behind an incriminating note spelling out the entire strategically coordinated, ruthlessly executed conspiracy to gut traditional lending standards and bring affordable housing to the inner city, whatever the cost, so long as it was off the federal budget and privately subsidized by industry. While everybody was worried about Clinton socializing the health care industry, he and his radical gang had successfully socialized the other 14 percent of the economy—housing.

Reno also gloated as the administration winded down. "Lenders have listened and learned," she said. "Bank commitments . . . have increased."

Treasury undersecretary Gary Gensler, moreover, bragged that banks under the Clinton administration's new regulatory regime made home loans to minorities at "twice the rate" they had to other borrowers—and he credited subprime mortgages for facilitating the growth. "Several years ago, many borrowers were unable to access credit at any price," Gensler testified before Congress in 2000. "Today, due to the growth of subprime lending, more lower-income and minority families have the opportunity to buy homes, to refinance their debts, and to finance educational, medical and other important expenses." He added, "A subprime loan is a good option when the alternative is no access to credit." Gensler, a staunch Democrat, now serves as Obama's top commodities regulator.

Clinton also burst forth with pride, braying that he had compelled banks to issue virtually all the CRA loans ever issued up to that point. He calculated that they made a staggering $800 billion in home mortgage, small business, and community development loans to poor and minority communities on his watch. (See the chart in the appendix.)

"We've had great success . . . with vigorous enforcement of the Community Reinvestment Act—which has been on the books for 22 years," Clinton said in 2000, "but over 95 percent of all the investments have occurred in the last seven years, because it's good business to invest in . . . places that are underserved."

Not a few failed bankers would take issue with that assessment today. It decidedly was not good business for them to invest in areas where people could not repay loans.

It is plain that the former president viewed his nearly $1 trillion shakedown of banks as one of the signature achievements of his administration. He dare not trumpet it now, though, seeing how it led to a tsunami of inner-city subprime refinancings and bankruptcies. With subprime foreclosures now swamping Detroit, Atlanta, Cleveland, Baltimore, and other heavily black cities, the homeownership rate for African-Americans has slipped back below 50 percent—well shy of Clinton's goal. (See the chart in the appendix.)

## BUSH AND THE BARRIO

Clinton has tried to steer the scandal away from himself and his legacy by claiming the subprime boom arose from Wall Street greed that went unchecked by a Republican administration. While this is a popular notion, the Bush administration's culpability centers not on lack of regulation, but overregulation. More precisely, it made the mistake of continuing, almost seamlessly, the Draconian anti-redlining and affordable-housing regulations and policies instituted by the Clinton administration.

President Bush, the "compassionate conservative" from Texas who fancied himself the first bilingual president, poured tequila on the subprime fire with his affordable-housing program targeting Hispanic immigrants. He challenged the housing industry to help create 5.5 million new minority homeowners by the end of the decade as part of his America's Homeownership Challenge initiative. To help achieve the goal, Bush tasked his housing secretary, Mel Martinez, with putting together a coalition involving various segments of the housing industry, which Martinez dubbed the Blueprint for the American Dream Partnership.

"Last June, I issued a challenge to everyone involved in the housing industry to help increase the number of minority families to be homeowners," Bush reminded banking and housing executives gathered at a daylong housing conference the White House held at George Washington University in October 2002. At the same time, the Republican leader proposed helping people in the barrio overcome what he viewed as some underwriting "barriers" to buying homes. "A lot of folks can't make a down payment," Bush clucked. So he called on Congress to pass his American Dream

Down Payment Assistance Fund to subsidize down payments for 200,000 low-income minority homebuyers. The fund, approved by a Republican-control Congress, gave qualifying families up to $1,500 in matching funds toward down payments on homes.

During the George Washington University speech, Bush singled out Franklin Raines for praise, thanking him for his commitment to affordable housing at Fannie Mae. Raines remained at the company's helm through the first part of 2005, when he was forced to resign under an ethical cloud. Bush also praised Freddie Mac for its own work to "dismantle barriers and create greater opportunities for home ownership." One praiseworthy Freddie program, he noted, "is designed to help deserving families who have bad credit histories to qualify for home ownership loans." The president appeared oblivious to the oxymoron of families with "bad" credit histories "deserving" home loans.

Under pressure from affordable housing activists, the Bush administration in 2004 proposed bumping up HUD's goals for Fannie and Freddie even further. NCRC's Taylor, by now the most powerful CRA lobbyist in Washington, demanded that the mortgage giants "step up their performance" in serving "first-time homebuyers, especially minority first-time homebuyers [and] credit impaired borrowers." He also wanted them to underwrite even more unsafe "CRA loans."

## ANATOMY OF A SCANDAL

Activists pressed HUD to set a 2008 target of 57 percent, but the Bush administration thought that was too aggressive and counter-proposed a target of 56 percent, a 12 percent increase over the 50 percent goal set by the Clinton administration. The final six-point boost, set in 2004 and phased in over the following four years, was more gradual than Cuomo's three-year, eight-point goal hike, which was not instated incrementally and sent Fannie and Freddie into panic. By far the largest jump in HUD's required goals occurred in 2000 (see the chart in the appendix). And analysts agree it triggered the sudden spurt in subprime investment by Fannie and Freddie from 2001 to 2004.

The Justice Department under Bush, meanwhile, was less aggressive against banks but still carried on Reno's legacy by continuing to prosecute "disparate impact" cases involving lending discrimination, at least through 2004. Prosecutors that year, for example, settled redlining charges against a Chicago lender for not serving "the credit needs" of minority neighborhoods. In another case resolved in 2004, they ordered a Detroit bank to invest $3 million in special minority financing to settle charges that it committed redlining in "the totality of the bank's policies and practices." The consent decree noted that the bank, which denied any wrongdoing, failed to open branches in heavily African-American neighborhoods.

While Bush did next to nothing to overturn the affordable housing agenda set by Clinton, analysts agree the real financial damage was done under Clinton, who fundamentally changed the home finance market.

Today, there are approximately 27 million subprime and other nonprime loans—chiefly Alt-A loans (often called "liar loans" because borrowers provide little documentation)—festering on the books of Fannie, Freddie, and other financial institutions. These junk loans, which total more than $4 trillion, account for almost half of all mortgages in the United States.

"The number and percentage of weak mortgage loans on the balance sheets of banks is an unprecedented situation in this country," Wallison says. "In all other housing bubbles in the past, we have never had anything like it."

"It looks to me," the commissioner told me, "that the huge number of subprime and Alt-A mortgages generated by government policy are the cause of the financial crisis."

Wallison figures government accounts for more than two-thirds of the risky mortgages outstanding, whether by virtue of being held or guaranteed by government-sponsored Fannie and Freddie, held by the Federal Housing Authority, or held by private institutions under the requirements of the CRA and HUD.

Helping shape the bad government policy that generated most of the bad debt were radical housing-rights activists, and one in particular. He is the ACORN official mentioned at the beginning of the chapter, Deepak Bhargava, a former union organizer who believes "housing is a human right." And though he has since left ACORN, he has helped craft the housing agenda of the Obama administration in his new lobbying role in Washington.

First, it is instructive to look back on Bhargava's influence over housing and banking policy as ACORN's top Washington lobbyist during the Clinton years. He had a major hand in amending the CRA. ACORN, which had a direct line to the White House, proposed 16 specific changes to the regulation, many of which were incorporated into the final rules, include adding a lending test based on market share. The changes were called "radical" even by some banking regulators at the time.

## "STEALTHY AGENDA"

Bhargava's influence was not limited to the CRA. He also urged Clinton officials to tighten the screws on Fannie and Freddie, even proposing that they require them to devote half their portfolios to loans for low-income and minority borrowers—advice they eventually took in 2000. (The administration actually considered setting the 50 percent target several years earlier, in the mid-1990s, but decided against the idea, figuring a hike from 30 percent to 50 percent would be too drastic. Of course, in the end the delay did not matter; the move to 50 percent in 2000 was still severe, producing more loan defaults by pressuring the banks to accept more unsafe borrowers.)

Bhargava also convinced HUD officials that Fannie's and Freddie's underwriting criteria were biased against minorities and needed adjustments in their favor. He said their credit guidelines were "developed for the suburban market but the effect is discriminatory" in urban markets. He sneered at bankers in general, charging that they only lend to their "golfing buddies."

Besides the obvious ideological congruence, how did Bhargava come to have so much influence in the Clinton administration?

ACORN was founded in Little Rock, Arkansas, in 1970, and its founders developed close personal ties to Clinton, who became governor of the state. "ACORN kind of grew up with Clinton," Bhargava said, and could get him on the phone. So as banking policies were hammered out, Clinton was receptive to its lobbying efforts. So much so, in fact, that he hired a community activist and banking industry critic to coordinate White House policy with ACORN and other anti-banking groups. "I'm quite pleased," with the appointment of Michael Waldman, Bhargava said after learning of his appointment to the White House. Waldman provided unprecedented access to ACORN. "We all talked to him," Bhargava said, "and he was helpful in suggesting ways to get our basic positions in the loop." As a result, ACORN had "lots of access" to the

Clinton White House, he said, and together they made lending discrimination a top-priority issue.

Now back to the Obama administration.

## FULL CIRCLE

The 44-year-old Bhargava also happens to have close ties to President Obama, with whom he attended Harvard. Obama trained ACORN leaders in hardball Alinsky tactics as a Chicago organizer, and later represented the group as a lawyer. He also paid ACORN, which endorsed him for president, $832,000 for a get-out-the-vote effort.

But their connection goes beyond ACORN.

In 2005, Bhargava invited Obama, then a senator, to the headquarters of his new Washington employer—the ultra-radical Center for Community Change—to receive its Community Change Champion Award for Obama's service to poor and minority communities.

During the presidential primary campaign in 2007, moreover, Bhargava hosted Obama at a forum in Des Moines, Iowa, that was hosted by his center, which he now runs as executive director. Sharing the stage with Bhargava, Obama promised him and other community organizers gathered there that he would meet with them as he prioritized his domestic policies. "During the transition, we're going to be calling all of you in to help us shape the agenda," Obama said. "We're going to be having meetings . . . so that you have input."

Like Clinton before him, Obama vowed that "a central priority" of his administration "would be having an affordable housing agenda," claiming that the "federal government has really abandoned the field when it comes to affordable housing." This was welcome news to Bhargava, who complains of a "credit famine" in the "hood," which he believes results from "deeply structured racism." Now more than ever, he thinks banks have a social duty to free up mortgages and other loans for minorities.

"A genuinely progressive movement will insist that race does matter," Bhargava says, "and therefore we have to be race conscious in how we construct policies." To that end, he has lobbied for "a more robust role for the government through greater regulation" and "a radical economic agenda." This dovetails with Obama's own agenda, which Bhargava describes as both "courageous" and "stealthy."

## Easy Credit Chronicles

1992: Boston Fed issues "watershed" report coauthored by economist friend of Hillary alleging that banks "redline" minority neighborhoods and discriminate against minority buyers.

1992: Democrat-controlled Congress passes rule authorizing HUD to set Fannie Mae and Freddie Mac targets for "affordable housing" lending in such "underserved" neighborhoods.

1993: Boston Fed issues new lending guidelines encouraging banks to use "flexibility in applying underwriting standards" to minority borrowers. Endorsed by Fed Chairman Alan Greenspan, the new "flexible" standards are designed to "combat possible discrimination in lending."

1993: President Clinton puts Boston Fed economist Alicia Munnell—coauthor of the redlining report and new minority lending guidelines—in charge of Treasury's economic policy.

1993: Clinton announces his plan to overhaul anti-redlining regulations under authority of the Community Reinvestment Act, or CRA.

1993: Democrat Congress requires Fannie Mae and Freddie Mac to submit to HUD a study on their underwriting guidelines. HUD begins periodic reviews of those guidelines.

1993: Comptroller of Currency Eugene Ludwig launches probe of more than 100 financial institutions with poor minority lending records, referring race-bias cases to the Justice Department. Ludwig also authorizes use of undercover agents to test mortgage loan officers for disparate treatment of minorities, a tactic not employed by prior administrations.

1993–95: Attorney General Janet Reno aggressively prosecutes several banks for alleged racist lending, while encouraging private discrimination lawsuits against banks—including one filed against Citibank by civil-rights lawyer Barack Obama.

1994: Clinton unveils ambitious National Homeownership Strategy to boost minority homeownership.

January 1994: Clinton issues executive order affirming support for the Justice Department's efforts to eliminate lending bias, while citing Boston Fed study alleging that minorities are more likely to be rejected for mortgages.

January 1994: Clinton issues Executive Order No. 12,892, enhancing HUD's powers to administer and enforce fair-lending laws regulating mortgage lending companies and Fannie and Freddie.

1994: Under the executive order, Clinton establishes the President's Fair Housing Council, comprised of the heads of the bank regulatory agencies and chaired by HUD's secretary, who is authorized to promulgate fair lending rules.

1994: Clinton sets up Inter-agency Task Force on Fair Lending—convened by the HUD secretary, attorney general, and comptroller of the currency—to coordinate a strategic crackdown on biased lenders.

1994: Under threat of expanded regulations and investigations, Countrywide Financial, the country's largest subprime lender, signs "voluntary" agreement with HUD, promising to relax underwriting standards for uncreditworthy minorities. The deal sets numerical targets for minority loans.

1994: Mortgage Bankers Association, representing thousands of independent mortgage companies unregulated by the CRA, signs first-of-its-kind "master agreement" with HUD, pledging to adopt "flexible underwriting standards" "for members of the minority community."

1994: For the first time ever, federal regulators reject bank applications for charter changes because of poor CRA grades. "These denials are a signal that this agency intends to fully enforce fair lending laws, including the CRA," announces the Office of Thrift Supervision.

April 1995: Clinton approves new CRA rules setting strict numerical lending targets for banks in "underserved" neighborhoods, while ordering regulators to crack down on alleged bank redlining. The new regulations mandate that banks use "innovative" or "flexible underwriting practices," adopting Munnell's earlier language. Compliance requires banks to pass a heavily weighted "lending test" or suffer holds on mergers and acquisitions and other penalties. Another new rule—public posting of the list of banks scheduled to undergo CRA performance exams—gives ACORN and other activists advance notice to organize anti-redlining protests against banks up for evaluation.

1995: HUD slaps Fannie and Freddie with higher affordable-housing targets to guarantee more loans to low-income and minority borrowers.

1995: In a first, HUD authorizes Fannie and Freddie to purchase mortgage-backed securities that include subprime and other risky CRA home loans as credit to help satisfy HUD's tougher affordable-housing goals.

1996: Clinton orders the IRS to issue individual taxpayer identification numbers (ITINs) to foreigners who are not eligible for a Social Security number.

1997: Clinton's beefed-up CRA regulations are fully implemented and enforced by a wave of new bank examiners deployed by four federal agencies.

1997: Freddie and Bear Stearns securitize first public offering of CRA mortgages "guaranteed" by Freddie through the U.S. Treasury.

1997: Fannie also dives into the CRA market, launching its Community Reinvestment Act Portfolio Initiative and financing $1 billion in CRA loans by the end of the year.

1998: Fannie rolls out high-risk loan program requiring ultra-low, 3 percent down payment, but no matter how hard it tries, HUD keeps raising the affordable lending bar.

1999: HUD investigates allegations of racial discrimination in the automated underwriting systems used by Fannie and Freddie to determine the creditworthiness of borrowers. Senior HUD official William Apgar subsequently initiates first-ever review of their underwriting systems in a "massive and historic undertaking."

2000: Banks begin accepting ITIN numbers from foreign mortgage applicants in lieu of Social Security numbers.

2000: HUD sets even higher affordable-housing goals, mandating that Fannie and Freddie dedicate fully half their mortgage business to "affirmative-action" lending for HUD's targeted population of poor and minority borrowers.

2001–04: Under Clinton's stiffer HUD mandate, Fannie and Freddie are obligated to continue meeting the 50-percent targets. The mortgage giants dutifully gobble up some $300 billion in subprime mortgage securities to count toward the higher mandates.

2001: Fannie CEO Franklin Raines, Clinton's former budget director, announces Fannie's "American Dream Commitment"—a ten-year, $2 trillion pledge to lend to "underserved" communities.

2002: Responding to urban housing activists, Bush holds "White House Conference on Increasing Minority Ownership" in which he pledges to help make homeowners of an additional 5.5 million minorities by the end of the decade, with a special focus on Hispanic immigrants. Bush directs HUD secretary Mel Martinez—as well as Fannie and Freddie—to help "families who have bad credit histories to qualify for home-ownership loans."

2003: Bush signs the American Dream Down Payment Act, setting aside a proposed $200 million a year to help thousands of poor minorities buy starter homes.

2004: Internal Freddie Mac e-mails express worry that it is leading the market in high-risk so-called NINJA loans.

2004: Adopting Clinton's goal of closing the "mortgage gap" between whites and minorities, the Bush HUD proposes raising affordable-housing goals for Fannie and Freddie, while suggesting they adjust "current underwriting standards to better reflect the special circumstances" of new immigrant households. HUD mandates additional annual hikes for each of the next three years.

2005: HUD ratchets up the main affordable-housing goals for Fannie and Freddie to 52 percent, but the mortgage giants throttle back on subprime securities as subprime loan delinquencies rise. The cutback proves too little too late.

2006–2007: In a suicidal move, Fannie takes one more shot at meeting its HUD goals by making more than $350 billion in subprime and other high-risk investments.

2008: HUD's main affirmative-lending targets for Fannie and Freddie level off at 56 percent.

2008: Treasury takes over Fannie and Freddie as the mortgage giants collapse under the weight of bad loans. Also collapsing is subprime giant Countrywide, the pioneer non-bank lender to sign on to HUD's affirmative-lending regime and the nation's largest minority lender. HUD's poster boy becomes the national whipping boy.

# FIVE

# THE NEXT HOLD-UP

Less than 1 percent of the 250 billion in venture capital dollars invested annually nationwide has been directed to the country's 4.4 million minority business owners. We are going to change that.

— President Obama

"I consistently believe that when it comes to . . . reparations," Barack Obama told a gathering of minority journalists in 2008, "the most important thing for the U.S. government to do is not just offer words, but offer deeds."

A few days later he clarified his remarks, saying he was not calling for direct cash payments to descendants of slaves, but rather, indirect aid in the form of government programs and regulations that will "close the gap" between what he sees as white America and black America.

Obama and the community organizers he has worked with on the south side of Chicago have a name for that inner-city gap: "American Apartheid." They genuinely believe there is a government conspiracy to "force" blacks "into geographically separate and grossly unequal communities"—a plot on par with such urban legends as the government cooking up AIDS and crack to destroy blacks, which have been peddled from the pulpit by Obama's longtime preacher, Jeremiah Wright. "Artificial lines of race jurisdiction . . . have been created to insure that people remain divided," say Obama's community organizer pals at the radical anti-redlining group Gamaliel Foundation, where Obama worked as a consultant and trainer. "Racism is masked and concealed inside a system of spatial segregation." As the theory goes, blacks are "trapped" in government-created ghettos, and therefore must be bailed out through "reinvestment" under the CRA and other federal anti-redlining laws (never mind the impressive numbers of middle-class blacks who have resettled in the suburbs without government help). Reinvestment demands massive new housing subsidies so blacks can move into the gated and guarded communities of the suburbs.

Claiming in his memoir that "blacks were forced into ghettos," Obama is certainly sympathetic to the idea of reparations. His longtime South Side Chicago church has actively petitioned for them for decades. And he has strongly suggested there is a legal case to be made for them.

"So many of the disparities that exist in the African-American community today can be directly traced to inequalities passed on from an earlier generation that suffered under the brutal legacy of slavery and Jim Crow," he said. "We still haven't fixed them."

He assumes the mortgage gap, and the broader economic gap, are legacies of discrimination and largely unrelated to personal responsibility. He also makes it seem as though things have not gotten better for blacks, when statistic after statistic shows strong growth in the black middle class over the past several decades, as more African-Americans escape the crime-ridden inner city for a better life in the supposedly "racist" suburbs.

Such stats undermine Obama's case for stealth reparations. Even if it were true, he argues, "better isn't good enough."

## STEALTH REPARATIONS

To fully understand where Obama is going with his "stealthy agenda," as Bhargava calls it, it is instructive to look back on a relatively unguarded, and little-noticed, radio interview Obama gave in Chicago long before he took the national political stage.

As an Illinois state senator, Obama told a friendly local radio talk-show host that he sought "major redistributive change" for the benefit of fellow blacks. He was speaking in the context of the civil-rights movement and how it had fallen short of "economic justice." He was speaking, if indirectly, of economic reparations for slavery and Jim Crow.

In that 2001 interview, Obama said it is a "tragedy" that the Constitution was not radically interpreted by the courts to justify and mandate redistribution of wealth for blacks, and it is still an issue of concern for him today. And he suggested he wants to effect major "redistributive change" through legislation.

He complained that during the civil-rights era, "the Supreme Court never ventured into the issues of redistribution of wealth" for blacks, and that the Warren Court was not "radical" enough:

"One of the tragedies of the civil-rights movement was . . . there was a tendency to lose track of the political and community organizing activities on the ground that are able to put together the actual coalitions of power through which you bring about redistributive change," he said while serving as a state lawmaker and University of Chicago lecturer. "And in some ways, we still suffer from that."

## THE COLOR OF MONEY

Now flash forward to the Obama presidency. In laying out his financial reform proposals for Congress, Obama asserted that the mission of a consumer finance watchdog agency should be to ensure that "traditionally underserved consumers and communities have access to lending, investment, and financial services."

The Dodd-Frank Act does that and more. It is affirmative-action legislation masquerading as financial reform, and it ensures that federal regulators, as never before, put racial lending at the top of their checklist. This federal statute gives regulators at the newly formed Consumer Financial Protection Bureau the power to autonomously write lending rules for all financial institutions—banks and non-banks alike—along with "primary . . . enforcement authority," including the power to subpoena executives and internal records. In that capacity, they will independently—or jointly with HUD and the attorney general's office—investigate major banks, credit unions, and mortgage lenders for alleged lending discrimination.

And the muscular new agency will field a steady stream of racism complaints generated by its Office of Fair Lending and Equal Opportunity, which will work with "consumer and community advocates on the promotion of fair lending compliance."

In addition, the bureau will hear at least twice a year from a Consumer Advisory Board made up of "fair lending and civil rights" activists, who no doubt will be the usual radical suspects—NPA, NCRC, NACA, Greenlining Institute, La Raza, MALDEF, and other ACORN clones.

But that is not all.

Representative Maxine Waters—one of several Congressional Black Caucus leaders invited to hammer out the final text of the bank reform bill—snuck in a provision unleashing an army of diversity cops on the Federal Reserve and all its regional banks, along with the FDIC, Treasury, and other federal financial agencies. Waters's amendment is now the law of the land, despite any evidence of racial discrimination at these agencies.

All told, some 20 government agencies will have to set up offices for "minority inclusion," regulating both their work forces and those of their contractors. This creates an unprecedented—and redundant—layer of Equal Employment Opportunity bureaucracy that financial analysts worry will have the end result of injecting affirmative-action decision making in financial transactions, slowing the flow of money and economic growth.

According to the text of the new law, the director of each so-called Office of Minority and Women Inclusion "shall develop and implement standards and procedures to ensure, to the maximum extent possible, the inclusion and utilization of minorities[,] . . . women, and minority- and women-owned businesses . . . in all business and activities of the regulated entity at all levels, including in procurement, insurance, and all types of contracts."

For the first time, the nation's central bank may have de facto racial hiring "quotas" imposed on it: "With the new financial regulation law, the federal government is moving from outlawing discrimination to setting up a system of quotas," said Diana Furchtgott-Roth, senior fellow at the Manhattan Institute. "Ultimately, the only way that financial firms doing business with the government would be able to comply with the law is by showing that a certain percentage of their workforce is female or minority."

## RISKY SMALL BUSINESS LOANS

Also buried inside the new financial reform law is a scheme to gradually force affirmative action on small-business lending—another "reform" with ominous implications for the economy.

Aimed at curtailing supposed discrimination, the race-based lending mandate is guaranteed to have perverse effects—just like the drive for racial "fairness" in *mortgage* lending paved the way for the subprime crisis and the 2008 financial meltdown.

The new Dodd-Frank banking law sets up a "data-collection" system to monitor small-business loans for racial bias. Lenders must report if a business that applied for a loan is minority-owned, and whether the application was rejected. Bank examiners will use that data to enforce CRA provisions governing more than 1,500 banks. And as noted previously, the Obama administration plans not only to toughen CRA testing of lending to minorities and communities of color, but also to impose those tests on nonbank institutions—independent mortgage companies, credit unions, insurers, securities firms, and investment banks.

In short, the administration will use the small-business-loan data as a cudgel to beat *everyone* into lending more to minority businesses.

Advocates have promised as much. NCRC's Taylor, who works closely with the White House, testified before the FDIC, "Upon passage of the Dodd-Frank bill to improve small-business data, CRA exams could scrutinize lending to minority small businesses."

Problem is, all this will redirect private investment to minorities—whether or not it is a wise investment.

The president thinks he is just overcoming prejudice. "Less than 1 percent of the 250 billion in venture capital dollars invested annually nationwide has been directed to the country's 4.4 million minority business owners," Obama has complained. "We are going to change that."

Yet the evidence for discrimination boils down to the fact that black-owned firms are twice as likely to have a loan application rejected as white-owned firms.

But that overlooks the fact that black owners are more likely to have bad credit and default on loans than white owners, as Federal Reserve data show and we shall see in full detail shortly. In fact, black owners are three times as likely to have bankruptcies and judgments against them as white owners. (They are generally less creditworthy than their Latino counterparts as well.)

In other words, statistically, black owners are less likely to repay loans and therefore pose a greater risk to commercial lenders. The "credit gap" is a function of rational business decisions, not racism.

But Obama and his fair-lending crusaders do not care; they are already moving ahead with their witch hunt against banks, evidenced by the flurry of lawsuits alleging small-business-lending discrimination filed by attorney general Eric Holder.

## OBAMA'S WITCH HUNT

In the 2009 case against First United Security Bank, the Justice Department ordered the tiny bank to "ensure that residential and

CRA small business loan products are made available and marketed in majority African-American census tracts," while offered on terms "more advantageous to the applicant than it would normally provide." Moreover, this demand was to be met even if the applicant "would ordinarily not qualify for such [a lower] rate for reasons including lack of required credit quality, income, or down payment."

In other words, do not worry if black borrowers are not qualified. Just give them the money—at a discount.

Holder's beefed-up Civil Rights Division was able to wring these concessions out of First United without proving its charges of discrimination. Remarkably, it presented no evidence to back its case. "There has been no factual finding or adjudication with respect to any matter alleged by the United States," states the 25-page order for resolution. This order was signed by Loretta King, the Obama-appointed black prosecutor who recommended dropping the case against a nightstick-wielding New Black Panther for intimidating voters at a Philadelphia poll during the 2008 election.

First United operates branches just outside Birmingham, Alabama, which is ground zero for the 1960s civil-rights struggle, a symbolic link not lost on the race-obsessed Holder.

The case appears as groundless as many of the lending discrimination cases prosecuted by Reno in the 1990s. Holder is following his old boss's playbook: Pick off a small bank with no political clout and make a big example of it so all banks, big and small, will get the message to open their lending windows even wider to minorities.

The point is driven home by his civil-rights chief. "We have identified large, mid-size and small lenders as targets of enforcement efforts," warns assistant attorney general Thomas Perez, echoing Reno's war cry. "Industry has much to gain in policing itself."

Other banks are scrambling to comply with the new anti-redlining offensive—creating de facto affirmative-action programs in small-business lending.

All of this means more bad news for the U.S. economy.

Small businesses are vital to economic growth. The more trouble they have expanding, the worse off we all are.

Yet business loans to small firms (which total some $670 billion) are risky; half of small borrowers fail in the first five years. Default rates, which have been hovering around 7 percent, are higher than junk bonds.

Now the administration has taken steps that will lead to increased defaults—obliging banks to charge more to their faithful paying borrowers to make up the difference, while diverting capital from more productive businesses trying to expand and create jobs. It is one more burden on a private sector struggling to recover.

Plus, the zealots' drive for lower underwriting standards for minority commercial loans could eventually lower standards across the board, as we saw play out in the mortgage bubble.

And do not rule out dangers we cannot yet predict: After all, nobody thought the drive for "fair" *mortgage* lending would wind up bringing the global economy to a halt. Even former bank regulators and bureaucrats agree that extending credit based mainly on skin color, rather than on an individual's ability to repay, is a recipe for a rotten economy.

"Under Dodd-Frank, [Obama] and his agents will control all credit and financial transactions, rewarding friends and punishing opponents, discriminating on the basis of race, gender and political affiliation," two former Treasury officials—Ernest S. Christian and Gary A Robbins—warned in the national newspaper *Investor's*

*Business Daily.* “Credit and liquidity may be choked by bureaucracy and politics—and the economy will suffer.”

▼

Obama and Democrats sold their reform bill as restoring America’s financial health. But it is really about restoring the kind of social engineering and race-based lending mandates that led to the financial crisis in the first place. It is a blueprint for a new bank heist, justified as punishment for the last one, which was blamed on the banks (aka “predatory lenders”), who were actually the victims.

“As we emerge from this recession, it is critical that we not only look for ways to hold those who discriminated in the past accountable. We must also find ways to repair some of the damage done to families and to communities,” Perez, a former Clinton appointee, recently told a friendly audience at the Brookings Institution in Washington. He concluded, “We must use the power of the law to encourage innovative strategies for rebuilding,” Obama’s top civil-rights cop added, “and be sure that decades of investment have not been permanently lost.”

What he is calling for is reparations by another name—“major redistributive change,” as Obama put it. The hold-up artists are itching to pull off another major theft. And there are a lot of them, all working in concert to pilfer your hard-earned money. On the following pages, I will identify the leading masterminds, past and present, and examine their radical rap sheets.

SIX

# THE BANK ROBBERS: TEN MOST WANTED

We believe that there are a lot of loans to black Americans that could be safely purchased by Fannie Mae and Freddie Mac if these companies were more flexible [in their underwriting requirements].

— William Apgar, former top aide to HUD secretary Andrew Cuomo, now top aide to HUD secretary Shaun Donovan

They may have boxed up their Birkenstocks and cut their hair, but make no mistake: the people you are about to meet are no less radical than they were in the 1960s. This gang of coat-and-tie radicals has snuck behind "enemy lines," infiltrating the Washington "establishment" they once railed against, to redistribute your hard-earned money in the name of "economic justice."

All the bad policy manufactured in Washington does not happen in a vacuum. Bad actors with bad ideas make bad policy. And too often they are crusading zealots with irrational notions about the way the world—particularly the business world—should work.

Yes, they may look like harmless policy wonks now, with their ill-fitting hairpieces, dark suits, and Ivy League pedigrees. But do not be fooled by appearances. These are hard-core leftists. And they have done, and are continuing to do, serious harm inside the warrens of Washington. Beneath the nerdy exteriors are ideological hacks with the power to destroy whole industries—and the economy and your wealth with them.

Does putting radicals in power really matter? Former attorney general Janet Reno was a big, honking radical, and look what she did to the banking industry. We are only now seeing the full extent of the damage she caused. She leads the Ten Most Wanted list of bank "robbers." They include the crusading zealots who wrote and implemented the reckless banking policies and regulations that led to the worst financial crisis since the Depression, as well as the overzealous regulators and prosecutors who enforced them. Here are their rap sheets:

## NUMBER 1: JANET RENO

Reno was the longest-serving attorney general of the 20th century. Her reign of anti-bank terror lasted from 1993 to 2000. In 1994, she held an extraordinary press conference at the U.S. Department of Justice, in which she announced her plans to file discrimination charges against banks that fail to lend as much in black neighborhoods as they do in white ones.

Reno warned that she would not look at whether banks refused service to blacks, but whether they "failed to make services *available* in predominantly African-American neighborhoods" (emphasis added)—a radical reinterpretation of discrimination laws. She made it clear that she wanted to see more branches operating in black areas, no matter how blighted, and more loans offered there, no matter how unprofitable.

Hers was a novel approach to fighting discrimination, to say the least. In fact, she was not even enforcing civil rights laws. The nation's top cop was enforcing the Community Reinvestment Act, which fell under the purview of bank regulators. Reno even cited the CRA during her press conference, saying banks in her crosshairs were ignoring their "obligation under the Community Reinvestment Act."

At the time, her remarks, jarring as they were, got little notice. But it was the start of a major "witch hunt" against the banking industry that lasted nearly a decade, and is still reverberating today. In fact, a new witch hunt has begun, led by her deputy (more on that in a minute).

Reno and her crusaders at Justice, some of whom still work there as prosecutors, filed a series of bruising lawsuits against mostly small banks, using these easy targets to set an example for the entire industry of what they were up against if they crossed her and refused to open their lending windows wide to minorities, no matter their creditworthiness. Or if they failed to open branches in crime-infested areas, even though no civil-rights law on the books requires banks to build branches in minority neighborhoods.

Instead of fighting the federal government, the banks agreed to pay tens of millions of dollars in fines and settlements to minority borrowers. This does not include the millions in legal fees (and higher insurance rates) they incurred defending themselves against her trumped-up charges of racism. Of course, they in turn passed on these punitive and legal costs to you and other customers in the form of higher fees and financing costs.

When she was not bullying small, defenseless thrifts, Reno went gunning for high-profile banks, such as Chevy Chase Federal Savings Bank in Washington, to throw a scare into other firms, who dutifully paid ransom to ACORN and other radical housing-rights groups in the form of loan commitments to get the aggressive attorney general, along with CRA bank regulators, off their backs (more on that in the next chapter).

Under Reno's reign of terror, banks were bullied into, among other things:

- opening new branches in unprofitable, high-risk areas—including, in the case of Chevy Chase, the crack- and crime-ridden Anacostia ghetto in the District of Columbia, at the time the murder capital of the United States
- offering minority applicants loans at 1 percent below the prevailing interest rate
- granting minority borrowers a portion of their down payments and closing costs
- hiring additional minority staff and paying them higher commissions
- retraining personnel to closely follow "fair lending" guidelines
- creating "fair lending" committees within their boards

- advertising on black radio stations and in black-owned community newspapers

"Such tactics amount to a tax on lending," said former FDIC and Federal Reserve official Vern McKinley at the time. "Even those innocent of discrimination will be willing to pay such a regulatory tax in order to avoid the costs of investigations and adverse publicity.

Minority outreach programs are not cheap—and all bank customers end up paying for them. Funds for these unprofitable loans come not from banks but from depositors and investors, McKinley explained. And losses are absorbed by shareholders and those holding securities backed by such shaky mortgages. If losses grow to a critical mass, as they did in the subprime crisis, taxpayers ultimately eat them in the form of bank bailouts.

Also in the name of "social justice," Reno and her anti-redlining zealots pushed lenders onto Indian reservations, where they were ordered to make home loans despite credit risks and collateral issues due to tribal land status and sovereignty. Banks were ordered to dole out risky loans in the Indian nation—or else. Reno issued her reservation-lending edict during a 1994 keynote speech at the National Community Reinvestment Coalition's annual conference in Washington, where some 250 community organizers had gathered to debate proposed reforms to the Community Reinvestment Act.

She was treated like a Hollywood celebrity. After pledging to continue her crusade against bank redlining, the crowd gave her a standing ovation. This attorney general was different—she was one of them.

In less than a year under her leadership, she had already prosecuted and settled five major lending discrimination cases—four more than in the previous 16 years that the Community Reinvestment Act had been on the books.

Continuing her speech at the Marriott, Reno delivered a pointed warning to banks who refused to lower their qualifying standards for minority borrowers with poor credit. She said she would give them a chance to comply with her multicultural lending edict. "But where cooperation fails, where discrimination continues," she snarled, "I intend to attack lending decisions on all fronts."

It was a chilling warning coming from the nation's top prosecutor: loosen lending for minorities—or else. Woe to those who do not cooperate, for they will feel the full weight of the United States government bearing down on them.

She promised to prosecute "unfair lending" wherever she could find it—even in Indian country. "No loan is exempt, no bank is immune," Reno added. "We will investigate in cities, towns, on reservations."

"This administration is dedicated to reaching out to Native Americans," she stressed, "to learn from them, and, yes, to enforce the law."

Or at least her radical interpretation of it.

### *Mantra of Economic Justice*

Four years later, Reno spoke again to the NCRC, proudly reporting back to her surrogates gathered in the Westend Ballroom of the Washington Marriott Hotel that banks had loosened their lending standards following her coordinated attacks. Bankers, she said, were "nudged in the right direction by the NCRC members and by Justice Department lawyers who care and want to do the right thing" by the poor and minorities. "Together," Reno added, to ringing applause, "we must work together for economic justice in this nation."

It was not the only time she used that curious phrase that morning. She mentioned "economic justice" nearly a dozen times throughout her speech. Again, "economic justice" is code for economic equality, which is socialism by another name. Repeating the phrase like a shared secret among fellow travelers suggests that public claims of correcting lending discrimination and opening up minority access to credit are just cover stories for redistributing your money. The end game appears to be reparations.

Reno's physical stature made her assault on banks appear all the more ham-handed. When she wagged her finger at bankers in press conferences, her targets could not help but notice her imposing six-foot, one-inch frame, which made her harangues even more intimidating.

This nuance was not lost on syndicated political cartoonist Howard Payne. He poignantly captured the thuggish nature of Reno's anti-bank shakedown in a 1994 cartoon distributed by Scripps-Howard.

In the illustration, Payne pictured a menacing-looking Reno and one of her diversity cops, both carrying nightsticks, towering over a nerdy little banker outside his small storefront bank. Reno is holding a brick behind her back, labeled "lawsuits." Her other hand is outstretched, palm up, before the petrified banker, who clearly can see that if he does not fork over more protection money to her, he can expect a shattered window or two, and perhaps a lump on the head.

In the cartoon's caption, Reno says, "We knows we can count on yous for minority community loans dis year, don't we, friend?"

Reno's tough anti-banking crusade lives on, through her star understudy.

## NUMBER 2: ERIC HOLDER

In 2009, Holder paid tribute to his old boss and mentor by presenting her with the American Judicature Society award. He is so fond of Reno that he has her portrait hanging in his office at the main Justice building, where he now serves as the nation's first black attorney general.

Holder acted as Reno's deputy in the 1990s and is now reasserting her authority over banks. He, too, has cast them as bigots, and plans to make them pay penance for perceived racism. His role in the bank theft began in 1994.

At a Washington press conference that year, Holder announced details of Reno's smackdown on Chevy Chase, which agreed under duress to make more than 1,000 subsidized loans, totaling $140 million, to African-Americans living in the District of Columbia who normally would not have qualified for mortgages under universally applied standards. He accused the bank of "redlining" predominantly black neighborhoods, a charge Chevy Chase strenuously denied. The Justice Department never proved its case, which at the time was unprecedented in its scope, because for the first time, a lender was accused not of discriminating against loan applicants but of violating fair-lending laws by failing to market services in minority neighborhoods.

So how did Holder justify such a harsh punishment? What evidence did he possess?

In a dramatic moment, the then deputy attorney general finally produced the purported smoking gun. He held up photographs of four homes, all similar in size and appeal, and asked the reporters gathered in the room to study them closely.

"Two of these homes are located in predominantly white

neighborhoods in Montgomery County [Maryland], where Chevy Chase aggressively sought out loans," Holder pointed out to the rapt reporters. "The other two homes are in majority black neighborhoods here in the District, where Chevy Chase made virtually no loans. I challenge anyone to distinguish between these homes," he added. "Just take a look at them."

Huh? This was the sum total of his evidence? Industry observers remarked that the only thing it proved was how little Holder understood about the mortgage business.

### *American Apartheid*

Shockingly, the number two prosecutor in the nation was using photos of houses to speculate about the qualifications of borrowers in the surrounding areas. It was plain that Holder had little, if any, clue about the complexities of the credit evaluation process. Houses do not buy houses. People do. And people have to be screened for risk.

Yet there Holder was, standing up and dictating how lenders should operate. As divorced as he was from the day-to-day realities of their industry, he still felt confident enough to tell them where they should advertise, even where they should build branches; and who they should approve for loans, even who they should hire.

Later, Holder acknowledged that the credit barriers Chevy Chase allegedly erected around black neighborhoods were "invisible." But these "invisible barriers" still keep him up at night. He thinks the mortgage gap is a vestige of America's segregationist past, something he calls "American apartheid."

"This nation has still not come to grips with its racial past," Holder said in a strikingly confrontational speech he gave in 2009 during Black History Month. "In things racial we have always been and we, I believe, continue to be, in too many ways, essentially a nation of cowards."

Ouch.

"Corrective measures" must be taken, he asserted, lest the problems of the inner city spill over into the "padlocked suburbs." This is where his muscularized Civil Rights Division comes in. In the off chance that Holder was not up to relaunching Reno's anti-bank crusade—which, of course, he is (bank lawsuits are already flying on his watch, as documented in an earlier chapter)—he has his marching orders from the president.

"I want Eric Holder as the next attorney general to reinvigorate that office and its mission," Obama has said of the civil rights unit.

Reno's pitchfork has been passed. Lenders beware.

## NUMBER 3: PAUL F. HANCOCK

The bank robbers are not just the political zealots who set the bad banking policies and rules. They also include the overzealous regulators and prosecutors who enforce them. Paul Hancock falls into that camp.

Working as Reno's key henchman during her assault on banks, he was the chief of the housing and civil enforcement section inside Justice's Civil Rights Division. In fact, he originated the department's fair-lending enforcement program, serving as its director for nine years. One of his treasured awards is one from Reno—a certificate giving him special recognition for developing the program.

Bank officials have slammed his aggressive enforcement approach as an effort to pursue social goals at the expense of banks, and their criticism has merit. Hancock is no stodgy career bureaucrat. A 1960s civil-rights crusader, he grew doctrinaire in his distrust of bankers, and was just as much a zealot for "economic justice" as his politically appointed bosses.

"Mortgage lending discrimination is probably the most serious problem in race discrimination we face today," he told a group of housing-rights activists in 1993. "We need to bring a lot more lawsuits in this area."

To that end, Hancock scanned local newspapers across the country for articles about banks running afoul of community organizers who complained about alleged racist lending. He zeroed in on the smallest and weakest thrifts to prosecute, figuring they would be less likely to fight the charges of discrimination. The department could make easy examples of them, cowing others into submission.

For example, articles he read in the obscure publication *Indian Country Today* led Hancock to investigate tiny Blackpipe State Bank of Martin, South Dakota. He sued it for discriminating against Native Americans by rejecting them for loans and for charging them higher interest rates and finance charges than white customers.

Blackpipe denied wrongdoing, explaining it was reluctant to make secured loans where the collateral was located on reservation land. And it argued, reasonably, that the Indian borrowers who were charged higher fees posed a far greater credit risk than other borrowers; therefore it had to charge them more to cover the added costs of processing and carrying their loans.

What's more, Blackpipe had passed anti-redlining tests, earning "satisfactory" CRA ratings from federal bank examiners. "There is no evidence that low- or moderate-income areas are excluded from the bank's marketing efforts," an FDIC exam report stated in 1990. The report explained why the bank was begging off reservation loans:

> The bank no longer makes these types of loans because of legal problems encountered pertaining to the foreclosure process when the property involves Native American trust land located within the bank's delineated lending area. Bank management has attempted to resolve this legal impediment with the Bureau of Indian Affairs, but no remedy was achieved. The bank refers all consumer real estate mortgage inquiries to federal agencies that would be able to meet these credit needs.

Some racist.

But the small, $18 million-in-assets bank did not have the resources to engage in a protracted legal battle with Reno's Justice Department. So it agreed to a government settlement that, among other things, required it to:

- expand its services to the reservations
- grant loans involving collateral located on reservation land
- reduce finance charges on existing loans to Indians
- revise its definition of a CRA-delineated community to include parts of two reservations
- revise its underwriting policies to accommodate Native Americans with flawed credit
- recruit and hire Native American employees
- market its products to Indians on the reservations
- hold regular meetings with tribal chiefs
- pay a $50,000 fine
- locate and pay past rejected Indian applicants $125,000 in compensation

Hancock assumed there were a number of "victims," and broadcast the easy money bonanza awaiting them. "We want to get the word out to the reservation areas," he told the Indian press.

Blackpipe was just one of many banks Hancock mugged. "Small banks shouldn't feel they have a safe harbor," he warned. "We're not eliminating anybody from the mix here."

And he was mighty proud of the persecution he led.

## *"Everyone Shares"*

While watching Clinton's first State of the Union address, Hancock became giddy with anticipation of Clinton throwing down the gauntlet against allegedly racist banks. "We must continue to enforce fair lending and fair housing and all other civil-rights laws," Clinton said, "because America will never be complete in its renewal until everyone shares."

Hearing the president make his job a top priority on national television sent a thrill through Hancock, who had been watching the speech with his wife in their Northern Virginia home. He turned to her, smiled and said, "That's us."

In the wake of the subprime meltdown, the silver-haired, bespectacled Hancock remains unrepentant. He thinks prosecutors should continue pressuring banks to make social loans, regardless of the risk they pose. "If we go back to the time when you had to put a 20 percent down payment down, for example," he said in an October 2007 interview with *Mortgage Banking*, "it's going to be very difficult for racial and ethnic minorities to purchase homes. We know that one of the major barriers to minority homeownership is the lack of wealth."

Another barrier, he maintains, is the credit-scoring system used by banks. On average, African-Americans have lower credit scores than other racial groups, at all income levels. He blames their low scores on racism, even though studies show no bias in credit scores. "It is very troubling for me, as someone who has been an advocate for fair lending for many years, "Hancock says. "It shows some very serious social inequities attributable to our history."

He also thinks more banks should be charged with lending bias: "I think we all recognize that there is some discrimination in the industry."

Hancock suggests his strategy all along was to bully banks into voluntary compliance by threatening to give them a black eye in the press. "If you are going to be sued by the Department of Justice, the damage that it would cause to the reputation of the lender is much more severe than any remedies that the department will obtain," he said. "So that's a starting point to take [fair lending] very seriously and to give good support to the compliance department of an organization."

And in that department—fair-lending compliance—Hancock is now cleaning up as a private attorney. He works with lenders on such bank regulations, which, thanks in part to his crusade, is now big business. Glad to see it has paid off for someone.

## NUMBER 4: EUGENE LUDWIG

Though the balding, button-down Ludwig may look like a banker, he is, in fact, a rabid anticapitalist advocating for the "democratization of credit," which is doublespeak for reallocation of credit to the uncreditworthy—which ultimately means redistribution of risk to taxpayers.

Ludwig was a classmate of Clinton at Yale Law School and one of his Rhodes Scholar buddies. After Clinton tapped him as his comptroller of the currency, regulating thousands of national banks, Ludwig spearheaded Clinton's drive to strengthen the CRA. And he carried out the task with the passion and vigor of the political activist that he is. During his five years as comptroller, Ludwig marshaled his 2,400 bank examiners to expose biased lending, even using undercover testers to try to catch loan officers treating black customers differently—a tactic not used by prior administrations. He, in turn, referred dozens of cases to Reno for prosecution.

"The CRA is about our better instincts," Ludwig says dreamily. "It's about a better world." (If not better business.)

These days, Ludwig is advising the Obama administration on ways to turn the CRA into a more potent weapon against the financial industry. "At a minimum," he says, the CRA should be broadened to cover credit unions and insurance companies. But "ideally," he says, it should "include all other major financial institutions, such as hedge funds and private equity funds."

"Hedge funds could hold community development-related debt instruments," Ludwig proposes. "And private equity funds could invest in community development projects or instruct firms in which they have ownership stakes to fund CRA projects in the communities they serve."

Do not worry, he says unconvincingly; doing business in these neighborhoods "is not about losing money."

He also suggests investment funds could earn CRA credits by offering "pro bono financial, accounting, and tax analysis to community organizations and low-income families in targeted neighborhoods." In other words, Wall Street could help anti-bank clones of ACORN stay in business so they could be in a better position to shake down Wall Street.

To help enforce the expanded law, Ludwig proposes "capping the percentage of executive salary and bonus that is tax deductible if a firm fails to maintain at least a Satisfactory CRA rating." Bonuses currently are deductible and so is executive pay up to $1 million.

### *Big Brother Database*

What Ludwig is proposing, in short, is reallocation of credit on a massive scale.

But wait, he has even bigger dreams. "Corporate America that is not covered by the CRA should be covered by a federal statute that does two things in the social responsibility area," he says:

- First, it should contain language that encourages all companies to serve their communities in a fair and equitable way, and in particular low- and moderate-income communities, and to affirmatively support these communities' well-being with time and money as appropriate.
- Second, companies should be obligated to report to a government-mandated and publicly transparent database what actions, if any, they do take to serve their communities, and in particular low- and moderate-income Americans.

"We will learn from the database," he says, who among corporate America is not living up to their "social responsibilities."

In other words, Ludwig wants Big Brother to keep tabs on corporations who are not making the requisite social investments, effectively turning the Fortune 500 into public utilities.

Prior to joining the Clinton administration, Ludwig was a partner at Covington & Burling LLP, a Washington law firm that also counts Eric Holder among past partners.

Since leaving office, Federal Election Commission records show that Ludwig, fittingly, has donated heavily to the reelection campaigns of representative Barney Frank and senator Chris Dodd, the banking committee chairmen in Congress who championed the CRA and affirmative-action lending targets at Fannie and Freddie and who co-sponsored financial reform legislation.

## NUMBER 5: ALICIA MUNNELL

The myth of the racist white lender was built from a fundamentally flawed and biased Boston Fed report authored by this radical activist posing as a scientist. As litigated earlier, Munnell's shoddy 1992 study was riddled with errors and slapped together in such a way as to do violence to professional scholarship. She followed up her report with politically correct lending guidelines that set the mortgage industry on its path to destruction.

Munnell was not just instrumental in manufacturing the redlining crisis. She helped Clinton socialize mortgages as a top official in his Cabinet. In 1993, after inviting her to speak at his post-election "economic summit" in Little Rock, Clinton tapped her to head economic policy at the Treasury, and then brought her into the White House as a top economist from 1995 to 1997. She had a role in strengthening the CRA and bending industry lending rules.

HUD, moreover, used her thoroughly repudiated study on biased lending to justify raising the Affordable Housing Goals that plunged Fannie and Freddie into the subprime market.

Thanks to Munnell, the myth of structural racism in lending is repeated as an article of faith among the left and continues to influence banking and housing policy even today.

Munnell was a friend of Hillary, as well. In fact, the 1960s Wellesley College graduate served on fellow alumna Hillary Rodham Clinton's secret task force on health-care reform. Federal records show she supported Hillary's run for president, donating $2,300 to her campaign, before contributing to Obama's campaign following his primary win.

Munnell, a well-coifed Beacon Hill Bostonian married to a corporate lawyer, resembles the prototypical salon socialist. While she does not come right out and say she is "socialist," critics certainly can be forgiven for questioning her devotion to the American free-enterprise system. She has problems with Americans getting too rich and wants to soak those who do with punitive taxes. "I don't want to live in a society where the top 1 percent control 37 percent of the assets," Munnell says. "I am really stunned by the increase in the wealth of the wealthy."

To her, income inequality is "unfair." She thinks most wealth has been acquired by "flukishness and luck."

### *15 Percent Tax on 401(k)*

Munnell has such an ax to grind against American capitalism that she once proposed a massive tax on employee pensions and individual retirement accounts to help redistribute wealth to the poor (namely for affordable housing), arguing that pensions benefit mainly the affluent and provide little benefit to minorities and the poor. To that end, she has proposed imposing a onetime 15 percent tax on private pension assets and an annual 15 percent tax on pension contributions. "The time may have come to . . .

introduce some form of . . . taxation" on such retirement funds, she says.

"It is difficult to understand why such a large source of potential revenue is allowed to go untapped," she wrote in the *New England Economic Review* in 1989.

For a supposedly mainstream economist, Munnell has some really extreme—some might say kooky—ideas. In fact, they were so radioactive that she was passed over for a seat on the Federal Reserve Board. It was clear she was too radical to ever be confirmed. Of course, she managed to do ample harm as a Fed research director.

Now a Boston College professor, Munnell has spent virtually her entire career in the public sector, which explains a lot. Before joining the Federal Reserve, she worked for the Brookings Institution, a liberal think tank in Washington. She has coauthored several papers with Peter Orszag, Obama's former budget director, while ensconced in her ivory tower.

Looking back, does she feel any responsibility for the collapse of the mortgage industry? After all, her bombshell study alleging mortgage lenders systematically discriminate against minorities led to the regulations that weakened lending standards and fed the subprime bubble.

Not at all, Munnell says. "The point of that study was never to say, 'Let's go out and lend to people who aren't going to be able to carry the debt,'" she maintains.

Whether it was or not, that is the effect her work had on lending.

What does she say to those older Americans whose nest eggs have been miniaturized to the point where they will have to work, on average, another two years to make up for the investment losses caused by the subprime crisis?

"Suck it up." Seriously, that is what she told *Forbes* in 2009.

## NUMBER 6: ANDREW CUOMO

As demonstrated previously, the former HUD chief was obsessed with closing the "mortgage gap" between blacks and whites, and as a result, pressured Fannie and Freddie to boost minority lending.

Seeing how blacks make up the lion's share of subprime borrowers, Cuomo encouraged the mortgage giants to tap into that market, loading up on subprime mortgages, even though they performed poorly. Cuomo figured that Fannie and Freddie would not be able to find enough "goals-qualifying" mortgages to meet his tougher multicultural mandates, which remained in effect through the 2007 subprime bust, unless they dove into this risky market.

Cuomo encouraged Fannie and Freddie to in fact dominate the subprime market, in both loans and securities, blithely proclaiming that expanding their customer base to credit-impaired minorities made "good business sense." Their underwriting guidelines were too "rigid" to allow such a risky plunge, however. So Cuomo, as their chief regulator, insisted they relax their qualifying standards—to accommodate "minority borrowers who have lower incomes and wealth."

Reluctantly, Fannie and Freddie developed lines of "flexible" mortgages requiring no money down and weaker credit. Soon, the nation's largest subprime lender, Countrywide Financial, became their largest customer. The dodgy loans they underwrote are the source of today's housing calamity.

In a 2000 HUD report, Cuomo cited Munnell's error-ridden study to support the reckless social goals he foisted on Freddie and Fannie. He readily bought into the notion of racist banks.

But castigating bankers for alleged redlining was nothing new to Cuomo, son of liberal Democratic icon Mario Cuomo, former governor of New York. Before joining the Clinton administration, the younger Cuomo served tirelessly as a housing-rights advocate in New York, heading the New York City Commission on the Homeless and the Housing Enterprise for the Less Privileged.

Cuomo, 53, aspires to return to Washington one day as president.

## NUMBER 7: WILLIAM APGAR

Say hello to the new race regulators, same as the old regulators. As Cuomo's senior adviser, William Apgar was convinced banks were subtly discriminating against black borrowers. He could not prove it, but he just knew it was going on.

"Housing discrimination is much more insidious today than it was two to three decades ago," he surmised.

He also suspected Fannie and Freddie were erecting invisible barriers to African-Americans. "There are a lot of loans to black Americans that could be safely purchased by Fannie Mae and Freddie Mac if these companies were more flexible" in their underwriting requirements, argued Apgar, whose official title at the time was "assistant HUD secretary for policy research and development."

Apgar hoped to boost black homeownership into the mid-50 percent range. And to reach that ambitious mark, he helped craft the HUD policy that pushed the mortgage giants' affordable housing targets to 50 percent, which eventually pushed Fannie and Freddie into the subprime abyss. He also was behind the decision allowing the companies to count subprime securities as credit against those aggressive new goals.

"It was a mistake," Apgar said of the securities part of the policy. "In hindsight, I would have done it differently."

He does not, however, regret setting the higher lending goals, which made the securities allowance necessary. His moment of partial regret came in a 2008 interview with the *Washington Post* while he was lecturing at Harvard University—where he taught a course titled "Policy-Making in Urban Settings," and where he directed the Joint Center for Housing Studies' evaluation of the Community Reinvestment Act.

Now Apgar advises Obama's HUD secretary Shaun Donovan. In his new capacity as "senior adviser for mortgage finance" at HUD, Apgar has developed and implemented the Obama administration's "Making Homes Affordable" program and other programs pushing for more politically correct lending.

At 64, Apgar is older but not necessarily wiser. He also proposes extending the Community Reinvestment Act to include independent mortgage companies and other nonbank lenders. "Congress should . . . consider expanding the CRA to include the residential mortgage lending operations of a diverse set of nondepository organizations now playing an increasingly important role in lending," Apgar suggests. "Reform could come either as a result of new rulemaking by federal regulators or new legislation."

### *Sweaty Radicals*

Apgar is fond of housing-rights activists—comfortable around even the most radical among them. In 1999, for example, he met with leaders of National People's Action at the radical group's conference in Washington. NPA had been pressing for more urban loans from Freddie and Fannie, among other demands.

"The night before [the] conference, he came to our hotel, stayed a long time by himself—at one point the air conditioning went out, everybody was sweating, but we all stayed—and he negotiated a very good agreement," said then NPA leader Gale Cincotta.

Apgar is himself a longtime social activist, standing up for the "housing have-nots," as he calls mortgage-less minorities. He cofounded the Leadership Institute at Harvard's Divinity School to help black churches agitate for housing benefits for their communities. The institute includes among its teaching staff Cornel West, an avowed black Marxist.

Apgar's newsletter for the fall of 2007 features Trinity United Church of Christ and its then pastor, Rev. Jeremiah Wright, a militant black nationalist who has damned America in his fiery sermons. "Trinity is known for its inspiring mission work," the institute newsletter gushes, "and as the home church of U.S. Senator Barack Obama."

Apgar also helped found the Committee for Boston Public Housing. His wife, Kristen, a longtime social worker, serves as a Massachusetts state welfare official.

Now back at HUD, this veteran social engineer, well-intentioned or not, may be helping to socially engineer another financial disaster.

## NUMBER 8: ROBERTA ACHTENBERG

Achtenberg is a hard-core San Francisco housing activist who, as a top Clinton HUD official, did everything in her power to turn banks into public utilities. She demanded they make social loans at the expense of profits. Why? She, too, thinks housing is a right—no different from "the right to vote," she argues—and is convinced that banks have a social obligation to underwrite that imagined "right."

She also believes banks are racist. Citing Munnell's spurious work, she said that "the Boston Fed study demonstrated there was definitely a problem of fair lending that the industry needs to address."

At the time the highest-ranking openly homosexual official in federal government, Achtenberg was one of the key HUD officials involved in setting affordable housing goals at HUD and enforcing laws against lending discrimination. And she left an indelible legacy at the department. As an assistant HUD secretary, she completely reorganized the fair-housing enforcement section, ramping up its staff and retraining career investigators to aggressively pursue lenders for alleged discrimination. In fact, she created the department's first office dealing exclusively with banking-related issues, as well as an interagency task force coordinating the administration's anti-redlining campaign.

"I did get a presidential order . . . that created a presidential fair housing council that made it clear to other agencies of the federal government that they, too, had fair housing responsibilities," she said.

Working with the NAACP, moreover, Achtenberg set up a strike force at HUD headquarters and ten fair-housing enforcement centers around the nation to root out alleged lending discrimination using "energetic, imaginative enforcement of civil rights laws." The centers actively solicited complaints from minorities denied loans, and Achtenberg referred many of them for further prosecution to her pal Reno at the Justice Department.

Most key, Achtenberg established historic fair-lending agreements between HUD and Countrywide and several hundred other mortgage lenders unregulated by the CRA, committing them to setting aside greater volumes of subprime and other risky mortgages for minorities with weak credit. In fact, she joined Countrywide chief executive Angelo Mozilo and HUD secretary Henry Cisneros in signing their flagship agreement in October 1994, which, among other things, bound the subprime giant to:

- "develop . . . underwriting standards that broaden credit opportunities for traditionally underserved groups"; and
- "target advertising and marketing efforts to reach potential low-income and minority customers."

Liberalizing lending policies in such a way "gives people who have been disadvantaged a little bit of a better start," Achtenberg rationalized.

### *Punishing Boy Scouts and Bank of America*

Before joining the Clinton administration, Achtenberg directed the National Center for Lesbian Rights. In that role, she championed efforts to force the Boy Scouts of America to accept gay scoutmasters. As a member of the San Francisco Board of Supervisors, Achtenberg sponsored a resolution urging the city to pull $6 million in deposits out of Bank of America to protest its donations to the Boy Scouts.

Before joining the board of supervisors, she served as dean of law at the now-defunct New College of California, a small alternative college in San Francisco that focuses on the study of social activism. The school's motto was: Education for a Just, Sacred, and Sustainable World.

As for Achtenberg's own academic background, she studied at Berkeley University before enrolling in law school, which she did because, in her words, "I thought it was a way of doing social justice." She worked for 15 years as a civil-rights attorney.

Upon her nomination to HUD, former San Francisco mayor Art Agnos said Achtenberg would draw from her own experience of fighting prejudice as a lesbian. "She will bring an insight into what discrimination feels like," Agnos said. "It gives her an extra sensitivity for those who are vulnerable in our society, . . . because she has felt the lash herself." And indeed, she pursued that victimhood agenda with a militant passion.

The 60-year-old Achtenberg is now a fair-housing consultant to the Bank of San Francisco. A major Obama supporter, who according to FEC records donated $2,300 to the Obama Victory Fund and another $2,300 to Obama for America, she helped lead Obama's presidential transition, recommending personnel for key posts in his administration.

As disclosed earlier, Achtenberg's old HUD office and position as assistant secretary for fair housing and equal opportunity is now occupied by former Clinton colleague and fellow San Franciscan, John Trasviña, who formerly headed the radical Latino group MALDEF.

## NUMBER 9: ALLEN FISHBEIN

Another crusading zealot for fair lending, Fishbein was Apgar's adviser at HUD; however, he is less repentant than his old boss.

Fishbein says the Bush HUD should have used its regulatory power to stop Fannie and Freddie from loading up on so many subprime loans—the very mortgages that he and other higher-ups at the Clinton HUD got them addicted to underwriting.

"They chose not to put the brakes on this dangerous lending when they could have," Fishbein argued, even though it was Fishbein who'd cut the brake lines.

In a recent interview with the *Village Voice*, he was reluctant to say anything critical about the regulations he helped develop while at HUD. That's because he's a radical housing-rights activist who's never seen a banking regulation he did not like. Before joining the Clinton HUD, Fishbein was a big CRA booster who lobbied to expand the regulation to cover insurers and credit unions. In fact, he helped found and run the notorious NCRC, the most aggressive CRA lobbying group in Washington. Fishbein also served as general counsel for the Center for Community Change, the socialist group in Washington that ACORN's former top lobbyist now runs.

## NUMBER 10: MEL MARTINEZ

The Bush administration for the most part continued Clinton's housing polices, only with greater emphasis on affordable housing for Hispanic immigrants. Spearheading these efforts was HUD secretary Mel Martinez, who, like his predecessors, believed in universal homeownership for minorities.

Following President Bush's own directive to boost minority homeownership, Martinez further strengthened HUD's authority over Fannie and Freddie, ratcheting up the main Affordable Housing Goal to 52 percent from the 50 percent set by the Clinton administration. He also added new subgoals. "The administration strongly supports retaining and enhancing the housing goals at HUD," Martinez told Congress in 2003.

In addition, he championed the so-called American Dream Downpayment Initiative, calling it a major achievement of HUD during his tenure. Congress allocated $163 million for the federal program to subsidize low-income and minority homebuyers.

▼

These were the masterminds of the greatest heist of all time. Next you will meet the hold-up men with whom these suits in Washington conspired—the inner-city activists, agitators, and street toughs who actually provided the muscle for the operation.

# SEVEN

# THE BANK "TERRORISTS"

Who's on your hit list, NPA?
Who's on your hit list for today?
Take no prisoners, take no names.
Kick 'em in the a— when they play their games.
Fight! Fight! Fight! Because housing is a right!

— anti-bank battle cries of Chicago-based National People's Action

In 1999, as chairman of the Senate Banking Committee, Phil Gramm strenuously warned that President Clinton's tightening of Community Reinvestment Act rules had given license and means to anti-redlining groups to blackmail banks for "kickbacks and bribes," something I call "redmail." A proviso Clinton added to the law urged banks to donate to such groups to earn Brownie points with regulators. Gramm, whose home later was trashed by thugs sent by the groups to silence him, called the process "little more than extortion."

Little did he know how right he was.

Terrified of similar threats and protests over their merger plans, which require approval by CRA regulators, banks pledged billions of dollars in urban loans to ACORN and other radical community organizers to make them go away. The size of these "commitments" mushroomed in the run-up to the subprime crisis.

For example, Chase, in its 1995 merger with Chemical Bank, announced a five-year commitment of $18 billion. But in its 2004 merger with Bank One, Chase committed a whopping $800 billion over 10 years—a 40-fold increase.

All told, community organizers have shaken the banking industry down for an eye-popping $6.1 trillion (yes, that is trillion with a *t*) in total CRA agreements and commitments to poor and minority communities (and yet they still grumble about "systematic redlining and disinvestment" in such communities). The dubious achievement is proudly brayed by the National Community Reinvestment Coalition, the nation's top CRA lobbyist, which tallied the figure. To put it into perspective, the entire gross domestic product of Japan, the world's second largest economy, is $5 trillion.

As if this mugging of the $13 trillion-in-assets banking industry were not enough, now these groups are lobbying for a bigger club and eyeing banks for bigger inner-city subsidies—even though the industry is in virtual full compliance with current CRA requirements. They are demanding tougher and more frequent CRA exams, along with stiffer penalties for noncompliance, now that they have less leverage against banks in the drought of merger activity. Under the CRA, they can block a bank's ability to expand by crying racist redlining. But the largest banks in the country have become much larger and will likely be involved in fewer mergers in coming years, leaving the CRA examination process as the only way activists can wring more unprofitable loans from banks.

Regrettably, such pay-offs are the price of doing business in a post-Clinton banking world, financial industry analysts say. If you want to play, you have to pay these goons protection money or you will be picketed as a racist and suffer poor CRA ratings.

Bank executives know they are going to be held up for more and more risky loans, and they have simply learned to write them off as "strategic losses." "Most bankers have learned to make it a business," says Janet Lamkin, former head of Bank of America's operations in California. "They've learned to adapt."

What's truly sad is that this multicultural protection racket has cost banks literally hundreds of billions of dollars that could have been plowed back into business operations. Such strategic investments would have made them stronger and helped them weather today's credit crisis.

On the other hand, the race racket has been very lucrative for community organizers. They have pocketed more than $10 billion from the corporate commitments they have extracted over the past decade. These bank profits have gone to pay for just the salaries and services (such as "credit counseling") of the nonprofit organizers. Many of their honchos pull down six-figure salaries, as we shall see further on.

Like a host sustaining parasites, the banking industry is effectively bankrolling its enemies. Here are the five most dangerous bank hold-up gangs—the street muscle who helped the masterminds in Washington clean out your retirement fund in the name of "fair lending":

## NEIGHBORHOOD ASSISTANCE CORPORATION OF AMERICA

Commonly known as NACA, this Boston-based nonprofit is run by a self-described "banking terrorist," who has essentially "blackmailed banks into making bad home loans in inner cities. Now those loans are defaulting by the millions, and he is blaming banks," according to *Investor's Business Daily.*

NACA founder Bruce Marks, who grew up in an affluent suburb of New York City, started NACA during the Clinton years to fulfill his own "warped sense of the American dream. He thinks owning a home is a right, not a goal. And he thinks every American should have a house—even those who cannot afford one." He also thinks banks are racist.

Critics say Marks sees victims wherever he sees a bank.

"Bruce has a Messiah complex," says Boston real estate analyst John C. Anderson. "He refuses to differentiate between people suffering discrimination and people who are legitimately bad credit risks."

The angry "pit bull," who boasts of "terrorizing" banks, has legally (thanks to the CRA) extorted billions of dollars from Citigroup, Bank of America, and other large banks to subsidize uncreditworthy borrowers in minority neighborhoods, where he has accused the banks of "redlining."

In 2004, for example, he threatened to blow up a merger deal between Bank of America and Fleet Bank by complaining to regulators that the banks were not making enough loans to minorities under the Community Reinvestment Act. The banks, in turn, paid him off with $6 billion in mortgage commitments for borrowers with weak credit.

Then Bank of America CEO "Ken Lewis announced this huge commitment at NACA's headquarters," NACA crows on its Web site. "This was televised live nationwide with hundreds of NACA members, community leaders and bankers in attendance." As Marks took the podium to announce the deal, Lewis and Fleet CEO Chad Gifford looked on, grimacing. Their pained looks told it all: they clearly were not happy having to share a stage with an "extortionist," as former senator Phil Gramm once called Marks, who had "targeted" them for massive shakedown.

The nonprofit NACA uses such ransom money to fund its own mortgages to high-risk borrowers without requiring down payments or good credit. Marks considers such underwriting requirements "patronizing and racist."

He boasts that 99 percent of the mortgage applications taken through NACA are approved, giving new meaning to the term "easy lending." Listen to NACA's pitch as Marks tells it: "Come to NACA, and regardless of how bad your credit is, regardless of how little you have saved, we will work with you for as long as it takes, until you are prepared for a mortgage better than what the wealthiest, most connected borrowers get."

"These are the ['liberal underwriting'] standards NACA and ACORN and other bank terrorists foisted on the banking industry, using as their cudgel the [CRA], which mandates (under threat of severe penalty) that banks make inner-city loans to people who cannot afford them," *IBD* notes. "Now these groups have the nerve to demonize the banks for the inevitable foreclosures."

NACA, a nonprofit group certified by HUD to counsel deadbeat borrowers, rakes in more than $5 million a year in administrative fees from banks and the government to service high-risk loans. In 2007, the year before they collapsed, Fannie Mae and Freddie Mac donated a combined $3.5 million to the group.

Marks, a former union activist, "makes a good living shaking down banks for loans to deadbeat borrowers that he thinks are entitled to homes." Federal tax records show he pays himself a healthy $150,000 salary, not including what he pays his lawyer wife, who is employed at NACA as a top officer.

How many of NACA's borrowers default on NACA's own loans? We do not know. Marks will not disclose his internal data.

But by the end of the 1990s, when Marks made high-profile announcements of megapledges from banks in the presence of Clinton staffers, more than 8 percent of the mortgages NACA had arranged through Fleet Bank were delinquent, compared with the national average of 1.9 percent, according to a review of foreclosure proceedings against loans made for banks by NACA at that time. In other words, long before the mortgage crisis, NACA's loans underperformed at a rate four times the industry average.

And NACA bails delinquent borrowers out with a so-called "stabilization fund." Those who cannot make their mortgage payments can tap into this pool of assistance. Delinquencies would be even higher without it.

Congress's banking committee chiefs, Senator Chris Dodd and Representative Barney Frank, have demanded banks stop foreclosures; and guess who they have invited to testify about it? That's right: Marks, who has proposed stopping all resets on subprime adjustable mortgages and allowing late payments for up to 90 days.

"Marks insists that regulators 'force' lenders to restructure their loans to prevent foreclosures from going forward. 'For noncooperative lenders,' he says, 'the regulators can and must impose "cease and desist" orders.'"

In 2008, as Fannie buckled under the weight of politically mandated loans, he and about 100 urban protesters stormed Fannie's headquarters in Washington, demanding it stop foreclosures on subprime houses—the same homes his group pressured Fannie to fund.

"As usual, the bullying tactics worked: Fannie Mae is now reviewing every foreclosure, while increasing the number of mortgages it restructures by lowering interest rates and extending loan terms to make payments more affordable."

Now Marks, flush with millions in shakedown fees, is recruiting an "army" of 1,000 new full-time bank terrorists for deployment against "predatory lenders" and bank executives who he says "have amassed huge fortunes on the backs of hardworking American families [w]hile living in their many luxurious homes."

NACA's current nationwide staff of around 500, along with hundreds of thousands of members, are more than 90 percent people of color. Their aggressive street-fighting tactics are legendary. Nobody is off-limits, not even children. In fact, they have sent goons to picket outside the schools attended by the kids of bank CEOs they have targeted for attack, badgering the tots about their daddies' actions. The thuggish tactics usually work. Hounded CEOs eventually sit down with the bank extortionists and sign deals.

"Every aspect of their lives is open to attack—their friends, neighbors, coworkers, employees, family," NACA openly boasts on its Web site. It says it is proud of its "junkyard dog approach." When banks hold their annual shareholders meetings at hotel ballrooms, NACA rents rooms for protesters so they can get inside the hotel. Once past security, they then "infiltrate" and disrupt the meetings by jumping up and demonstrating as CEOs speak.

NACA brags that it has extracted in excess of $10 billion in loan commitments from banks—money they could have used to protect their balance sheets against insolvency instead of protecting themselves from such bank terrorists.

With 31 offices throughout the country now, NACA hopes to double in size over the next few years under the friendlier Obama administration.

> For future underwriting practices, Marks urges lenders to adopt the NACA model.
>
> "NACA has done lending the right way," he maintains. "No down payment. No closing costs. No fees. No perfect credit. At a below-market fixed rate."
>
> And no repayment or profit. Call it Marksism.

## NATIONAL PEOPLE'S ACTION NETWORK

Taking ACORN's place as the left's rent-a-mob for "racial and economic justice" is Chicago-based NPA, originally named the National People's Action on Housing. It bussed in the goon squad that trampled Gramm's private property after he threatened to scale back the CRA.

The NPA gang sings a charming battle hymn before ambushing victims and their families:

*Who's on your hit list, NPA?*
*Who's on your hit list for today?*
*Take no prisoner, take no names,*
*Kick 'em in the a—when they play their games.*

The swarming thugs even turn on their own. In the late 1990s, NPA bussed some 800 angry protesters to Washington to picket the home of Clinton's second housing secretary, Andrew Cuomo, when it felt he was not doing enough in the way of housing subsidies. Cuomo promptly ratcheted up minority lending targets at Fannie and Freddie. Fannie also caved in to NPA's demands by lowering credit standards. To guard against future threats, the mortgage giant began sponsoring conferences organized by NPA. Anything to appease such bank terrorists.

One of NPA's founding board members is none other than Obama's longtime mentor and trusted adviser in Chicago, Northwestern University professor John McKnight. Known as the father of the CRA, he helped Obama get into Harvard Law School. (It's also worth noting that First Lady Michelle Obama is listed with McKnight as a current "faculty member" at the Asset-Based Community Development Institute in Chicago. ABCD was co-founded by McKnight.)

With a fellow community organizer in the White House, NPA says the time is ripe to "take the lead on advancing a national racial and economic justice platform on housing and banking issues." It says the mortgage crisis has turned people off to free-market principles and made them more receptive to public restructuring of financial markets.

"As a result of this crisis, conservative ideas and policies are being discredited," NPA advises its members. "We now have a chance to push for fundamental changes in housing, banking, and credit markets," including "sweeping regulatory reforms." And with the "first African American president," the group says, they have a chance to "correct the injustices of the past."

To that end, NPA's chairman Eugene Barnes has met with administration officials, and even joined Obama as he signed the bank reform bill into law. The law includes a consumer protection agency pushed by NPA.

Next up: expanding the CRA to the insurance and securities industries in order to "gain greater public control of economic decision-making," according to NPA's 2008 platform statement.

To keep pressure on Washington to advance its radically anti-capitalist agenda, the group has organized battalions of street agitators through its 135 affiliates across the country.

"Housing is our right, and we gonna take it!" a black woman shouted into a megaphone at an NPA rally in Washington in 2009. A sign at the rally read: "Neighborhoods, not banks."

One particularly popular NPA training session provides "hands-on techniques for organizing anger," according to one of the group's brochures. NPA is the militant wing of the National Training and Information Center, or NTIC, an Alinsky group started in the 1970s.

The HUD-funded NPA lists among its larger goals using "the government as our tool to . . . correct the injustices of the past and redistribute resources equitably." Also on its wish list: "a Constitutional amendment that guarantees the right to housing—safe, decent, affordable housing," a dream shared by White House regulation czar Cass Sunstein.

During a breakout workshop at NPA's 2009 conference in Washington, NPA leaders spoke of "reparations." On a large wipe board, they listed under the heading "Targets" the names of politicians standing in their way.

Among its accomplishments, NPA lists "passage of the Community Reinvestment Act" and striking national lending agreements with Fannie Mae. "In the 1990s," it adds, "NPA worked with then-Attorney General Janet Reno to reform regulations to allow community groups to receive up to 15 percent of assets, as well as real property, that can be used to benefit the community."

## NATIONAL COMMUNITY REINVESTMENT COALITION

Known by the acronym NCRC, the National Community Reinvestment Coalition is the top CRA lobbyist in Washington. The nonprofit group states that its mission is to "increase fair and equal access to credit, capital, and banking services and products," adding that it is "at the vanguard of a growing economic justice movement" in which community organizers are redirecting the "flow of capital" to urban areas using "fair lending" tools such as the CRA.

NCRC's president, John E. Taylor, has huddled with key Obama Cabinet officials, including the secretaries of Treasury and Housing and Urban Development, over the issues of affordable housing, "predatory lending," and overhauling the nation's banking regulations. Taylor, in fact, joined the president at the ceremony in which he signed the recent landmark financial-reform bill, which adopted many of Taylor's ideas. (It was Taylor's scheme, for example, to collect data on minority small business lending to police banks for racism in commercial loans.) He now is lobbying hard for regulatory changes that would pump the CRA full of steroids. Among other things, he wants regulators to attack "reverse redlining" by pressuring banks to "promote borrowers from the subprime to prime mortgage market," even if they have "less-than-perfect credit."

NCRC maintains its own "civil rights enforcement division," which engages in what it calls "mystery shopping." This involves NCRC staffers, both black and white, going into banks posing as loan seekers. Their goal essentially is to entrap mortgage loan officers and brokers into making discriminatory statements or decisions (or at least treating black customers differently than white customers), then report what they find back to federal regulators and prosecutors.

Boston-educated Taylor proves there is big money to be had in shaking down banks in the name of civil rights. He has come a long way from the days when he advocated for the homeless in Beantown. He does not mention it in his bios or his press appearances, but he is now chairman of the board of a CRA-qualified investment mutual fund with close to $1 billion in assets under management.

In 1999, as his nonprofit group was lobbying HUD to hike affirmative-lending targets at Fannie and Freddie, where he served as an affordable-housing adviser, he helped start the CRAFund to invest in Fannie and Freddie securities backed by riskier nonprime loans. Banks that invest in his fund, managed by Community Capital Management, earn credit for CRA investments. The mutual fund, in turn, pays his NCRC lobbying group a .05-percent cut of the fund's average net assets. The racket has netted NCRC and Taylor hundreds of thousands of dollars.

SEC records show that Taylor also has a personal vested interest in the fund that he set up to exploit federal banking regulations. He beneficially owns an equity stake worth tens of thousands of dollars—on top of his compensation as chairman of the board.

And that is all in addition to the generous compensation he receives from NCRC, which in 2007 totaled more than $530,000, according to the group's latest reported federal tax filing.

In short, Taylor, who also serves on the board of Jesse Jackson's Rainbow/PUSH Coalition, is personally profiting from the social policies for which he lobbies.

He says the CRA is good for minorities. But it has been very, very good to him.

## GREENLINING INSTITUTE

Another housing-rights group militating against banks is the San Francisco–based Greenlining Institute, which actually advised Financial Crisis Inquiry Commission chairman Phil Angelides on where to invest California state funds last decade when he was state treasurer. Greenlining provided Angelides with its own CRA report card, giving high marks to banks that greenlined loans for minorities beyond even the strict requirements of the CRA.

"This helps us spot the banks that are great players in community reinvestment," an impressed Angelides said in an interview with the *American Banker* at the time. "It helps us make judgments about where to put our resources."

Angelides, in turn, steered billions of dollars in state funds to CRA-friendly banks that loaded up on subprime and other risky investments. Beginning in 1999, he sank billions more into subprime securities backed by Freddie Mac. And he did not let up until he left office in 2007, the year the subprime bubble burst.

It marked the first time a state had bought mortgage-backed securities based on home loans made under CRA guidelines. "There's a first time for everything," Angelides blithely responded at the time. He insisted the state's investment in such loans was a sound one.

But that hardly was his justification. Echoing Greenlining's battle cry, Angelides argued that "the gap between America's rich and poor threatens the fabric of our society," and that more financial resources needed to be targeted to underserved communities through the CRA. He remarked that banks are a "ballast" for investment in such communities. He urged the state's two biggest pension funds—the California Public Employees Retirement System and the California Teachers Retirement System—to invest more in the state's urban communities. They took his advice and have suffered huge losses as a result.

In short, the head of the commission tasked with solving the subprime crime joined forces with one of the worst bank shakedown gangs in the country to fuel the subprime crisis as California's investment chief.

For the past decade, Greenlining has bled even financial giants like Wells Fargo and Bank of America for billions of dollars in affirmative-action "commitments" for its clients—money that the $18 million-in-net assets Greenlining turned around and used to finance the staff and operations they need to conduct even greater bloodsucking. They also used their blood money to pay deadbeat borrowers millions in down payments. These borrowers, in turn, use the down payments to go back to Wells Fargo and Bank of America and secure loans they never should have gotten in the first place.

In effect, these banks have been paying customers to borrow money from them, all in the name of diversity.

Think about that for a moment: The banking industry has forked over billions to these race-baiting parasites for down payments, the very cornerstone of the lending business. Not only do the deadbeat borrowers who use them really have no stake in the houses they buy, but the banks essentially forfeit their profits in those loans.

Greenlining, which recently gave an award to House Financial Services Committee Chairman Barney Frank, used the CRA to leverage Bank of America and Wells Fargo for record loan set-asides for uncreditworthy minorities, then demanded even more money when they announced merger plans, filing protests with the Federal Reserve to delay their bids. Now with the subprime foreclosure crisis draining wealth from urban areas, it demands broadening the CRA from credit allocation to "wealth creation." Never mind that the CRA sped foreclosures by promoting such loans.

"For every dollar of wealth owned by a white family, an African-American or Latino family owns just 16 cents," Greenlining complained to federal regulators during a CRA hearing held in Los Angeles in August 2010. "Expanding the CRA is the best way to . . . address the large and growing racial wealth gap," because right now the regulation "lacks the power to truly address the inequities."

To close the wealth gap, Greenlining's executive director Orson Aguilar proposes going well beyond mortgages. He insists Washington regulators monitor all financial firms to ensure that they are promoting racial diversity in:

- business ownership;
- business contracts;
- equity investments;
- checking accounts;
- savings accounts;
- retirement accounts;
- ownership of stock; and
- employment.

"We also urge that every industry that benefits in any way from federal government fiscal or monetary policy be subject to [the] CRA," argues Aguilar, formerly a fellow with the Congressional Hispanic Caucus Institute. That, of course, would include all of corporate America.

Aguilar says the CRA's goal should be focusing on "creating wealth building opportunities" in communities of color. But his proposals have nothing to do with building wealth and everything to do with redistributing it. He sees the financial sector as a pie, and the CRA as a knife, albeit one in need of sharpening.

Federal tax records show that Greenlining's former executive director, John Gamboa, pulled down a cool $167,958 in compensation. Interestingly, the records also show that Washington Mutual Bank held the mortgage to the nonprofit group's headquarters. The bankrupt WaMu is now considered a "predatory" subprime lender.

The same 2006 filing also lists among other Greenlining liabilities an unsecured $500,000 note issued by Wells Fargo. The interest rate: 2 percent. Talk about a sweetheart loan!

## ASSOCIATION OF COMMUNITY ORGANIZATIONS FOR REFORM NOW (ACORN)

Reeling from scandal, ACORN reportedly is on the verge of bankruptcy and folding its national operations. But the damage this Obama-tied group already has done to banks is deep. In the 1990s, ACORN lobbyists had remarkable influence over banking and housing policies in Washington. It was their idea to lower Fannie's and Freddie's underwriting guidelines, charging they were "discriminatory." It was their idea to count food stamps and other welfare as qualifying income. And it was their idea to pressure Fannie and Freddie to package subprime and other CRA-eligible mortgages to reduce originators' risk and free up more money to lend to minorities and others with weak credit.

"For over two decades," the group crows on its Web site, "ACORN has waged a campaign against redlining; worked to increase access to credit for low-income and minority neighborhoods; and fought for greater community reinvestment by financial institutions."

"Fought" is putting it mildly. ACORN has used the CRA as a club to beat money out of banks. It has staged in-your-face protests in bank lobbies, drive-through lanes, and even at bank executives' homes to get them to issue risky loans in the inner city or face charges of racism. In short, ACORN has made a career of stalking bank "bigots" for billions of dollars in affirmative-action loans.

Take for example its coordinated attack on Wells Fargo and Norwest Corporation. As the financial giants were attempting to merge in the late 1990s, ACORN complained to federal regulators that they discriminated against minority loan applicants—charges that, as usual, proved unfounded.

"Why reward this racist, classist performance?" ACORN spokeswoman Marcia Erickson hissed.

Outside a Federal Reserve hearing on the planned merger, militant ACORN protesters chanted: "Norwest and Wells Fargo, Hey, Hey, Say No" and "Ripping off the poor: We won't take it anymore." They also carried placards reading: "Stop Redlining: Community Reinvestment Now."

The swarming shakedown tactics worked. Wells Fargo set a goal of making a minimum of 35 percent of mortgage loans to minority homebuyers. The bank later committed to making $1 billion in riskier CRA loans.

"ACORN knows that corporate America has no starch in their shorts and, therefore, what they try to do is buy peace from groups that agitate against them," said black conservative Robert L. Woodson at the time. "The same corporations that pay ransom to Jesse Jackson and Al Sharpton pay ransom to ACORN."

As more and more banks agreed to underwrite risky subprime loans, ACORN switched tactics and complained about "predatory lending." It attacked the banking industry for doing too well what it blamed them for not doing a decade earlier. "They drove us into minority communities, and now they say we're too aggressive," one exasperated HSBC Bank executive told me, throwing up his hands. "We're damned if we do, damned if we don't."

HSBC's subprime mortgage unit a few years ago got full-frontal ACORN. After the group accused HSBC of using "loan shark" tactics with minority customers, it deployed rowdy picketers to its branches, waving inflatable plastic sharks. ACORN continued to harass the bank until it agreed to pay settlements totaling more than half a billion dollars.

In 2004, ACORN also went gunning for Wells Fargo in a "shark hunter caravan," alleging it was targeting African-Americans for high-cost subprime loans. "There is not a shred of truth in ACORN's allegations" of "predatory lending," a Wells Fargo spokesman said at the time. The bank said the group was deliberately trying to "distort and misrepresent our business practices."

"Pricing for consumer loans is just like pricing for insurance," the San Francisco–based company explained. "The greater the risk the higher the price." Every one of the so-called victims of predatory lending whom ACORN trotted out for the press melted away under the facts, which showed these black borrowers brought to the negotiating table a lot of debt or delinquencies on past loans—negatives that weighed heavily in the type of mortgage they received.

But such facts do not matter to ACORN. A sign that ACORN goons hammered into the front lawn of a harassed banker's home in Philadelphia reveals its real agenda. The sign said: "Foreclosed for non-payment of moral debt!" In other words, banks owe blacks, not the other way around.

ACORN was founded in 1970 in Little Rock, Arkansas, by Wade Rathke, a welfare-rights activist and friend of Bill and Hillary. Thanks to generous federal grants and corporate donations, he grew the local organization into a national powerhouse with more than 850 chapters and 350,000 members.

ACORN developed a strong presence in Chicago, its main chapter, and Obama trained its leaders there in the hardball street tactics of Alinskyite organizing. "Barack has proven himself among our members," said then ACORN director Madeline Talbott. These ACORN leaders, in turn, trained the group's mostly black members, who stormed banks by the busloads as CRA shakedown artists, using "body power" to make their point—whether it was conducting sit-ins at Citibank's headquarters or dumping uncollected trash in the offices of targeted executives. Their intimidation tactics were feared and resented by bankers.

"I've been fighting alongside ACORN my entire career," Obama proudly said in a 2007 speech to ACORN. ACORN endorsed his presidential campaign, and Obama funneled more than $830,000 to ACORN and its subsidiaries to help him get out the vote. "We accept and respect him as a kindred spirit, a fellow organizer," said Talbott, who's bragged of dragging bankers "kicking and screaming" into Chicago's West Side and other ghettos.

The Obama connection put ACORN in the national spotlight, exposing for the first time its corrupt practices. Rathke was accused of covering up an embezzlement scandal involving his brother, Dale Rathke, who allegedly pilfered almost $1 million in ACORN funds. ACORN did not inform the police. A whistleblower revealed the fraud in 2008, leading to the departure of the

Rathkes. (Despite a pattern of malfeasance, ACORN has received at least $53 million in federal grants and other funds since 1994, according to an analysis by the *Washington Examiner.*)

Interestingly, ACORN's board retained First Lady Michelle Obama's former law firm in Chicago to represent it in the case. The Obamas met at the firm, Sidley Austin LLP, when Barack interned there after his first year at Harvard Law School.

Despite all the bad press during the campaign, ACORN did not miss a beat in its shakedown. In 2008, Bank of America, which previously set up (under ACORN threat) "flexible underwriting" programs for minorities, pledged to give ACORN another $2 million in donations. This helped the organization's local chapters from New York to Arkansas stay open despite mounting corruption charges and financial woes. (Bank of America says it since has stopped donating to ACORN.)

ACORN's influence has not gone away. In fact, it has permeated the White House. Obama appointed an SEIU union official with close ties to ACORN as his national political director. Patrick Gaspard, an African-American who runs the White House office of political affairs, worked closely with ACORN boss Bertha Lewis. His brother Michael, moreover, has done communications work for ACORN.

And Lewis has said she continues to have a close working relationship with Gaspard in the White House, as well as with HUD secretary Shaun Donovan. This should come as no shock, as ACORN officials had a direct line to the last Democrat White House. And they met monthly with Clinton's first housing secretary, while helping revise the 1995 CRA regulations to aid their own shakedown efforts.

Also, then HUD chief Henry Cisneros made sure HUD-regulated Fannie and Freddie contributed to ACORN. Fannie alone has donated more than $800,000 to the group. HUD itself has directed millions of dollars in grants to ACORN, a HUD-certified "credit counselor." In 2006 alone, according to federal tax records, ACORN received $2.3 million in government grants, which means taxpayers helped fund their own plunder.

"What has ACORN accomplished?" its Web site asks. Among other things, it has "forced Fannie Mae to establish a precedent-setting program to buy community reinvestment mortgages."

▼

ACORN wormed its way into the mortgage business through the CRA, which it helped draft and protect. "ACORN has fought every threat to the CRA" by the banking lobby, it boasts on its Web site, and "stands ready to repeat the fight whenever the threat reappears."

In effect, Clinton's brawnier CRA created a multitrillion-dollar shakedown industry that has devastated the financial industry. The graveyard of banks bullied into making unsafe loans by ACORN and its clones piles higher and higher. These financial concerns have imploded trying to meet the government's social goals and not their own business goals.

And many of the survivors have merged with other banks to form bigger and bigger conglomerates. So the real loser is the average bank customer denied the lower fees and rates and other benefits that come with healthy competition. All because of a stubborn myth, which we debunk next.

EIGHT

# MYTH OF THE RACIST WHITE LENDER

The picture for Asians differs greatly from that for blacks.

— Federal Reserve report on minority lending

Like her husband, Hillary Clinton is conveniently now a critic of subprime lending. She has tried to portray whites as the main beneficiaries of prime mortgage lending and every minority group as "victims" of "predatory" subprime lending. As subprime mortgage foreclosures began to mount during her presidential run, she claimed that the financial pain of such borrowing "falls disproportionately on African-Americans, on Hispanics, on a lot of Asians."

This certainly is the prevailing wisdom among the East Coast elite and the underprivileged classes they deign to protect. It assumes racist bankers automatically lend to whites and offer them the best deals on loans, while parking all other ethnic groups in "abusive loans"—or no loans at all.

"The reality in our country remains one of a dual lending marketplace in which white and affluent communities enjoy a wide range of product choice, while minority and working-class communities are stuck with the high-cost home mortgage lenders," says the aforementioned John Taylor. (Recall that Taylor is president of the National Community Reinvestment Coalition, the radical Washington lobby group that has done much to shape conventional thinking—and legislation—on the issue.)

But conventional wisdom has not looked at the numbers, which paint a far different reality.

Data collected by federal regulators show that Asian-Americans—not whites—are the preferred bank customer, if there is such a thing. Contrary to Clinton's assumption, Asians decidedly are *not* victims of high-cost subprime lending. In fact, they get the best loans of all—better even than whites. They also are the least likely ethnic group, on average, to be rejected for any kind of loan.

"Whereas statistics are touted that the African-American [loan] denial rate is twice the white denial rate and that means discrimination, those very same statistics indicate that the white denial rate is almost double the Asian denial rate," points out Andrew Sandler, a Washington lawyer specializing in the CRA and other bank regulation compliance. "So these statistics, if they're read that way, would also be suggesting that whites are discriminated against vis-a-vis Asians."

Does this mean the banking industry is racist against whites?

Of course not. It simply means Asians are better qualified for prime loans. The lower the risk, the better the rate, and Asian applicants tend to present the lowest risk of defaulting on loans.

**DEFAULT RATES BY RACE**

Asian-Americans typically default least on loans

| | |
|---|---|
| Black | 9% |
| Native American | 6% |
| Hispanic | 5% |
| White | 4% |
| Asian | 3% |

Source: Federal Reserve Board

"The picture for Asians differs greatly from that for blacks," confirms a recent Federal Reserve report on minority lending disparities, which takes credit histories into account. The study found that Asians on average enjoy the highest credit ratings of all races, which is the key variable lenders use to set mortgage interest rates. They also exhibit the lowest default rates. Blacks, in contrast, tend to have the worst credit records, along with the highest default rates. In fact, they typically are three times as likely as Asians to default on their loans.

These trends have played out in the housing bust. The *New York Times* looked at census tracts in the Tri-State area, for example, and found that black areas had three times more foreclosures than others. Meanwhile, Asian-Americans not only held on to their homes but took out new mortgages. In 2007, as the number of new mortgages fell sharply for blacks in New York City, the number of Asian borrowers rose by 6 percent.

## 1 IN 2 BLACKS HAVE BAD CREDIT

Lost in all the knee-jerk outrage over banks allegedly discriminating against blacks is the fact that almost half—47 percent—have poor credit, according to a major study by Freddie Mac. And they pose the highest risk to lenders, who in the past protected themselves by either denying loans or charging higher rates for them (now they are loath to do either for fear of being branded racist).

Even black banks reject risky black borrowers. The largest black-owned thrift—Seaway Bank and Trust Company—which happens to be based in President Obama's hometown of Chicago—and Carver Federal Savings Bank—which is based near former President Clinton's office in Harlem—have been cited by anti-redlining regulators over the years. "Such institutions have come under criticism primarily because they have not been aggressive enough in lending to low-income borrowers within their community," says former FDIC and Federal Reserve official Vern McKinley.

Federal statistics show that even at minority-owned banks, the loan-denial rate for blacks and Hispanics is significantly higher than the rate for whites and Asians.

**LOAN DENIAL RATES AT MINORITY-OWNED BANKS**

| | |
|---|---|
| Hispanics | 26% |
| Blacks | 25% |
| Whites | 16% |
| Asians | 7% |

Source: Federal Reserve Board

Are black bankers racist too? Of course not. They are just businesspeople making business decisions. And bad credit is bad business.

Bad credit also explains the even wider "credit gap" in minority small-business lending, a major concern of the Obama administration, which like the Clinton administration has launched a multifront offensive against banks to close it, as detailed in an earlier chapter.

While black-owned firms are more than twice as likely to be denied loans as white-owned firms, they are also likelier to have bad credit and default on loans than white owners, as Federal Reserve data show. In fact, black owners are three times as likely to have bankruptcies and judgments against them as white owners. They also tend to pose substantially greater risk to commercial lenders than Latino owners.

## MINORITY BUSINESS LENDING

Black-owned firms are twice as likely to get rejected for a loan as white-owned firms . . . *

| | | |
|---|---|---|
| % of small-business loan applications denied, by race of owner | Black – 62.3% | White – 28.8% |

. . . but are nearly twice as likely to default than firms owned by other racial groups . . . **

| | | | |
|---|---|---|---|
| % of firms posing significant-to-high risk of loan default, by race | Black – 45.1% | White – 27.6% | Hispanic – 37.3% |

. . . and black owners are generally less creditworthy in every category.***

| | | | |
|---|---|---|---|
| % of firms delinquent in business obligations, by race | Black – 21.2% | White – 13.3% | Hispanic – 16.1% |
| % of owners delinquent on personal obligations, by race | Black – 30.4% | White – 11.6% | Hispanic – 13.1% |
| % of owners with judgments against them, by race | Black – 9.7% | White – 3.3% | Hispanic – 6.6% |
| % of owners declaring bankruptcy in past 7 years, by race | Black – 6.0% | White – 2.2% | Hispanic – 4.6% |

* Source: Federal Reserve

** Source: Dun & Bradstreet

*** Sources: Federal Reserve, National Survey of Small Business Finances, The Review of Economics and Statistics (November 2003)

"Black-owned firms were generally less creditworthy than firms owned by other racial groups," notes National Bureau of Economic Research economist David Blanchflower in a major study on small-business credit conducted last decade.

Some argue that bad credit is a function of chronic poverty, which affects blacks to a greater degree; therefore loan officers should cut blacks some slack. "Blacks have been disadvantaged in many ways for a long time, and that is going to show up in credit reports," argues former Clinton official Alicia Munnell. (Munnell is the economics professor whose fundamentally flawed study on lending discrimination at the Boston Fed ignited the movement to socialize mortgages and ease bank credit for risky customers.)

Only, the credit problem is not limited to lower-income blacks. Even wealthier blacks are more likely to miss payments or default on loans, suggesting the issue is more cultural than economic. This is corroborated by a comprehensive study by Freddie Mac, which found that even among higher-income earners, far more black people have bad credit than Asian minorities or whites. Slightly more than 1 in 3 African-Americans earning as much as $75,000 a year have impaired credit, compared with 1 in 5 whites—and fewer than 1 in 8 Asian-Americans—at that income level. The study showed a larger share of upper-income blacks had worse credit than even whites or Asians with incomes below $25,000. (It is worth noting that the NAACP and other black groups collaborated with Freddie Mac in its study, and endorsed, if reluctantly, its findings.)

While blacks are denied home loans more often than Asians, those denial rates generally track the bad-credit rates reported by Freddie Mac—at all income levels—as the following chart reveals.

## CREDIT MATTERS

While blacks are more likely to be rejected for a home loan . . .

| Share of home-loan denials by race | Blacks 54% | Hispanics 39% | Whites 26% | Asians 12% |
|---|---|---|---|---|

. . . and more likely to get a bad deal on a home loan . . .

| Share of high-cost home loans by race | Blacks 32% | Hispanics 20% | Whites 9% | Asians 6% |
|---|---|---|---|---|

. . . they are more likely to have bad credit . . .

| Share of consumers with bad credit, incomes under $25,000 | Blacks 48% | Hispanics 39% | Whites 31% | Asians 22% |
|---|---|---|---|---|

. . . even at higher income levels.

| Share of consumers with bad credit, incomes $65,000–$75,000 | Blacks 34% | Hispanics 27% | Whites 20% | Asians 12% |
|---|---|---|---|---|

Sources: Federal Reserve, Freddie Mac.

The Federal Reserve confirmed the corollary in a 2005 report. It concluded that credit data also likely explained disparities in mortgage-interest rates paid by racial groups. On average, Asian-Americans were the most likely among ethnic groups to have good credit and were least likely on average to get saddled with high-priced loans, such as subprime mortgages, which charge a risk-related premium.

Higher-cost loans compensate lenders for the added risk of lending to borrowers with credit blemishes and poor track records of repaying loans. The "price discrimination" of which fair-lending activists like NCRC's Taylor complain is really *risk* discrimination, which every insurer in the country does every day (of course, now the Obama administration wants to change that too).

Would an insurer charge a black man with high-blood pressure and diabetes the same premium as an Asian man with normal blood pressure for the same term life insurance policy? Of course not. So why should banks charge the same interest rate and fees to a high-risk borrower with bad credit who happens to be black as they would a low-risk borrower with good credit who happens to be Asian?

Banks are not public utilities, as much as the credit-reallocation crowd would like to change that. They are in business to make money, not lose it; and they cover risk by charging premiums, much like insurance companies.

So when you look at *all* the pieces to the lending puzzle—not just loan denials and loan pricing by race, but also credit history by race—the picture that emerges reflects not racism but rationalism. On average:

- Asians have the best credit and pay the lowest rates.
- Whites have the next best credit and get the next best deals.
- Hispanics tend to have worse credit than Asians and Whites, but better than blacks, and they get better deals than blacks.
- Blacks tend to have the worst credit and get the worst deals.

The politically incorrect truth is, racism is not the hurdle most blacks face when they walk into a bank. It's their own damaged credit.

According to LaTanya M. Johnson, a black loan officer in Ohio, blacks, on average, pay their bills "sporadically," which hurts their credit scores—and their chances of getting a good loan. This explains much of the mortgage gap. What's worse, she said, "We live day to day. We have the finest clothes but no assets in our back pockets to fall back on." African-Americans, she added, "look at all these people buying or building new houses and they want to attain what everyone else has. [But] then they get in and they can't afford it."

Kenneth Grimes, a black banker in Michigan, backs up Johnson's statements. "Blacks spend more money than any other ethnic group. Yet we have the least assets." The solution, he says, is for African-Americans to "change their cultural attitudes regarding spending money."

## TRUTH IN LENDING

So even black underwriters agree that the main reason black loan applicants are denied prime loans more often than whites is the same reason whites are denied choice loans more often than Asians: their credit simply doesn't measure up. Even the poorest Asians had credit records comparable to the wealthiest whites surveyed by Freddie Mac.

The mainstream media almost never point this out, even when credit score statistics are available in the loan-approval process. They are content hewing to the progressive narrative of white corporate America taking advantage of blacks, even though every lending study that has taken into account minority applicants' credit histories—along with other key underwriting criteria, such as household assets—has failed to demonstrate racial discrimination.

Of course, this is a very inconvenient truth for race racketeers, such as NCRC, who resort to trumpeting their own biased studies claiming structural racism in lending.

In 2005, for example, NCRC found that African-Americans of

all income levels were twice as likely to receive high-cost loans as whites in 171 metro areas. It publicized its "Income Is No Shield" study as proof that bankers discriminate against black applicants. The media, wedded as they are to the same black-exploitation narrative, lapped up the report.

However, the NCRC report was widely panned by the lending industry as a simplistic study that failed to control for creditworthiness and other key underwriting factors.

"The technical validity of their criticism is, to some extent, accurate," NCRC's Taylor reluctantly confesses, "but the point is nevertheless meaningless to public policy." In other words, he and other activists are not going to let a few inconvenient facts get in the way of "good" social policy if it helps achieve their ultimate goal of "economic justice." And so they studiously avoid mentioning such facts when they solicit blacks and Hispanics to join class-action discrimination lawsuits against banks, or join bus caravans to Washington to demand banking "reforms" guaranteeing more minority loan set-asides.

They tell them they are victims of racism. What they do not tell them is that loan underwriting programs—as well as loan pricing systems—are automated and color-blind, and exclude personal bias from the process. Loan officers do not sit around, pen in hand, just itching to redline minorities out of cheap loans or greenline them into pricey ones. "Our pricing is automated, is absolutely colorblind," says Terry Theologides, spokesman for Irvine, California–based New Century Mortgage Corporation, a national subprime lender accused of targeting minorities. "The program they [minorities] are offered is identical to the program that would be offered if they were white and lived in the suburbs."

Brown, black, or white, each applicant is qualified based on uniform, sterile factors, irrespective of race. "We consider each applicant by the same objective criteria, which are blind to race," says Bank of America spokesman Terry Francisco.

There also is nothing arbitrary or unreasonable about the credit-scoring system lenders use to help evaluate applicants. It, too, is standardized and computer-based.

If your credit-history score is between 580 and 620, you probably will not get a good deal and will have to settle for a subprime loan, no matter who you are. If your score is over 700, chances are you will qualify for a prime loan—whether you are black, white, or purple.

## AUTOMATED AND COLOR-BLIND

Skin color does not factor into the score; only your paying history, which is almost flawless in predicting your ability to repay a loan. And this is why banks pay so much attention to it.

Only, now there are efforts under way to undermine even this bedrock indicator of financial risk.

For starters, the head of the Department of Justice's civil-rights division has ordered his prosecutors to force alleged "predatory lenders," who made subprime loans in minority neighborhoods, to "repair damage to borrowers' credit scores." Delinquencies? Default? Foreclosure? Doesn't matter. Wipe their credit history clean. Also, the financial overhaul law directs the Federal Reserve to craft regulations to "prohibit mortgage originators from mischaracterizing the credit history" of underserved borrowers. The newly formed federal consumer watchdog bureau, meanwhile, is studying whether credit scores are flawed and "disadvantage" such borrowers.

Clearly a movement is afoot to try to demonstrate that the

credit scoring process itself—not just the underwriting process—is biased against blacks and other minorities. But there is no conspiracy among credit scoring agencies or bankers to snub them, and some black pundits are fed up hearing such excuses.

"Many American blacks falsely and unfairly accuse whites for black America's 'plight,'" says black radio talk-show host Larry Elder. "Crime? White racism. Underperformance on standardized tests? Racist or 'culturally biased' tests. Can't get a loan for a home or a new business? Racist lending officers, who would rather reject profit than give a black man a loan."

Elder, tongue in cheek, makes a poignant point. Loan officers want to make money, and they do that by making sound loans (at least that used to be the case, before the CRA and other federal regulations mandated "flexible underwriting"). It is not in their interest to discriminate against borrowers so long as their credit is good and their money is green.

They also look closely at assets during the loan evaluation process. And Asians tend to save more of their income—even more than whites—which is one of the reasons their 60-percent homeownership rate is a full 10 points higher than that of blacks and Latinos.

Asian-Americans also put more stock in education. As recent Census Bureau data bear out, inner-city poor tend to spend what little money they have not on educational tools, but on video games and big-screen TVs. In contrast, personal computers are a relative scarcity in such households, even though they cost less and provide a gateway to vast stores of free information and potential career opportunities.

Unfortunately, shaking down corporations over imagined racism has become a rewarding alternative career path.

▼

Despite what race demagogues would have us believe, there is no systemic racism in lending. For discrimination to occur, a loan officer would have to impose *different* standards for evaluating a minority customer's application, and that would require, for starters, processing the application outside the color-blind computerized programming and rejecting the applicant based on personal prejudice. That would be a serious and egregious violation of civil rights—and one that should be prosecuted to the fullest extent of the law.

But that is just not happening as the NCRC and other fair-lending advocates claim. Statistics show their charges of institutional racism are groundless—and reckless. In fact, the only ones judging loan applicants by different terms are the race racketeers and regulators who compel affirmative-action lending in *preference* to otherwise uncreditworthy minorities. If anyone is racist, they are. They were the ones who pressured banks to set up two standards for underwriting loans: an easier one to, in effect, reward people with bad habits, just because of their skin color; and a tougher one for the rest of Americans. Now, depending on what neighborhood you live in, you can be compensated for walking on a loan you could not afford and should never have signed, then have your bad credit history scrubbed clean as if it never happened.

If there is a "dual lending marketplace," as Taylor contends, this is how it really works—thanks to him and his ilk. The rest is myth.

Instead of calling for more banking reforms and prosecutions to combat phantom racism, ethnic leaders and activists would better serve the minority community by pushing more effective programs to combat financial illiteracy, and educating minority borrowers about the importance of paying bills on time and maintaining good credit. This would do more to close the "credit gap" than all their race-based government nostrums combined.

# NINE

# DEADBEAT BORROWERS IN BLACK AND WHITE

I will crack down on predatory lenders—who all too often target the African-American community, target the Hispanic community—with tough new penalties that treat mortgage fraud like the crime it is.

—President Obama

Amid the financial wreckage of subprime hot spots like Detroit and Chicago, President Obama has vowed to punish banks that made loans to minorities who could not afford them, forgetting that he and other community organizers once pressured them into making such loans. He has made it clear that subprime lenders are the villains, and subprime borrowers are the victims.

To hear Obama, there is no gray area on this issue.

But are all minorities really victims of "greedy" bankers who took advantage of them? Or are some of them victims of their own greed?

It is instructive to peel back some of the sob stories inner-city activists and the media have trotted out regarding these borrowers.

A popular one involves April Williams of Detroit. She lost her two-story colonial to foreclosure, another victim of "predatory lending" by subprime mortgage brokers—or at least that's how her story, like so many others, has been told in the media.

Even the *Wall Street Journal* could not resist using Williams, an African-American, as a poster child for "reverse redlining," a practice whereby supposedly racist lenders aggressively target inner-city minorities for high-cost loans with hidden fees. In this case, as the tale of woe is spun, a greedy lender took advantage of the poor, 49-year-old Williams and her husband.

"Subprime mortgages and the brokers who peddle them are helping to take families out of homes in which they've lived for years," the front-page article in the *Journal* lamented.

While there are genuine cases of borrowers abused by unscrupulous brokers, the Williamses are not one of them. When you peel back their story, you find that the couple is hardly a hardship case worthy of our sympathy.

It turns out that they have lived in a middle-class neighborhood and owned a $50,000 Lincoln Navigator. And the loan they took out was a mortgage refinance for the purpose of cashing out equity funds.

They already owned the house and used cash from the bigger loan to buy toys—including stainless-steel kitchen appliances and a koi pond—that they ultimately could not afford once their adjustable interest rate reset at a higher rate. The Japanese fish pond and luxury SUV were left out of the *Journal*'s story, which cited "a community organizer for ACORN" among key sources.

The Williamses could not afford the bigger loan, and the bank had to foreclose on their property. And now they are angry at the bank; and so are several of their neighbors who also took out higher-cost subprime loans, which charge above-market interest rates to cover the higher risk of such shaky borrowers. Most of them already owned their homes and used the refinancing cash to renovate them or pay off credit cards.

The Williamses at the time were grateful to get their loan, which was approved in spite of their high debt, poor credit, and admitted financial problems.

Such subprime refinance lending, which now accounts for the majority of all subprime lending, shot up 1,000 percent from 1993 to 1998, when Clinton plunged lenders into the subprime market to better serve minorities. As a result, black neighborhoods were five times more likely to receive subprime refinance lending than those living in white neighborhoods, according to a HUD study.

Then there is Veronica Peterson, who was profiled on the front page of the *Baltimore Sun* as another foreclosure "victim." The 46-year-old single mother of four could not keep up with her mortgage payments and was about to be thrown out of her home with her children.

While her story sounds tragic, hold the violins. The *Sun* failed to mention that Peterson had made, at most, one payment since buying her $545,000 home in the Maryland suburbs. In effect, she had been squatting there for two years.

With income of $50,000 a year plus child support, she had ambitiously taken out two loans on the half-million-dollar property from subprime lender Washington Mutual, and owed a combined mortgage payment of $4,450 a month. As high as the notes were, she repaid virtually none on them, and made no real effort to make good on her debt.

After receiving an eviction notice, Peterson joined ACORN in protesting subprime lending at rallies in Baltimore and Washington. Holding herself up as a victim of "predatory lending," she claimed the thrift used the subprime loans as "weapons of mass destruction" to ruin her life.

"We've come to a heck of a place where the people on Wall Street can make a mess, and those who are the victims of the mess have to pay for it," chimed in Gloria Swieringa, ACORN'S Maryland chairman, who exalted Peterson and other local "victims."

The Robinsons of Charlotte, North Carolina, have claimed a similar plight. According to a sympathetic piece in the *Charlotte Observer*, the middle-class black family lost their $171,000 home in the leafy suburbs of the city because an unscrupulous mortgage broker steered them into a high-cost loan. They took out a 30-year mortgage with a fixed interest rate of 9.99 percent, though the average fixed rate on a 30-year loan at the time was 6.64 percent, the newspaper pointed out.

"The couple fell behind on their monthly mortgage payments and the lender foreclosed," the *Observer* mourned. "A sheriff's deputy posted an eviction notice on their front door."

The article, headlined "A 10% loan, a job loss, their first home gone," was part of an *Observer* "investigation" into lending discrimination. The newspaper series suggested that African-Americans get stuck with higher-cost subprime loans due to racism. "Bias looks to play a role," it concluded, "as blacks pay higher mortgage rates."

The paper portrayed James Robinson as a victim of discrimination. "I try my best to provide for my family, and what I had to provide for my family was a good income and good credit," he was quoted as saying. "That didn't seem to be enough."

It was not enough, because Robinson provided neither such thing. He could not prove he had good, steady income, and he clearly did not have good credit—critical details he and the *Observer* left out of the larger story.

In fact, Robinson's credit score was a weak 648. Borrowers with scores below 680 typically do not qualify for prime-rate loans, irrespective of skin color. Lenders charge higher rates to cover the higher risks and costs of qualifying such uncreditworthy borrowers for loans.

And Robinson, who came into the deal already carrying large debts, did not provide documentation of his ability to repay the new loan, such as proof of steady employment, according to his lender, New Century Mortgage Corp., a subprime operator.

Hedging against such risk proved a good call by the lender. Robinson lost his job a little over a year after closing on the original loan. He filed for bankruptcy twice before New Century foreclosed on his home.

Still, the *Observer* pressured New Century to issue a statement insisting the company "does not consider race in lending decisions."

It is never good when anybody loses their home, but nobody held a gun to these borrowers' heads when they signed the loan papers at the title company—which, by law, included a HUD settlement statement, spelling out all terms and conditions, that must be reviewed and initialed before closing.

Even if they signed prematurely, they still had three postal days to change their minds and rip up the contract. (In their case, they had *six* days to carefully review details of the loan and decide whether to cancel it. Federal law at the time required lenders to provide additional disclosures to borrowers of such high-cost loans three days before they even close.)

But someone does hold a virtual gun to the heads of lenders to pressure them to make such risky loans in the first place, and that someone is the federal government, which today cares more about the genetic history of borrowers than their credit history.

## WHITE DEADBEATS

Of course, not all deadbeat borrowers in the subprime crisis have been black. Meet the Mahers.

Rick Maher moved his middle-class white family from Miami to the Charlotte suburbs, where they bought a $289,900 new home in the Taylor Glenn subdivision—one they ultimately could not afford.

They soon fell behind on their mortgage payments to subprime giant Countrywide Financial. And they stopped paying their homeowners' association dues, which the subdivision uses to pay for the community pool and utilities, and even basic cable TV for all residents.

After the Mahers racked up $3,367 in back dues and other fees, the homeowners' association threatened to foreclose on their home. The couple claimed they did not know about the dues when they bought into the development, even though an annual estimate appeared on the settlement papers they signed at closing.

The Mahers went to the local press to drum up sympathy for their plight. Photos of the couple standing on their front porch with their small children in their arms appeared in the community newspaper. Accompanying articles painted them as an honest American family down on their luck, while portraying the mortgage company and homeowners' association as heartless money collectors.

Soon donations from good Samaritans began pouring in, and a fairy tale ending seemed near.

But then neighbors started telling a much different story about the Mahers. They described a couple who spends too much and does not pay their bills. For instance, it was revealed that the Mahers threw lavish parties, including a birthday party with ponies and a petting zoo for their toddler.

Rick's wife, April Maher, says the bill for the petting zoo, which came to $200, was covered by a grandparent as a birthday gift. "Was I supposed to take that money [and pay bills with it]?" she asks. "That's stealing from a 3-year-old."

It was also learned that the Mahers used the subdivision pool almost daily during the summer, even though their security entry card was deactivated for lack of payment.

"They have no scruples at all about abiding by the development's rules," one neighbor complained.

Neighbors also said the Mahers never attended any homeowners' association board meetings to address the issue, and failed to make a good faith effort to meet their financial obligations.

"We didn't feel that getting up in front of everyone at the board meeting would solve anything," Rick Maher explains.

But that's not all. It turns out that when he and his wife closed on their new house, after moving from Florida, they chose to relax at home for over a year before looking for work. Rick Maher eventually took a job with Home Depot, but the initial gap in income put them behind on their mortgage payments.

To avoid defaulting on their mortgage, the Mahers turned to the Neighborhood Assistance Corporation of America, or NACA, the notorious "banking terrorist" group discussed earlier that has shaken down banks for billions of dollars in loan set-asides and other subsidies.

In the end, the couple took advantage of a deal struck between the state attorney general's office and Countrywide, allowing some 5,000 North Carolina families to receive mortgage payment relief. The deal cut the couple's monthly payment by nearly two-thirds to $1,200.

The Mahers say their neighbors' negative reaction to their plight caught them by surprise. "I can't help it if our neighbors hate us or not," April Maher says. "They don't pay our bills."

Apparently, neither do the Mahers. And therein lies the whole problem.

▼

Echoing the Maryland ACORN activist, Obama nonetheless claims that "millions of innocent homeowners" have been "tricked" into expensive mortgages by "Wall Street predators" employing "unscrupulous lending" practices.

But that story line, powerful class-warfare rhetoric as it is, dissolves upon closer inspection. As these cases reveal, many subprime "victims" were not innocent first-time homebuyers duped into taking out expensive mortgages, but rather seasoned homeowners, albeit with damaged credit and a lot of debt, who chose subprime loans to refinance their mortgages so they could cash out equity and buy more toys, using their homes as ATM machines without considering the risk. Others took out subprime loans because prime loans would have required steady employment.

These are hardly sympathy-deserving characters.

As for those first-time homebuyers who bought—and lost—their first homes after taking out expensive subprime loans, many were disadvantaged only by their own deficient credit and premature timing. They clearly bought more than they could afford at their early stage in life and career.

And many did so while living here *illegally*, as we shall see next.

# TEN

# HANNIE MAE: CASAS FOR ILLEGALS

Espanol.hud.gov is another step towards achieving the Bush administration's goal of helping more minorities achieve the dream of homeownership.

—former HUD secretary Mel Martinez

President George W. Bush also had a dream of universal homeownership. Rivaling Clinton's dream, his included an additional 5.5 million minority homeowners by 2010. Only, Bush was trying to purchase the loyalty of a different constituency—Hispanic immigrants. If Clinton was America's "first black president," then Bush was its "first Hispanic president," or at least that is how the self-proclaimed bilingual president viewed himself. And he had a soft spot for immigrants who could not afford or qualify for a home.

Wrapping up a daylong White House Conference on Increasing Minority Ownership at the capital's George Washington University, Bush in 2002 listed a number of "obstacles" facing Hispanic immigrants applying for mortgages—from a lack of income for down payments to a shortage of bilingual information. "You can imagine somebody newly arrived from Peru looking at all that print and saying, 'I'm not sure I can possibly understand that,'" Bush said during the event. He cited the Arias family, who had just moved from Peru to Baltimore. He also mentioned Luis Cortez of Nueva Esperanza in Philadelphia, who "understood that a home ownership program is incredibly important to revitalize this neighborhood."

Bush, whose sister-in-law Columba Bush emigrated from Mexico, then promoted his $200 million American Dream Down Payment Act, which he said was a down payment on his "compassionate" society. He also praised affordable housing programs offered by Fannie and Freddie. "Freddie Mac recently began 25 initiatives around the country to dismantle barriers and create greater opportunities for home ownership," he noted. "One of the programs is designed to help deserving families who have bad credit histories to qualify for home ownership loans."

The president's message to Hispanic immigrants: *Bad credit? No hay problema. You deserve your own casa too.*

Bush's point man for closing the Hispanic "mortgage gap," as he called it, was HUD secretary Mel Martinez, a Cuban American. For Bush's housing conference, Martinez commissioned Cuban-American artist Xavier Cortada to paint a mural depicting Latino families signing mortgage papers and entering the front doors of their new homes. In 2003, he launched a new Spanish-language

Web site—www.espanol.hud.gov—to cater to the housing needs of the nation's 35 million Hispanics. "To reach this growing population," Martinez said, "last year President Bush announced a goal to create 5.5 million new homeowners."

Most important, however, Martinez pushed Fannie and Freddie to purchase higher volumes of loans for low-income immigrants with damaged credit or no credit histories, building on the already Draconian affordable-housing requirements inherited from the Clinton administration. "Changing demographics will create a need for the primary and secondary mortgage markets to meet nontraditional credit needs, respond to diverse housing preferences, and overcome information and other barriers that many immigrants and minorities face," HUD said in a 2004 report proposing higher affordable housing goals for Fannie and Freddie. The HUD proposal also directed the mortgage giants to adjust "current underwriting standards to better reflect the special circumstances of these new households."

Martinez took his marching orders from the White House. "It is compassionate to understand there is an ownership gap in America, and we must use our resources to close that gap by encouraging minority ownership of homes," Bush said at the time. "One way to do that is to work with Freddie Mac and Fannie Mae to encourage capital. We need billions of more dollars available for those who want to realize the dream."

Bush's casas crusade produced rapid results. Fannie and Freddie invested hundreds of billions of dollars in subprime loans and securities; and by 2005, Hispanic homeownership had climbed to nearly 50 percent from 47 percent in 2000—a major leap historically.

Running for the United States Senate in Florida in late 2004, Martinez took credit for the gains. "More Hispanics in America own a home than at any other time in our history," he boasted. "I was connected to that as HUD secretary."

In fact, he and Bush got a lot of help from Congress and the Hispanic housing lobby.

## LATINO PRESSURE GROUPS

The Congressional Hispanic Caucus fanned the flames of the easy credit bonfire. Led by Democratic representative Joe Baca, whose California district is 60 percent Hispanic, the caucus teamed up with lobbyist groups to pressure Fannie and Freddie into making risky subprime loans to uncreditworthy Hispanic immigrants, waiving both income and asset documentation.

By 2006, before the bubble burst, Hispanics surpassed African Americans as the fastest-growing segment of the subprime market, taking out some 40 percent of all subprime loans. And they were aggressively pushed into that market by a Hispanic lobbying group advised by former HUD secretary Henry Cisneros, who in 1995 originally set the minority lending targets at Fannie and Freddie. Even as defaults mounted, the Washington-based National Association of Hispanic Real Estate Professionals, known as NAHREP, lobbied lenders, as well as Freddie and Fannie, to ease down payment and credit standards for immigrants, arguing for "flexible" and "culturally appropriate" home loans tailored to the needs of Latino immigrants. It pressed mortgage underwriters, for instance, to allow Hispanic applicants to "pool their income" with other tenants to satisfy household cash-flow requirements, since Hispanic households tend to be occupied by multiple adults and extended families.

"NAHREP maintains that California, Texas and other states

with large numbers of immigrants could see a dramatic jump in homeownership if a greater number of major lenders adopted alternative credit-scoring systems," NAHREP said in a 2007 report, which included a foreword written by Cisneros, urging the closing of the homeownership gap between Latinos and whites.

NAHREP sponsored an "affordable housing" initiative called *Hogar*, Spanish for "hearth." It was launched in 2003 by Baca and his caucus to work with lenders and the radical group National Council of La Raza to boost lending to Latinos and ease underwriting guidelines. (*La Raza*, Spanish for "The Race," has advocated the *reconquista* [reconquest] of the Southwest. In 2006, the group hosted top Bush adviser Karl Rove at its annual convention, while receiving more than $15 million in federal grants.)

Eventually, Countrywide Financial and other subprime lenders donated $2 million a year to NAHREP, which the association used to build an army of 16,000 Latino agents and mortgage brokers. The Hispanic Realtors, in turn, marketed in Spanish to day laborers, janitors, busboys, nannies, and other low-income immigrants. Countrywide also gave generously to Baca and other members of the Hispanic caucus.

Giving new meaning to *chutzpah*, NAHREP and the caucus now blame subprime lenders for the flood of Hispanic foreclosures, claiming Hispanics fell prey to their "predatory lending practices."

Not so fast. According to a recent Federal Reserve report, the problem centers on bad credit. Hispanics, on average, "have lower credit scores than non-Hispanic whites and Asians," the study found. Not surprisingly, they have higher default rates on mortgages—and not just higher-cost subprime mortgages, but all types of loans, the Fed noted.

Hispanics for the most part defaulted for the simple reason that they were less likely to qualify to own a home and repay a mortgage in the first place.

## MADNESS GATHERS PACE

Least qualified were illegal immigrants, but that did not faze NAHREP and the Hispanic caucus on Capitol Hill. They actually encouraged lending to aliens. No Social Security? No problem. NAHREP pushed the use of ITINs—Individual Taxpayer Identification Numbers—in conjunction with the Mexican-issued *Matricula Consular* card in lieu of Social Security numbers.

"NAHREP currently estimates that about 375,000 undocumented immigrant households are eligible for mortgages," the association said in its 2007 report.

By law, banks do not have to check immigration status; and after aggressive lobbying by such Hispanic housing advocates, they made loans to illegals—lots of them. By some estimates, millions of undocumented workers became undocumented borrowers almost overnight during the subprime boom.

Until recently, ITIN mortgages could not be sold on the secondary market; Fannie and Freddie would not touch them as a matter of policy. So with the support of NAHREP and the Hispanic caucus, "Hannie Mae" was created—the Hispanic National Mortgage Association, based in San Diego. And it began buying ITIN mortgages from lenders, helping them spread the risk, while packaging the pools of mostly subprime loans it bought into securities for investors.

Now Hannie Mae, which lists Cisneros as a board member, itself risks choking on the more than $200 million in loans it has acquired. Foreclosures have put Hannie in the same bind as Fannie, her *gringa* counterpart. Today, the company's main phone number is out of service, and its Web site has not been updated in more than a year.

How in the world did so many illegal immigrants qualify for American home loans? Two words: Bill Clinton.

## ILLEGAL LOANS

In 1996, Clinton opened the housing market up to potentially 12 million illegal aliens by ordering the IRS to issue nine-digit Individual Taxpayer Identification Numbers to immigrants in lieu of Social Security numbers. Lenders soon after began accepting the so-called ITIN number from undocumented foreign mortgage applicants, while "verifying" their creditworthiness in some cases merely by checking on their utility payments or asking their priests how regularly they drop cash in the collection plate.

One bank that catered to illegal Hispanic immigrants was Second Federal Savings and Loan in Chicago, which typically took at least six hours to underwrite such loans, commonly known in the industry (fittingly) as "TIN mortgages." "We have to go to local churches to find out if they're paying weekly," Mark Doyle, Second Federal's president and chief executive, told Chicago Public Radio in 2007. "If they've borrowed money from an uncle to buy a pickup truck, there's a paper trail behind that, so we look for the check, we take a look at the title, we make sure they paid him back. If they're a tenant, you know, we look for receipts, proof they've been [paying] rent to their landlords."

Citibank also courted undocumented immigrants, partnering with ACORN Housing to provide mortgages to more than 900 illegals nationwide in the years leading up to the subprime bust.

Countrywide, meanwhile, advertised in Spanish in the barrio

and hired bilingual counselors to prequalify Hispanic applicants over toll-free phone lines. Before long, it became the biggest lender to the Hispanic community—and the biggest loser in the subprime bust.

Ads soliciting undocumented Latino immigrants for mortgages popped up across the country, proclaiming: "*Sin verificacion de ingresos! Sin verificacion de documento!*"—which loosely translates as "No income tax forms required! No immigration papers either!" As a result, poor immigrants ended up with mortgages they ultimately could not afford. Flagrant examples include Gerardo Cadima, a 23-year-old from Bolivia, who secured a $330,000 loan for a home in suburban Virginia with no money down and a part-time electrician's income. Then there were the Ramirezes from California. They earned $14,000 a year picking strawberries, yet qualified to buy a home for $720,000, thanks to a no-questions-asked mortgage they got from Washington Mutual, which also catered to such Spanish-speaking immigrants. Not surprisingly, they fell behind on their payments and defaulted on their loan.

What had been a tiny underground market for illegal loans grew into a multibillion-dollar legitimate industry that, by 2007, grew so big it helped crash the home finance system.

## BUSTED DREAMS IN THE BARRIO

While the subprime crisis has heavily affected black neighborhoods, it is not confined to them. Thanks to the same misguided housing policies, the barrio has also seen its share of subprime loans go bust—along with the dreams of millions of Hispanics. It is no coincidence that foreclosures have hit heavily immigrant states like California, Nevada, and Florida hardest. In fact, according to a recent Pew Hispanic Center study, 25 of the 33 counties with the nation's highest foreclosure rates are located in these three states. They have experienced foreclosure rates of roughly twice the national average.

All told, an estimated 17 percent of Latino homeowners have lost their homes to foreclosure. As a result, the Latino "mortgage gap" that Bush was so determined to close has only widened. The Hispanic homeownership rate has retraced most of the gains made under his crusade, falling back to 48 percent, according to the latest Census Bureau figures. (See the chart in the appendix.) So much for Bush's "noble goal," as he called it.

Analysts say cultural differences explain the 20-point gap between Hispanic and white homeownership. They say it has little, if anything, to do with discriminatory "barriers" erected by lenders, as Bush suggested. "The lower [Hispanic homeownership] rate was perfectly understandable, given the lower educational levels, lower household incomes, and shorter tenure in the country of Latinos, compared with the average American household," points out Manhattan Institute senior fellow Steven Malanga. By trying to prop up the rate, he says Bush, like Clinton before him, moved it from its natural level to an artificial one that was ultimately unsustainable.

And Bush's failed social experiment has been as devastating to the barrio as Clinton's experiment has been to black neighborhoods. Foreclosures have invited more vandalism and other crimes. In predominantly Hispanic cities like San Diego and Los Angeles, vacant homes are plastered with graffiti. Gangs have moved in. Drug-dealing is rampant.

Still, the social engineers in Washington have not learned any lessons from the devastation their easy credit crusades have wrought. In fact, President Obama's new Consumer Financial Protection

Bureau is looking into ways to "enhance the . . . credit score" of Hispanic immigrants who apply for mortgages, including counting their "remittance transaction history," or payments to Mexico and other destinations south of the border. In other words, the administration wants lenders to give undocumented Hispanic applicants credit for wiring money home to relatives.

And as detailed previously, Obama has put in charge of HUD's fair-housing enforcement section the former president of the radical Hispanic-rights group known as the Mexican American Legal Defense and Educational Fund. Assistant HUD secretary John Trasviña has already launched several investigations of banks for lending discrimination, shaking them down for millions of dollars in loan set-asides for alleged minority victims.

NAHREP, for its part, is unrepentant about its role in fanning the flames of the subprime crisis. In fact, it is demanding even easier credit for Hispanics. "In the case of Latino borrowers," it asserts, "the housing industry must not revert to undue restriction of credit. Rather, it must forge ahead and continue to improve its evaluation of the true credit-worthiness of Latino borrowers through the use of more culturally sensitive underwriting criteria."

Congressman Baca remains equally unrepentant: "We need to keep credit easily accessible to our minority communities."

# ELEVEN

# RED HERRINGS

Redlining may have become a red herring.

— Federal Reserve Bank of Dallas

The White House, Congress, and their hand-picked commission to investigate the financial crisis have conspired with their friends in the national media to cover up government's role in the "great American bank robbery." They have used a number of red herrings to take the most steadfast truth hounds off the real culprit's scent.

But do not be misled. Using ironclad data, I will expose their clever but specious arguments in this final chapter. Let the litigation begin.

RED HERRING #1: Because the Community Reinvestment Act of 1977 was enacted long before the subprime crisis, "it is not tenable that the CRA could suddenly have caused an explosion in bad subprime loans more than 25 years after its enactment," the Obama Treasury has argued.

FACT: President Clinton rewrote the anti-redlining regulation in 1995, and the changes did not fully take effect until 1997—just a few years before the subprime explosion. Clinton's historic CRA overhaul—the first and only major change to the law in its 33 years on the books—toughened enforcement while mandating for the first time that banks use "flexible underwriting standards" to qualify more low-income and minority borrowers for home loans.

In fact, "flexible lending practices to address the credit needs" of such "underserved" borrowers is one of the five performance criteria banks must meet in the "lending test," which carries the most weight in the post-1995 CRA examination.

FACT: The amended CRA influenced subprime underwriting on the secondary market, as well as the primary market, in the 2000s. As banks bent their rules to comply with the new CRA rules, Fannie and Freddie also adopted greater lending "flexibility" by offering "mortgage products for borrowers with less than perfect credit."

"Secondary-market innovations have proceeded in tandem with shifts in the primary markets: depository institutions, *spurred by the threat of CRA challenges*, have pioneered flexible mortgage products," revealed a 2002 Fannie Mae report detailing a trillion-dollar commitment to affordable housing for low-income minorities, based on the "innovative" and "flexible" underwriting criteria codified in the new CRA. (Emphasis added.)

FACT: Also in 1995, Clinton for the first time authorized the securitization of subprime mortgages. The move was designed not only to help banks earn CRA credits against his tougher CRA lending targets but to help Fannie and Freddie earn credits against his tougher affordable-housing targets, which he raised starting in 1995.

FACT: Former Federal Reserve chairman Alan Greenspan confirmed, under oath, that the subprime securities market developed from the CRA reforms of the mid-1990s. Listen to this extraordinary exchange, unreported by the media elite, between Greenspan and Republican representative Todd Platts of Pennsylvania during 2008 congressional hearings on the subprime crisis:

> **PLATTS**: Back home I have had numerous banking officials address with me the Community Reinvestment Act. They're being forced by bank regulators to engage in making loans to risky applicants, loans they would not otherwise make and they know are at great risk of defaulting. So I'd be interested in your opinions on that role in this crisis, big or small.
>
> **GREENSPAN**: Well, you know, it's instructive to go back to the early stages of the subprime market, which has essentially emerged out of the CRA. The evidence suggests that this market evolved in a manner which if there were no securitization [of CRA loans], it would have been a much smaller problem and, indeed, very unlikely to have taken on the dimensions that it did.

RED HERRING #2: "The worst abuses were made by firms not covered by CRA," Treasury argues, pointing out that only "six percent" of subprime loans in 2006 were originated by banks subject to the CRA.

FACT: The "six percent" stat is worse than half-baked, since it fails to account for:

- subprime loans made by mortgage companies that were wholly owned subsidiaries or affiliates of banks (ten of the 25 largest subprime lenders were affiliated with bank holding companies);
- high-risk loans underwritten by ACORN Housing, NACA, and other CRA shakedown groups using "commitments" and other subsidies pledged by banks (institutions including Bank of America, JPMorgan Chase, Citibank, and Washington Mutual pledged some $2 trillion in such commitments from 2001 to 2008); and
- subprime loans and securities *bought* by banks to obtain "CRA credit."

Under the "investment test," CRA examiners gave banks credit for loans they purchased from Countrywide Financial and other subprime lenders, as well as loans they originated, which encouraged independent mortgage companies to undertake such lending. They also gave them credit for the billions of dollars' worth of subprime and other CRA-qualified mortgage-backed *securities* they bought directly through Fannie and Freddie or through the CRA Qualified Investment Fund (Citibank, Wells Fargo, Washington Mutual, and other large banks invested heavily in the $1 billion-in-assets fund).

CRA regulations do not differentiate between "direct" and "indirect" investments. Conveniently, however, the Obama Treasury in its analysis does not count the trillions of dollars in indirect subprime and other risky investments CRA-covered banks made before the crisis.

Fact: The Federal Reserve estimates that while independent mortgage companies not regulated by the CRA accounted for about half of all subprime loans, "it is . . . possible that the remaining share of higher-priced lower-income lending may be indirectly attributable to CRA."

Fact: Even though they were not covered by the CRA, mortgage companies were driven into the subprime market by political pressure. The Clinton HUD compelled the Mortgage Bankers Association to sign a "Fair Lending Best Practices Master Agreement" establishing a first-of-its-kind "lending code" among its 2,900 members. Under this historic deal, mortgage bankers pledged to aggressively seek business among minorities and "encourage development of flexible underwriting and appraisal standards." Countrywide inked a separate, more detailed contract with HUD, pledging performance targets of 5 percent annual increases in poor and minority lending, even though the lender was not covered by the CRA. The agreement included a commitment to establish "second review programs to ensure that underwriting standards are applied both flexibly and in a nondiscriminatory manner."

Fact: In a little-noticed report published in 2000, Clinton's own Treasury found that "the CRA may have had a positive 'demonstration effect' on lenders not covered by the Act, and thus indirectly increased lending by these institutions as well."

RED HERRING #3: "The CRA does not require banks to make loans that are inconsistent with safe and sound operations," the Angelides Commission insists in a staff report.

FACT: A Federal Reserve study found that CRA examiners give far more weight to lending flexibility than safety. In fact, banks with the highest CRA ratings tend to have the lowest safety and soundness ratings based on the so-called CAMELS formula, which takes into account capital adequacy, asset quality, management, earnings, liquidity, and sensitivity to market risks. "The safety and soundness criteria used in assigning CAMEL[S] ratings and the credit availability objectives of CRA are in opposition," asserts Fed economist Jeffery Gunther.

(Yes, Clinton's 1995 revision to the anti-redlining law states that banks "are permitted and encouraged to develop and apply flexible underwriting standards for loans that benefit low- or moderate-income geographies or individuals, only if consistent with safe and sound operations." But expecting banks to be more "flexible" in their underwriting while still making "safe and sound" loans is like expecting them to smoke but not inhale—a trick apparently only Clinton knew how to pull off. Banks have found it virtually impossible to downgrade standards to please regulators and still make safe loans.)

FACT: Even former Federal Reserve Board governor Lawrence Lindsey, a staunch CRA defender, acknowledges that the regulation "did contribute to a downgrading of credit standards."

FACT: HUD required Fannie and Freddie to buy CRA loans, *knowing* that CRA loans carry higher risks. At one point, CRA loans did not qualify for acquisition by Fannie and Freddie. "CRA loans . . . are likely to have a high LTV [loan-to-value ratio], high debt-to-income ratios [and] no payment reserves," HUD said in its final rules for 2000. As a result, "many do not meet the underwriting guidelines required in order for them to be purchased by" Fannie or Freddie. After HUD raised affordable housing targets that year, pressuring Fannie and Freddie to buy CRA loans to meet the higher targets, the mortgage giants watered down their guidelines to accept CRA loans, resulting in mounting losses. "Purchasing these loans could be an important strategy for reaching the housing goals," the same HUD regulations urged.

RED HERRING #4: CRA-mandated loans have been profitable for banks, and "it is possible that much of this lending would have been done even in the absence of the CRA," contends an Angelides Commission staff report.

FACT: A Federal Reserve study on CRA loan performance found that even during the 1990s economic boom, "nearly 90 percent of large banking institutions report higher 30–89 day delinquency rates for CRA-related home lending than for overall home lending."

FACT: Another Federal Reserve study found that only 29 percent of loans in bank lending programs established especially for "CRA compliance" purposes could be classified as profitable, meaning banks took a bath on the vast majority of these federally mandated loans.

FACT: In 2008, CRA loans acted as a significant drag on Bank of America's earnings. On an annualized basis, they accounted for just 7 percent of the bank's total lending but constituted an astounding 29 percent of its losses on residential mortgages. The situation was nearly as bad in 2009, says Bank of America chief financial officer Joe L. Price, with the CRA share of losses amounting to 24 percent.

FACT: Banks subsidize CRA loans by amounts as high as $8,000 per loan to write down the added costs and losses from such loans. "The process of justifying the credit quality of these loans has become continuous and unrelenting," complains Mark Willis, head of community development at JPMorgan Chase.

FACT: CRA loans default at a higher rate than conventional loans—a point even the Angelides Commission concedes. "To be sure," says a draft staff report from April 2010, "loans made by CRA-regulated lenders to low- and moderate-income borrowers in their assessment areas default at a higher rate than loans made to the typical borrower by these same lenders."

In its current efforts to "upgrade" the CRA, the government explains it wants to "ensure that the CRA remains effective for encouraging institutions to meet the credit needs" of underserved communities. Of course, if there were profitable loans to be made in these communities, banks would not need the government "encouraging" them to make them.

RED HERRING #5: The worst of the subprime mortgages were originated in 2005 and 2006, long after Clinton's regulations went into effect.

FACT: Subprime losses from earlier years, especially 2000 to 2004, are masked by appreciation in home prices, which often allowed subprime borrowers to sell their homes or refinance rather than default on their higher-cost mortgages. And a study of longitudinal performance of 6 million subprime mortgages in 2005 found that these loans still had a very high failure rate from the earliest vintages studied. Subprime loans originated in years 1998 to 2001 had already failed at a rate of one in four or one in five by 2005. And 2003 originations were already on that same trajectory by 2005.

FACT: The Clinton housing policies that helped create the subprime market were still in place in 2005 and 2006. Mortgage industry data show two distinct periods of expansion in subprime lending. The first expansion took place during the late 1990s, after Clinton allowed Fannie and Freddie to count subprime securities as credit against HUD affordable-housing goals. This special allowance remained in place through 2005 and 2006. And the second expansion started in 2002, after Clinton ramped up HUD's top affordable-housing goal for Fannie and Freddie to 50 percent. This dramatically higher baseline rate remained in place through 2005 and 2006. (See the chart in the appendix.)

RED HERRING #6: HUD's Affordable Housing Goals cannot be to blame for the subprime crisis, because HUD barred Fannie and Freddie from purchasing such risky loans.

FACT: HUD did no such thing. A careful reading of the voluminous final rules HUD entered into the Federal Register shows that HUD allowed Fannie and Freddie to take goal credit even on some subprime loans that carried high charges and prepayment penalties. Though generally discouraged as "abusive," these practices were not proscribed in the HUD regulations. (See also Red Herring #9.)

RED HERRING #7: The desire to increase profits drove Fannie's and Freddie's increased appetite for risk, not government mandates to support affordable housing. "We should be careful not to learn the wrong lesson from this experience," warns HUD secretary Shaun Donovan.

FACT: Officials from both firms swear their hands were forced by HUD. They testified they had to lower their underwriting standards and absorb substantial costs to meet HUD's ever-increasing Affordable Housing Goals. Internal communications written before the crisis confirm that profits were the last thing on their minds as they added more subprime and other nonprime loans to their portfolios. Executives said they were not making money on such social lending activity. They grumbled that it was expensive and they were straining to do it. "We had to absorb significant costs to meet the HUD purchase money goals," Fannie president Daniel Mudd noted in an internal 2007 report. "We are struggling to meet the goals."

RED HERRING #8: It was private-label securities that really drove the subprime and Alt-A markets.

FACT: Historical data show that Fannie and Freddie, the world's largest mortgage-backed securities issuers, were the catalysts driving demand for subprime and Alt-A securities and guarantees on Wall Street. Private-label issuance volume for mortgage-backed securities tracks volume generated by Fannie and Freddie, which guaranteed the private-label junk. And the trend toward higher volumes of subprime securities was set by the government-sponsored mortgage agencies starting in 2001. Together, they commanded a whopping 44 percent of the subprime securities market by 2004.

RED HERRING #9: The Clinton administration did not push subprime loans on bankers or Fannie and Freddie.

FACT: As detailed in earlier chapters, former HUD secretary Cuomo argued that Fannie's and Freddie's "expanded presence in the subprime market could be of significant benefit to minorities," and he therefore directed them to "play a significant role in the subprime market." That was in 2000. Two years later, the Urban Institute concluded in a report for HUD that "Fannie Mae and Freddie Mac are expanding their subprime business, partially in response to the higher affordable housing goals established by HUD." In 2004, furthermore, HUD revealed the following in its rules and regulations report for that year: "Partly in response to higher affordable housing goals set by HUD in its new rule set in 2000, the GSEs are increasing their business in the subprime market. In the 2000 GSE Rule, HUD identified subprime borrowers as a market that can assist Fannie Mae and Freddie Mac in reaching their higher affordable housing goals."

FACT: Also as documented earlier, top CRA regulator Seidman, another Clinton appointee, proudly brayed that the administration had created the booming market for both subprime loans and securities.

(Most Clinton officials were for subprime loans before they were against them. Former HUD secretary Henry Cisneros went on to gross more than $5 million in stock sales and board compensation from Countrywide Financial, the nation's largest subprime lender. Even former First Lady Hillary Clinton's chief of staff jumped on the subprime bandwagon. Maggie Williams, an African-American, made $200,000 serving on the board of New York-based subprime lender Delta Financial Corporation before it went bankrupt in late 2007. Williams defended her seven-year tenure with the discredited firm, explaining that the risky loans offered credit-impaired minorities the only option they had to purchase a home. "I joined the board because I understood that the subprime option, for all its challenges, was the only chance for many people to own a home," she said. "There are people who miss payments and have bad credit for all kinds of reasons.")

RED HERRING #10: CRA exams and HUD Affordable Housing Goals are unrelated to a borrower's race.

FACT: The Federal Housing Enterprises Financial Safety and Soundness Act, which authorizes HUD to set such goals for Fannie and Freddie, defines the "underserved areas" for loan targeting as "high-minority tracts."

FACT: Though technically the CRA does not enumerate race, the statute has its origins in concerns over racial redlining. And discrimination charges adversely affect CRA evaluations. More, the CRA's targeted assessment areas are "predominantly minority neighborhoods."

RED HERRING #11: "It wasn't the CRA" or HUD mandates or any other federal regulation that fueled the subprime crisis, House Financial Services Committee chairman Barney Frank insists. "It was the lack of regulation that did it." Senate Banking Committee chairman Chris Dodd, agrees, citing "deregulation that occurred on basically an eight-year coffee break by the administration."

FACT: Marsha Courchane, who worked as a Treasury regulator under Clinton, disagrees with Frank and Dodd. She argues that, though well-intentioned, federal housing policies under both Bush and Clinton played a key role in the crisis. "I do believe that public policy in general pushed us to try to erase homeownership gaps between white and minority neighborhoods," she testified before the U.S. Commission on Civil Rights in 2009. "And a variety of innovative products, some of which were toxic, were developed to try to do that."

FACT: Banking and finance are the most heavily regulated sectors of the economy, and they were subject to tougher, not weaker, anti-redlining rules over the past two decades. Typically, four federal agencies—the Federal Reserve, the FDIC, the Office of the Comptroller of the Currency, and the Office of Thrift Supervision—enforce the CRA. But Clinton extended enforcement powers to the Department of Justice and HUD, turning them into de facto CRA regulators. And these two agencies effectively expanded compliance beyond banks to include mortgage companies and Fannie and Freddie, who previously had been unregulated by the CRA. This regulatory regime remained in place during the Bush administration.

RED HERRING #12: It was all Bush's fault. "This was the Bush social policy. This was their compassionate conservatism," Frank claims, contradicting his earlier argument. "They were the ones pushing this. Fannie Mae and Freddie Mac were doing it at the orders of the Bush administration."

FACT: While the Bush administration continued to ratchet up Affordable Housing Goals, the Clinton administration made by far the largest hike in HUD's required goals. In 2000, the housing agency required Fannie and Freddie to devote half of their lending to support affordable housing through 2004, and that year they together commanded 44 percent of the subprime securities market. In a 2004 report, HUD attributed the sudden spurt of subprime investment to the earlier record hike, stating that it came "partly in response to higher affordable housing goals set by HUD in 2000."

FACT: Clinton's 20-point hike in affordable-housing goals over his two terms far exceeded Bush's six-point goal increase over his eight years. (See the appendix to view the chart.) Not only was Clinton's hike steeper, but it also had a greater impact, coinciding as it did with the biggest surge in Fannie and Freddie subprime securitization.

RED HERRING #13: It was Greenspan's fault. The central banker created the subprime bubble by keeping interest rates too low from 2002 to 2004.

FACT: The Fed's role in the housing bubble which began in 1997 has been overstated. Even if the Federal Reserve was too loose, home prices rose more than would be expected given historical links between Fed policy and home prices. There have been other periods when the Fed slashed interest rates and it did not lead to a mortgage crisis. Nor did prior easing result in unprecedented homebuying among minorities (half the 12 million new homeowners between 1995 and 2005 were minorities, according to a Harvard study). Clearly other factors were at play.

FACT: The Fed does not directly control mortgage rates. They are pegged to long-term bond yields, not the short-term federal funds rate the Fed uses as its key policy benchmark.

FACT: Lower rates had nothing to do with lower underwriting standards, the root of the problem.

(Although as noted in an earlier chapter, Greenspan gave his blessing to flexible underwriting guidelines. He also was a steadfast supporter of the CRA, even voting to deny bank mergers based on poor CRA report cards. Amusingly, Greenspan's mentor, 1970s-era Federal Reserve chairman Arthur Burns, opposed original passage of the CRA, arguing it would corrupt the market flow of credit.)

RED HERRING #14: It was Wall Street's fault. As Obama maintains, the subprime crisis was "due to the irresponsibility of large financial institutions on Wall Street that gambled on risky loans."

FACT: A breakdown of the aggregate mortgage data reveals that Wall Street is responsible for less than one-third of the risky loans, while government is responsible for more than two-thirds of them. More precisely, Washington accounts for 71 percent of the 27 million risky subprime and Alt-A mortgages outstanding. This overwhelming public portion of dodgy loans includes:

- 12 million held by Fannie or Freddie;
- 5 million held by the Federal Housing Authority, or FHA; and
- 2.2 million held by private institutions under the requirements of the CRA and HUD.

FACT: That leaves 7.8 million—or just 29 percent—of the high-risk home loans issued solely by Wall Street through private label issuers, according to calculations by former Fannie chief credit officer Edward Pinto and Financial Crisis Inquiry commissioner Peter Wallison. (See the pie chart in the appendix.)

So you see, the social engineers on Pennsylvania Avenue ran amok far more than the financial engineers on Wall Street.

Undeterred, Frank offers a metaphor to buttress his argument demonizing Wall Street. "Think of this as bullets and guns," he argues. "Those were the bullets—the bad subprime loans. The guns then were these very sophisticated instruments, collateralized debt obligation derivatives, that rocketed them all throughout the world, but it began with those guns."

Though Frank is correct to compare dangerous subprime loans to bullets, the guns that fired them were the CRA and HUD regulations Washington used to hold up private banks, and Fannie and Freddie. And it was government-sponsored Fannie and Freddie that guaranteed the Wall Street "derivatives" that ricocheted around the world.

In other words, the risk-taking was driven by government policies and spread by government policies.

This is not to say Wall Street did nothing stupid. It is just that the evidence fingering Washington in the subprime crime is overwhelming. The historical record on this is absolutely clear.

▼

For decades, Frank and other social engineers knocked lenders for not making enough loans to minorities. Then they went out and made those loans, and the bubble burst. Now the same people in Washington say, "Well why'd you make those loans?" It is a classic example of the government creating a problem and then blaming the private sector.

And they do not want to face the consequences. If government regulations caused the problem, deregulation, not reregulation, is the obvious solution. But they argue the CRA and HUD are easy "scapegoats" for flint-hearted critics who want to abolish anti-redlining laws, along with Fannie and Freddie and their affordable housing mission.

"The conservative view is stop trying to help poor people. That's it. Repeal the Community Reinvestment Act," Frank contends. "Our view is no, let's try to help poor people."

He and others insist that if anything, now is the time to *strengthen* anti-redlining regulations and fair-lending policies to help inner-city victims of foreclosures.

But these apologists are merely circling the wagons around government programs and policies they know are central to the problem. And they are trying to cover their own tracks in the financial crime of the century.

# AFTERWORD

In America, we have this strong bias toward individual action. You know, we idolize the John Wayne hero who comes in to correct things with both guns blazing. But individual actions, individual dreams, are not sufficient. We must unite in collective action, build collective institutions and organizations.

— Barack Obama, 1995

The late, great economist Joseph Schumpeter once lamented that capitalism would eventually succumb to socialism—not by violent worker revolution, as Karl Marx predicted—but by a slow strangulation at the hands of an elite class of critics and agitators that could never survive outside of capitalism if not for the great wealth it affords even those hostile to it. He predicted that blood-sucking bureaucrats, politicians, and lawyers, as well as professors, lobbyists, journalists, and social activists (including community organizers), would one day consume their generous host.

Schumpeter argued that unlike the business entrepreneurs they attack, such parasites have not a clue how to create wealth. But they know to a fare-thee-well how to divide it, redistribute it, loot it. They have lofty terms for their shakedown. President Obama, for one, calls it "economic justice." He thinks businesses have a societal obligation—a "social compact," as he says—to cater to and compensate ever-demanding minority rights groups.

But that social compact has become a suicide pact. And America is on the verge of fulfilling Schumpeter's prophecy.

This country is in very serious danger of transitioning from an entrepreneurial economy to a parasitic economy—whereby race racketeers, grievance mongers, and street agitators (or as the First Lady euphemistically calls them, "social entrepreneurs") align with group-identity politicians to suck the lifeblood out of the real entrepreneurs in private industry.

One leech on a host will not necessarily kill it. But if enough parasites attack it, collectively, they can destroy it—especially when it is as weak as it is now. Organized groups of parasites are shaking down corporate America, and they are emboldened and empowered as never before by this presidency.

The parasites are radical community organizing groups—clones of ACORN, such as NPA, NACA, NCRC, and the Greenlining Institute—who convince poor, inner-city minorities that they are victims of racist conspiracies led by the white establishment. These groups agitate minorities into "collective action" against an imagined enemy. They convince them that they are powerless as individuals and have to organize as groups to get ahead. They brainwash them into believing that their race is their only identity and their only worth; that they are entitled to that which they cannot achieve through merit; and that there is nothing demeaning about depending on government versus pluck. It is a pernicious lie, but the lie has become culture.

Hoover Institution fellow Shelby Steele, who grew up black in Chicago, says victim-focused racial-identity politics has choked black advancement more than racism itself has. "It's been ruinous," he said. "It's had the worst impact of anything short of slavery."

"There's more color-consciousness than ever, and that's sad," Steele adds. "'Individual' is a very negative word in black America today. People forget that Martin Luther King talked about blacks as individuals."

## DISQUIETING TREND

Our current decline in living standards is simply the end result of our long decline in cultural standards. The American Creed has been replaced by a militant, something-for-nothing groupism that has led to the tribalization of the American economy. Community organizing promotes such groupism. It tells people it is not their job as individuals to go out and pursue their life, but rather the government's job to do it for them.

Now a former community organizer sits in the Oval Office. Obama scoffs at the rugged individualism enshrined in the American's Creed, and he seeks to turn the creeping collectivism that plagues the nation into a full gallop.

"In America, we have this strong bias toward individual action. You know, we idolize the John Wayne hero who comes in to correct things with both guns blazing," Obama told a black

Chicago publication in 1995, during his first bid for public office. "But individual actions, individual dreams, are not sufficient. We must unite in collective action, build collective institutions and organizations."

This echoes his Alinskyite training. "We claim the value of a sacred community over isolating individualism," intones the vision statement of the Chicago-based Gamaliel Foundation, an Alinsky station of the cross, which gave Obama his start in community organizing.

"Every community organizer that I have known believes that . . . capitalism doesn't work," says former University of California regent Ward Connerly, a black conservative. "So any time someone tells you they're a community organizer, watch your wallet."

Their purpose is redistributing wealth. And they work with government to accomplish this through financial regulations, among other things. Business incentives have become so distorted in favor of politically protected classes—who then carve up the economic spoils based on their own parochial interests—that even time-tested business standards such as prudent mortgage-underwriting rules are trashed to placate them.

Before long, the number one industry in America may be the shakedown industry itself—the afterbirth of a decades-long obsession with multiculturalism and diversity. With each new race-based government regulation, the race racket becomes more lucrative, attracting more parasites to the host.

The last thing America needs is *more* regulations benefiting this race racket. Quite the opposite, we need to repeal race-based government mandates, starting with the left's sacred cow, the Community Reinvestment Act ("reinvestment" being code for redistribution).

Yet the administration plans to expand it to cover the entire financial spectrum, including insurers, possibly even adding a specific discrimination litmus test that banks will have to pass. Adding a new layer of financial regulations on top of the Dodd-Frank Act—which has already generated more than 5,000 pages of new rules from just three of its 16 titles—could cripple the financial sector and the economy with it.

It was government overregulation, in the form of the CRA and HUD's Affordable Housing Goals, that fueled the subprime market the regulators and activists complain about today. CRA social goals overtook good business sense. Washington's social engineers injected risk into an industry that lives or dies by its ability to manage risk. But the CRA encourages imprudent lending practices and actually invites risk in the name of "fair lending." Its social incentives are divorced from financial reality, and they result in bad loans that cumulatively harm the communities of color they are supposed to help.

No community, no matter how "disadvantaged," is ultimately aided by bad loans and struggling banks. Properly underwritten loans strengthen communities, while poorly underwritten ones undermine them.

The resulting mortgage crisis is a harsh reminder of the unintended consequences of good intentions. And it will have lasting repercussions. By trying to close the "mortgage gap" between races—a disparity that has little to do with racism and almost everything to do with personal initiative—the "fairness" agonists have mortgaged the financial security of all our children. The next generation quite possibly may be the first that fails to enjoy higher living standards.

## DIVERSITY TAX

Ignoring variables such as credit scores, NCRC president John Taylor claims high-cost mortgages are racist. "African-Americans and Latinos are being discriminated against in the marketplace," he has testified on Capitol Hill, "and being forced to pay a 'race tax' due to unequal access to credit."

In fact, he has it backward. The *majority of Americans* are being forced to pay a *diversity* tax proposed by CRA lobbyists like NCRC and levied by overzealous government regulators and politicians, who forget that the most important minority in this country is the *individual*.

Ironically, these agonists are neither of color nor poor. They are in fact privileged white men, like NACA founder Bruce Marks, who grew up playing tennis at Boston-area country clubs; and ACORN founder Wade Rathke, who attended a private New England college and whose complexion is as ruddy as his old pal Bill Clinton's. It was while enrolled at Williams College in Massachusetts—one of the most expensive colleges in the nation—that Rathke got the idea to start ACORN. There, he started a riot at an area welfare office that resulted in looting and the arrest of some 50 people, including him.

It is no coincidence that command central of the housing rights movement is Massachusetts, the Brahmin base of the East Coast upper-crust establishment. A remarkable number of the leading coat-and-tie radicals involved in the subprime scandal hail from there, including: Alicia Munnell, formerly of the Boston Fed, who has called tony Beacon Hill home; Democratic congressman Barney Frank of upscale Newton, Massachusetts; NCRC's Taylor, formerly of Boston; the Kennedy clan of Hyannis; NACA's Marks of Boston; and William Apgar of Cambridge. Former top ACORN lobbyist Deepak Bhargava also spent time in Cambridge while enrolled at Harvard.

And now add to the list the dowdy Elizabeth Warren, the interim director of Obama's new Consumer Financial Protection Bureau. She is another Boston denizen, a member of Harvard's law faculty.

Warren, who appears in Michael Moore's market-bashing film, *Capitalism: A Love Story*, is an anti-business crusader who favors nationalizing banks and capping the interest rates they can charge consumers. Federal Election Commission records show she has donated to the campaigns of some of Congress's most famous progressives, including Democrat senator Russ Feingold and the late Democrat senator Paul Wellstone. No wonder far left groups like Moveon.org and the Service Employees International Union, or SEIU, have petitioned Obama to name her to run the consumer watchdog agency.

These New England zealots all work in concert to shake down the banking industry on behalf of the poor minorities they deign to protect—and they make a pretty good living at it, as we have seen. Along with its ideological sister cities, San Francisco and Chicago, Boston seems to be the hatchery for all that is radical and wrong in America, with Washington serving as the catch basin for its nostrums.

So, do not blame individual minorities for this crisis. They did not water down time-tested underwriting rules. They did not knock the pillars out from under the banking industry. They did not turn the housing sector into a house of cards. Blame these guilt-ridden country club radicals with their Ivy League pedigrees, who exploit underprivileged minorities and enlist them as foot soldiers in their romantic revolution for "social justice" as atonement for their own privileged family status. Many of the minorities herded onto buses with bullhorns and pickets to shout down the alleged greedmongers are being used by the professional grievance-mongers as lab rats in their dystopian experiment. And when it fails, as it did in the housing bust, the minorities are the ones left picking up the pieces. They are the ones who suffer from boarded-up neighborhoods and damaged credit reports. The puppet masters just go back to their think tanks or take cushy jobs in the next administration, where they plot and scheme to exploit the "underclass" all over again. To be sure, some have genuinely good intentions in pushing for more affordable housing policies. But the road to serfdom is paved with good intentions. If the worst financial crisis since the Great Depression did not teach us that, nothing will.

## REDLINE THE CRA

One of CRA's biggest original critics was the late Emory University finance professor George Benston. He was one of a handful of economic prophets who last decade warned of the costly hazard the act posed in the hands of Reno and other left-wing zealots tilting at racist windmills in the lending business.

"There is no evidence that such discrimination exists," asserted Benston. But there is "lots of evidence that the act harms both banks and their customers," whether black, brown, or white.

Indeed, everybody would be better off if the pernicious CRA were simply . . . abolished.

This is not fringe thinking. Several respected economists are arguing to eliminate it, along with Fannie and Freddie—Harvard economist Jeffrey Miron, for one. "The fact that government bears such a huge responsibility for the current mess means any response should eliminate the conditions that created this situation in the first place, not attempt to fix bad government with more government," he argues.

So what should the government do? Eliminate those policies that generated the current mess.

"This means, at a general level, abandoning the goal of home ownership independent of ability to pay," Miron proposes. "This means, in particular, getting rid of Fannie Mae and Freddie Mac, along with policies like the Community Reinvestment Act that pressure banks into subprime lending."

"The CRA should be repealed," agrees Vern McKinley, a former FDIC and Federal Reserve official. Keeping it alive will only encourage "future administrations to utilize the statute as a government credit allocation scheme."

Another precrisis oracle, Financial Crisis Inquiry commissioner Peter Wallison, warned as early as 1999 that Fannie and Freddie were overleveraged on CRA and other risky loans and might fail in a recession, requiring the government to step in and bail them out. "This is another thrift industry growing up around us," Wallison told the *New York Times* at the time, referring to the savings and loan crisis earlier in the decade.

The CRA no longer has a moral leg to stand on. The subprime debacle has forever undermined it as a noble vestige of the civil-rights movement. It stands now as a failed social experiment on the scale of President Johnson's War on Poverty, and it should be pole-axed, not strengthened.

The CRA system, like affirmative action, robs the creditworthy among minorities of the satisfaction of qualifying for a first home mortgage on their own merits. "[Instead] it sends the message that this most important milestone has been provided through the beneficence of government, devaluing individual accomplishment," says Manhattan Institute scholar Howard Husock.

Worse, the CRA after Clinton's revisions in 1995 created a double standard for lending—an easy standard for protected and politically favored groups, and another, harder one for everybody else. This is the very definition of racism. Let's be clear: Minorities already have "access to credit." The CRA has merely compelled the private sector, by force of law, to effectively allocate credit based on government social goals—without regard for the merits of loan applications, which is unconstitutional.

Groupism leads to different standards for different people groups. That is what the heroes of the civil-rights movement fought against. Why are we backtracking?

## STOP THE MADNESS

Using the CRA as a weapon, community organizing thugs like NCRC, NPA, and Greenlining have already shaken down banks for a total of more than $6 trillion in set-asides and other commitments for minorities. Now they want to shake them down for business contracts, retirement funds, stock holdings, and jobs. Inner-city "wealth-building" is the new frontier for CRA lobbyists.

Next, these parasites will want banks to underwrite the government's entire welfare and jobs budget. That is not as far-fetched as it sounds. Facing record budget deficits, the Organizer-in-Chief in the White House is desperate to find other sources to fund his stealth reparations. By conscripting Wall Street, he can bypass the public appropriations process. And he can avoid enraging voters who do not like Washington using tax dollars to directly subsidize protected classes. This way he can indirectly subsidize them—with your *deposits* (and later, your tax dollars when more bailouts are needed). In effect, he can finance his social agenda off-budget.

If the White House and Congress want to continue subsidizing housing and other social projects, they should do it up front—where taxpayers and voters can see it—not by stealth, through expanding banking regulations.

Now that Republicans control one half of Congress, they must move quickly on this front, before the CRA can be refashioned into a more potent weapon to brandish against banks. They must also move to dissolve Fannie and Freddie and its affordable-housing charter, thereby removing the federal government from the mortgage business and denying Democrats their personal piggy banks.

As my *Investor's Business Daily* colleague Terry "Buck" Jones has opined, "Fannie and Freddie were created by Democrats, regulated by Democrats, largely run by Democrats, and protected by Democrats"—for the benefit of their Democrat constituents, I would add.

Abolish the 33-year-old CRA? Dissolve the venerable Fannie and Freddie, which sprang from the Great Depression? Sounds impossible! Can this ever really happen?

Sure it can. The bills have already been introduced in Congress. They are: the Reliable Economic Stabilization, Capital Utilization, Enterprise Reform Act of 2008 (H.R. 7264, which includes Sec. 105. Repeal of Community Reinvestment Act), and the Government-Sponsored Enterprises Free Market Reform Act of 2008 (H.R. 7094). All it takes is the political will to pass them.

The last thing we need is more banking reform. What we need now is *government* reform.

## FIRE FANNIE AND FREDDIE

Before Clinton's race-based loan targets wound up overexposing them to toxic subprime debt, Fannie and Freddie were rock-solid institutions. Now they are the biggest mortgage risk holders in the biggest mortgage crisis.

These quasi-federal disaster zones should have been treated like any insolvent bank—seized, wound down, their assets auctioned off, and debt restructured. Instead, they acted as a dumping ground for $1.8 trillion in toxic bank loans, and now serve as a mechanism for backdoor bailouts of the rest of the troubled banking sector.

Yet the most "sweeping" overhaul of the financial industry since the Great Depression does not touch either of them. The two companies at the heart of the financial crisis and most deserving of reform dodged the wrecking ball, which makes financial reform meaningless. And the Angelides Commission, tasked with identifying the root causes of the crisis, barely lays a glove on them or their "affordable housing" charter.

Instead of breaking up the government-subsidized duopoly, Washington is circling the wagons around it, even as it continues to hemorrhage losses from busted subprime loans, costing taxpayers billions more in bailout funds.

Overhauling the banking system without fixing Fannie and Freddie is like fighting terrorists without attacking the jihadist ideology motivating them. All that's changed with passage of the Dodd-Frank Act—which should be renamed the Fannie-Freddie Protection Act—is the size of government's hand in the economy, now bigger than ever.

"The bill does not respond at all to the causes of the financial crisis," Wallison says. By not addressing Fannie and Freddie, economist Brian Wesbury adds, "the government is taking no blame for the subprime crisis and is demanding more power over the U.S. financial system."

Chartered in 1938 by Congress, Fannie Mae will turn 75 soon. I propose making her 75th birthday her last. This Depression-era baby nearly caused a second Depression. Wind her and her brother down, and hold a joint funeral instead.

Because of their dual private-public mandate to please both Wall Street shareholders and Washington social engineers, Fannie and Freddie are demonstrably a failed social experiment on a massive scale. Yet the Democrats in Congress and the White House, which placed them into conservatorship in 2008, will not let them fail. That would mean abandoning their holy crusade of "affordable housing," which they financed through Fannie and Freddie.

## COVERING THEIR FANNIE

You cannot talk about the housing crisis or reforms without talking about the affordable-housing goals HUD slapped on Fannie and Freddie. That is, unless you are Congress. Or Timothy Geithner. The Treasury secretary hosted a summit in August 2010 to discuss redesigning the mortgage-finance system—which is still controlled by Fannie and Freddie. Even today, 9 of 10 new mortgages are backed by them, and the two agencies account for almost half the nation's $12 trillion in residential mortgages outstanding.

Geithner vowed to fundamentally "change" the failed government-sponsored mortgage giants. Yet, suspiciously, he did not offer how or rule out expanding their role in the housing market as a nationalized entity. Nor did he explain why they lowered their underwriting standards and collapsed under the weight of subprime loans and securities in the first place. So here is a refresher:

- In 1997, as part of Clinton housing policy, HUD required that 42 percent of Fannie's and Freddie's mortgage financing go to "underserved" borrowers with unproven or damaged credit.
- To help them meet that goal, HUD, their regulator, authorized them to relax their lending criteria.
- HUD also authorized them to buy subprime securities that included loans to uncreditworthy borrowers.
- Unhappy with the results—despite Fannie and Freddie already committing $1 trillion in risky low-income loans in the 1990s—HUD in 2000 raised its affordable-housing target again—to 50 percent, a 19 percent jump from the earlier level.
- By 2008, HUD's target had topped out at 56 percent. And Fannie and Freddie had drowned in a toxic soup of bad subprime paper.

HUD secretary Shaun Donovan insists the affordable-housing goals are not to blame. "We should be careful not to learn the wrong lesson from this experience," he warned skeptics, "and sacrifice an important feature of the current system: wide access to mortgage credit."

This, of course, is revisionist history. Fannie and Freddie internal communications written in the months leading up to the crisis confirm that executives were under enormous pressure to meet "our HUD goals."

But as Orwell warned, whoever controls the present controls the past. And right now, the people who pushed Fannie and Freddie—along with our entire financial system—off the cliff in the name of "affordable housing" are running the show. And it sounds as though they intend to double down on the failed government-backed mortgage agencies.

Just look at some of the expert panelists Geithner invited to his Potemkin summit.

Figuring prominently into the "debate" was Ellen Seidman, a former Clinton aide who became one of his top bank regulators. As former head of the Office of Thrift Supervision, she aggressively enforced Clinton's beefed-up Community Reinvestment Act, which codified the "flexible" underwriting that Fannie and Freddie eventually adopted.

Seidman, who headed Fannie's regulation office before joining the Clinton administration, argued that Fannie's and Freddie's support for "low-income and minority communities"—especially now amid a wave of urban foreclosures—is "absolutely critical." She proposes the government take an even larger role in promoting housing for "underserved markets."

"The private sector will not do it on its own," Seidman said, "and we should just stop having that debate."

She acts as if everybody agrees with her premise of universal home ownership. Homes are not a right. People who lost their homes can go back to renting; there is no shame in that. The shame came when government pushed them into homes they could not afford. And the housing bubble it created hurt everybody in the end.

Echoing Seidman, Geithner asserted that whatever replaces Fannie and Freddie must continue to "provide access to affordable housing for lower-income Americans." He added that it must also continue to guarantee loans.

In other words, Fannie and Freddie are not going anywhere. They will be absorbed into the government, most likely Treasury or HUD, or both. The proof will be in the administration's final proposal "on the future of housing finance." The report is scheduled for delivery to Congress by January 31, 2011.

Why must taxpayers continue subsidizing home ownership through a government-guaranteed secondary mortgage market run by a government-protected duopoly?

## WELLS FARGO'S PLAN

Within the proper framework, private firms can originate, purchase, and securitize mortgages more safely and efficiently—and do so without the politically injected risk or taxpayer liability.

Wells Fargo, for one, may have a viable plan. It proposes gradually replacing Freddie and Fannie with privately owned "mortgage conduits" that buy loans from the primary market and deliver the loans into a common mortgage-backed security. They would assume the risk on the underlying mortgages, while the government would guarantee only the mortgage-backed security. To protect taxpayers, the conduits would pay into an insurance fund, although setting a risk-based premium would be problematic.

The plan attempts to maximize the use of private capital while limiting Washington's role to assuming catastrophic risk in the event of conduit failure.

Other charter privileges enjoyed by Fannie and Freddie would be eliminated—including their Treasury line of credit, state and local tax exemptions, and weak capital requirements. Above all, the plan would curb HUD's interference in the mortgage market. No more unrealistically high affordable-housing goals. No more pressure to lower qualifying standards.

Canceling their legislative charters—and along with it, their "affordable housing" missions—would end not only the massive risk these charters pose, but also the corruption and cronyism they have spawned. It would bring an end to Fannie's and Freddie's

- accounting frauds and obscene executive bonuses;
- sweetheart loans for VIP politicians who protected them from due oversight;
- payola for the Congressional Black Caucus and Congressional Hispanic Caucus in the form of huge donations funded through campaign war chests Fannie and Freddie created through their charitable foundations (see the table in the appendix); and
- politically appointed boards of directors stacked with Democrat insiders like Franklin Delano Raines, now an informal housing adviser to Obama.

Raines, a Clinton appointee who ran Fannie for five years, described the mortgage giant as "a mediating structure that bends the financial system to create homeowners." It certainly became that way under his leadership, which ended amid scandal in December 2004.

Raines, an African-American upset with the stubborn mortgage gap between blacks and whites, has pooh-poohed individualism and argued that it takes a government-corporate village to improve society. "We live in a society where the boundaries of business and government are beginning to blur," he rejoiced, adding, "We have come to accept that government cannot and should not do it all. Corporations have a greater social responsibility today."

In fact, corporations have a singular responsibility to make profits and maximize shareholder value—period. End of story.

It is absolutely outrageous that the federal government—which has no business in the mortgage business in the first place—now controls virtually 100 percent of the secondary mortgage market. It is even more scandalous when you consider that the government, not the free market, caused the failure of its newfound wards, Fannie and Freddie. Our own national government, through its "affordable housing" mission, in effect, rigged the market to fail.

Breaking up Fannie and Freddie into smaller, private companies is the best way to protect taxpayers and homeowners from future harm. Otherwise, we will continue writing Washington a blank check to prop them up.

"The financial crisis was caused by U.S. housing policies and specifically the huge number of subprime and Alt-A loans called forth by government requirements imposed on Fannie Mae, Freddie Mac, and private lenders," Wallison warns. "If the government gets back in the business of distorting the private markets in order to stimulate housing growth in the future, we will have another financial crisis."

This is no academic debate. In the ideological battle between groupism and individualism, between statism and entrepreneurism, your money and livelihood are at stake. Winning is of towering importance to America's future financial health and living standards.

# APPENDIX

## WALL STREET DID IT?

Government accounts for more than two thirds of the 27 million risky subprime and other nonprime mortgages outstanding.

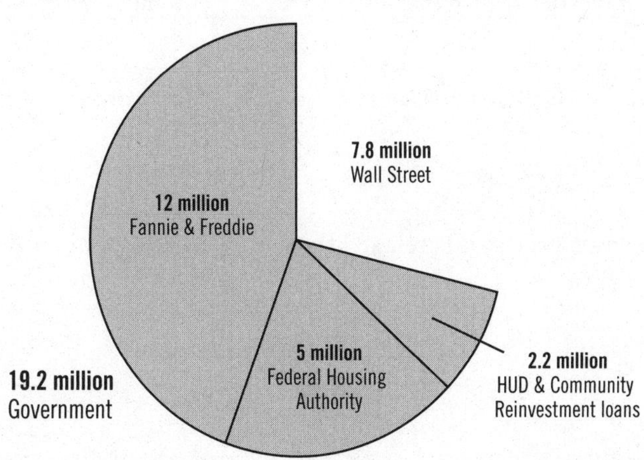


Sources: Edward Pinto, former chief Fannie credit officer; Peter Wallison, Financial Crisis Inquiry Commission member

## BAD INFLUENCE

As HUD pressured Fannie and Freddie to underwrite more home loans for low-income and minority borrowers . . .

| HUD affordable-housing goals, as a share of GSE mortgage purchases | |
|---|---|
| 1995 | 30% |
| 1996 | 40% |
| 1997 | 42% |
| 1998 | 42% |
| 1999 | 42% |
| 2000 | 42% |
| 2001* | 50% |
| 2002 | 50% |
| 2003 | 50% |
| 2004 | 50% |
| 2005 | 52% |
| 2006 | 53% |
| 2007 | 55% |

* New Clinton HUD goals went into effect January 1, 2001, and extended through 2004.

Source: Federal Housing Finance Agency

. . . the mortgage giants relaxed their underwriting standards . . .

## SHARE OF HOME LOANS PURCHASED WITH DOWN PAYMENT OF 5% OR LESS*

| | FANNIE | FREDDIE |
|---|---|---|
| 1997 | 3.3% | 1.1% |
| 2000 | 4.4% | 6.1% |
| 2004 | 14.1% | 6.4% |
| 2007 | 26.0% | 19.3% |

* Traditionally lenders require a minimum 20% down.

Sources: HUD Office of Policy Development and Research: "Profiles of GSE Mortgage Purchases in 1999 and 2000," April 2002; "The GSEs' Funding of Affordable Loans: A 2000 Update," April 2002; "Profiles of GSE Morgage Purchases in 2001–2004," April 2008; "Profiles of GSE Mortgage Purchases in 2005–2007," September 2008

. . . and gobbled up almost half the market in subprime securities sold on Wall Street to satisfy HUD goals . . .

## SUBPRIME MORTGAGE-BACKED SECURITIES PURCHASED BY FANNIE AND FREDDIE, IN BILLIONS

| | |
|---|---|
| 2002 | $38 |
| 2003 | $81 |
| 2004 | $176 |
| 2005 | $169 |
| 2006 | $110 |

Note: Pre-2002 totals unavailable.

Sources: Federal Housing Finance Agency, HUD, Office of the Federal Housing Enterprise Oversight

. . . triggering an explosion in overall subprime lending. . . .

## SUBPRIME LOAN ORIGINATIONS, IN BILLIONS

| | |
|---|---|
| 2000 | $126 |
| 2001 | $165 |
| 2002 | $204 |
| 2003 | $325 |
| 2004 | $513 |
| 2005 | $630 |
| 2006 | $591 |

Sources: HUD, Fannie Mae, Freddie Mac

## CRA SHAKEDOWN

Through 2000, over 90 percent of all bank loans mandated under the Community Reinvestment Act of 1977 were made during the 8 years of the Clinton administration.

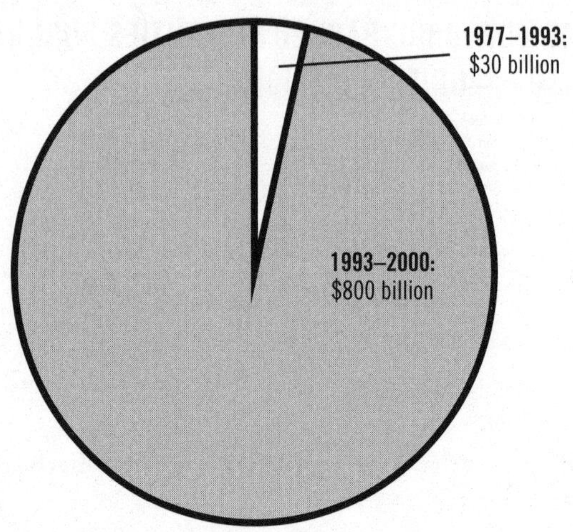


Source: Clinton Foundation, Center for Community Change

## MORE RACE REGULATORS

Number of federal bank examiners continued to grow under Clinton after resolution of S&L crisis.

| | |
|---|---|
| 1979 | 4,669 |
| 1984 | 3,931 |
| 1990 | 5,577 |
| 1994 | 6,452 |

Note: Totals include FDIC, Federal Reserve, and Comptroller of the Currency.

Source: FDIC

## BUBBA'S BUBBLE

Yale economist Robert J. Shiller created an index of American home prices going back to 1890. It presents housing values in consistent terms over 116 years, factoring out the effects of inflation. From 1997 to 2006, the index soared an unprecedented 83%.

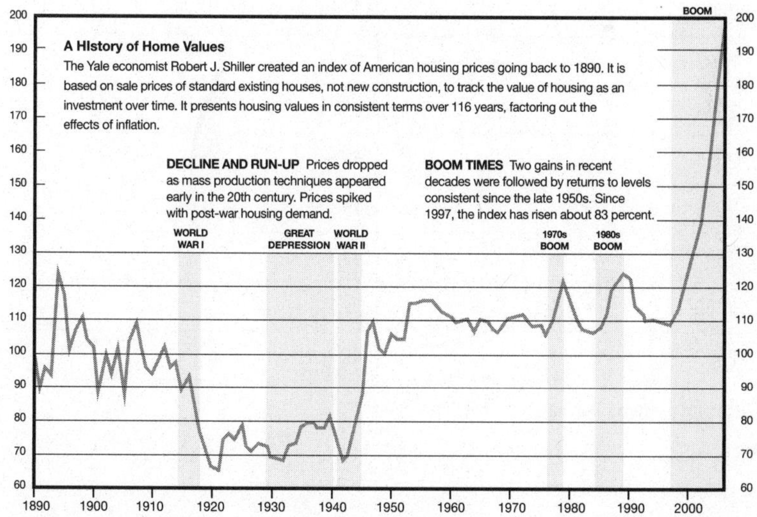


"Irrational Exuberance," Princeton University Press, 2006; *New York Times*

## LATINO HOMEOWNERSHIP

Easy credit policies boosted Hispanic homeownership rate to record highs

| | |
|---|---|
| 1990 | 41.2% |
| 1991 | 39.0 |
| 1992 | 39.9 |
| 1993 | 39.4 |
| 1994 | 41.2 |
| 1995 Clinton orders tough new bank anti-bias rules | 42.1 |
| 1996 Clinton orders IRS to allow ITIN numbers in lieu of Social Security | 42.8 |
| 1997 | 43.3 |
| 1998 | 44.7 |
| 1999 | 45.5 |
| 2000 | 46.3 |
| 2001 | 47.3 |
| 2002 | 47.0 |
| 2003 Bush signs law subsidizing immigrant down payments | 46.7 |
| 2004 | 48.1 |
| 2005 | 49.5 |
| 2006 | 49.7 |
| 2007 | 49.7 |
| 2008 | 49.1 |
| 2009 | 48.4 |

Source: Census Bureau

## REVERSAL OF FORTUNE

After Clinton pressured banks to ease lending rules for minorities in the mid-1990s, black homeownership rates shot up to record levels. The added demand fed the housing bubble, which eventually burst, sending rates tumbling back down.

| Black homeownership rate | |
|---|---|
| 1990 | 42.6% |
| 1991 | 42.7 |
| 1992 | 42.6 |
| 1993 | 42.0 |
| 1994 | 42.3 |
| 1995 Clinton orders tough new bank anti-bias rules | 42.7 |
| 1996 | 44.1 |
| 1997 | 44.8 |
| 1998 | 45.6 |
| 1999 | 46.3 |
| 2000 HUD pushes Fannie and Freddie into subprime market | 47.2 |
| 2001 | 47.7 |
| 2002 | 47.4 |
| 2003 | 48.1 |
| 2004 | 49.1 |
| 2005 | 48.2 |
| 2006 | 47.9 |
| 2007 | 47.2 |
| 2008 | 47.4 |
| 2009 | 46.2 |

Source: Census Bureau

## PROTECTION MONEY

Top recipients of Fannie and Freddie campaign donations, 1989–2008

| | |
|---|---|
| 1. Sen. Chris Dodd (D-CT) | $133,900 |
| 2. Sen. John Kerry (D-MA) | $111,000 |
| 3. Sen. Barack Obama (D-IL) | $105,849 |
| 4. Sen. Hillary Clinton (D-NY) | $75,550 |
| 5. Rep. Paul Kanjorski (D-PA) | $65,500 |
| 6. Sen. Robert Bennett (R-UT) | $61,499 |
| 7. Sen. Tim Johnson (D-SD) | $61,000 |
| 8. Sen. Kent Conrad (D-ND) | $58,991 |
| 9. Rep. Tom Davis (R-VA) | $55,499 |
| 10. Sen. Kit Bond (R-MO) | $55,400 |
| 11. Rep. Spencer Bachus (R-AL) | $55,300 |
| 12. Sen. Richard Shelby (R-AL | $55,000 |
| 13. Rep. Rahm Emanuel (D-IL) | $51,750 |
| 14. Sen. Jack Reed (D-RI) | $50,750 |
| 15. Sen. Tom Carper (D-DE) | $44,389 |
| 16. Rep. Barney Frank (D-MA) | $40,100 |
| 17. Rep. Carolyn Maloney (D-NY) | $38,750 |
| 18. Rep. Melissa Bean (D-IL) | $37,249 |
| 19. Rep. Roy Blunt (R-MO) | $36,500 |
| 20. Rep. Deborah Pryce (R-OH) | $34,750 |
| 21. Rep. Gary Miller (R-CA) | $33,000 |
| 22. Rep. Nancy Pelosi (D-CA) | $32,750 |
| 23. Rep. Tom Reynolds (R-NY) | $32,700 |
| 24. Rep. Steny Hoyer (D-MD) | $30,500 |
| 25. Rep. Darlene Hooley (D-OR) | $28,750 |

Note: Includes contributions from PACs and individuals. 2008 cycle totals based on data downloaded from the Federal Election Commission on June 30, 2008.

Source: FEC, Center for Responsive Politics

## CRA REPORT CARD

After Clinton's tougher CRA grading fully went into effect in 1997, the share of banks earning top scores on their CRA examinations plunged.

| % receiving "Outstanding" CRA rating | |
|---|---|
| 1995 | 24.3% |
| 1996 | 26.5% |
| 1997 CRA reforms take full effect | 22.4% |
| 1998 | 18.6% |
| 1999 | 18.6% |
| 2000 | 17.5% |
| 2001 | 10.6% |
| 2002 | 9.8% |
| 2003 | 10.1% |
| 2004 | 13.1% |
| 2005 | 16.0% |
| 2006 | 14.0% |
| 2007 | 11.9% |
| 2008 | 9.5% |

Source: Federal Financial Institutions Examination Council

# NOTES

Author's Note: If quotations within the text are readily available in multiple wire news reports, no attribution has necessarily been given here. Also, to avoid redundancy, facts, data, and studies attributed to their sources in the text may not be accompanied by notes. Uncommon quotations, including author interviews and data not readily available to the public, however, have been sourced.

### *A Note of Caution*

p. ix, Yes, the hardest-hit: Democracy Now Web Site, "Bush Offers an Umbrella When We Need a Tent"—Jesse Jackson Says President's Plan to Prevent Foreclosures Doesn't Go Far Enough" (interview with Amy Goodman), December 10, 2007, http://www.democracynow.org/2007/12/10/bush_offers_an_umbrella_when_we.

## Preface

p. xi, According to the Federal Reserve Board: According to the Federal Reserve System's statistical table, titled "Flow of Funds Accounts of the United States," American household net worth plummeted a record $14 trillion, or 28 percent, between 2007 and 2009. (This is also documented on *Wikipedia*, s.v. "Financial Crisis of 2007–2010," http://en.wikipedia.org/wiki/Financial_crisis_of_2007%E2%80%932010.) An all-time peak of $64.4 trillion was reached in the second quarter of 2007, followed by a low of $50.4 trillion in the first quarter of 2009. Household net worth measures the total value of real estate and financial assets, including stocks, bonds, and mutual funds. The 9 percent drop in net worth in the last three months of 2008 marked the biggest quarterly decline since record-keeping began in 1951.

p. xi, The president blames "fat cat bankers": Michael A. Fletcher, "Obama presses case for financial regulation," *Washington Post*, December 12, 2009.

p. xi, The people on Wall Street: Elizabeth Williamson, "Obama Slams 'Fat Cat Bankers," *Wall Street Journal*, December 14, 2009, http://online.wsj.com/article/SB126073152465089651.html.

## Introduction: The Angelides Commission

xiii, Old civic activists never: Transcript of Phil Angelides interview with Bill Press, *Bill Press Radio Show*, August 5, 2010.

p. xiv, Bitterly hostile was Wall Street: Ferdinand Pecora, *Wall Street Under Oath* (New York: A. M. Kelley, 1968), preface.

p. xiv, On January 13, 2010: Midsouth Bancorp Inc., "MidSouth Bank's Cloutier Testifying Before Financial Crisis Inquiry Commission on Causes of Financial Disaster," PR Newswire Web site, January 12, 2010, http://www.prnewswire.com/news-releases/midsouth-banks-cloutier-testifying-before-financial-crisis-inquiry-commission-on-causes-of-financial-disaster-81241592.html.

p. xiv, While commission chairman Philip Angelides: Brady Dennis, "In Capitol Hill hearing, bankers remain torn on their role in crisis," *Washington Post*, January 14, 2010, http://www.washingtonpost.com/wp-dyn/content/article/2010/01/13/AR2010011304834.html.

p. xv, "Subprime" refers to home: Fannie and Freddie also loaded up on so-called Alt-A mortgages, which, like subprimes, counted toward HUD's Affordable Housing Goals. Commonly known as "liar loans," Alt-A loans include borrowers with weaker-than-average credit scores and limited documentation. All loans with a FICO score below 660 are described as subprime, while those with loan-to-value ratios above 90 percent, or with certain loan features such as negative amortization or interest-only payments, are generally described as Alt-A. Both types are considered riskier than prime loans.

p. xv, It sounds like selling a car: Associated Press (AP), "Bank leaders: Sorry for behavior, bad decisions," *Times-Reporter.com* (Dover-New Philadelphia,

OH), January 13, 2010, http://www.timesreporter.com/business/x1409373858/Bank-leaders-Sorry-for-behavior-bad-decisions.

p. xvi, Even so, Angelides demanded: "D.C. Witness Protection Program: A financial inquiry hits the bankers, ignores the Fed and Fannie Mae," January 15, 2010, *Wall Street Journal*, http://online.wsj.com/article/SB10001424052748703414504575001103995916736.html.

p. xvi, Maybe this is like 'Murder on the Orient Express': AP, "Bank Leaders."

p. xvi, The group, like scores of: Andrew Breitbart, "US Blacks See 'Financial Apartheid' in Subprime Crisis," American Renaissance.com, January 27, 2008, http://www.amren.com/mtnews/archives/2008/01/us_blacks_see_f.php.

p. xvii, Now that those loans have: Testimony of Michael Calhoun, Center for Responsible Lending Before the U.S. House of Representatives Committee on Financial Services, April 23, 2009, http://www.house.gov/apps/list/hearing/financialsvcs_dem/crl_-_calhoun.pdf.

p. xvii, In fact, Angelides himself helped: Gilbert Chan, "Angelides gets behind urban aid," *Sacramento Bee*, January 6, 2007, D2.

p. xvii, In a 1999 speech: "State Treasurer Angelides Pledges New Partnership with Community Banks," PR Newswire, 3 May 1999.

p. xvii, He also vowed in a letter: Philip Angelides, "Impact of CRA," *Los Angeles Times*, September 22, 1999, B6.

p. xvii, The San Francisco–based Greenlining Institute: "More Is Better in His Version of CRA Grades," *American Banker*, October 27, 2000, 1.

p. xvii, The 57-year-old Angelides: Opening Remarks of Chairman Phil Angelides at the First Public Meeting of the Financial Crisis Inquiry Commission, Washington, D.C., September 17, 2009, http://www.fcic.gov/hearings/pdfs/2009-0917-OpeningRemarks.pdf.

p. xx, As Graham stated in: Transcript of hearing, Financial Crisis Inquiry Commission, Washington D.C., January 13, 2010.

p. xix, As he shared with: Angelides, *Bill Press Radio Show*.

p. xix, What's more, Angelides has stacked: John D. McKinnon and Louise Radnofsky, "Businesses Criticize Cast of Inquiry Panel," *Wall Street Journal*, January 13, 2010. Angelides hired Christopher P. Seefer, a partner with Robbins Geller Rudman & Dowd LLP, as a senior staff investigator. Seefer specializes in securities class-action litigation and operates out of the San Francisco office of San Diego–based Robbins Geller, formerly Coughlin Stoia Geller Rudman & Robbins. Another longtime lawyer with the firm, Byron Georgiou, sits on the Angelides Commission as a Democrat appointee. The law firm, which has filed dozens of lawsuits against major banks since 2007, including (according to its Web site) Angelides target Goldman Sachs, is connected to Angelides himself. As California state treasurer, Angelides was trustee of state pension funds that periodically retained Seefer and Georgiou's firm in securities litigation. More, the firm and its lawyers contributed some $250,000 to Angelides's Democratic campaign for governor.

As ranking minority member of the House Committee on Oversight and Government Reform, Rep. Darrel Issa (R-CA) has demanded a full investigation into the potential conflicts of interest on the commission. He says the panel reeks of "partisan Democratic politics." Angelides, who has stonewalled Issa's requests for documents, called his charges "bogus," contending that Issa's complaint is part of a larger effort by financial interests to keep the commission from investigating Wall Street.

p. xix, Public records show that Angelides: The ventures include: Canyon Capital Realty Advisors, Canyon Partners, River West Investments, Riverside Development, and Riverview Capital Investments. He's also partnered with Magic Johnson in various urban reinvestment projects. Angelides is chairman of the Canyon Johnson Urban Communities Fund. FEC records show that Angelides has donated at least $2,000 to Rep. Maxine Waters, D-Watts, a fierce defender of the Community Reinvestment Act and a Congressional Black Caucus leader. As one of the nation's most vocal banking critics, Waters has called mortgage lenders "egregious redliners" and accused them of systemic racial discrimination against blacks.

p. xx, I've been stunned . . . New York casino: Angelides, *Bill Press Radio Show.*

p. xx, Responding to Press's listeners: Ibid.

p. xxi, And nobody from HUD: In April 2010, chairman Angelides swore in past directors of the erstwhile Office of Federal Enterprise Oversight—the *other* regulator of Fannie and Freddie—but no witnesses from HUD itself. It was HUD that made the risky policies mandating that mortgage giants engage in more and more race-based lending. In January 2010, Angelides invited attorney general Eric Holder to testify, but he limited the discussion to his department's investigation of mortgage fraud, even though Holder was instrumental in pressuring banks to make unsafe loans as deputy attorney general in the Clinton Justice Department. Holder and his former boss, attorney general Janet Reno, sued a raft of banks for alleged racist lending and then ordered them to change their lending policies to accommodate more minorities, regardless of their creditworthiness. They also ordered banks to open branches in blighted urban neighborhoods and other unprofitable areas. The aggressive anti-redlining suits and related settlements had lasting repercussions for the banking industry, including deteriorated lending standards and greater risk exposure. Holder avoided any related questions by stating at the outset of his testimony, "We do not have the expertise, nor is it part of our mission, to opine on the systemic causes of the financial crisis. Rather, the Justice Department's resources are focused on investigating and prosecuting crime. It is within this context that I am pleased to offer my testimony and contribute to your review" (http://www.justice.gov/ag/testimony/2010/ag-testimony-100114.html). The commissioners, including GOP panelists, honored his request and did not stray outside that scope. Holder fielded no questions regarding his prior crusade against banks.

p. xxi, Yes, you are correct: Author interview by e-mail, September 2, 2010.

p. xxi, This is a serious fight: Author interview with Peter J. Wallison, commissioner, Financial Crisis Inquiry Commission, October 5, 2009.

p. xxi, The diagnosis determines the: Opening statement by Peter Wallison, Financial Crisis Inquiry Commission hearing, Washington D.C., September 17, 2009.

p. xxii, As Angelides recently remarked: Dale Kasler, "In home stretch, Angelides brings meltdown probe to Sacramento," *Sacramento Bee*, September 20, 2010, A1.

p. xxii, To help sell the report: Elizabeth Warren, the front-runner to permanently head the consumer watchdog agency, has been an editorial adviser to Little, Brown's law and business imprint since 1990, according to her curriculum vitae. A Harvard professor, Warren recently served as the top bailout cop in Washington monitoring the distribution of TARP funds to banks as chairwoman of the Congressional Oversight Panel, a position appointed by Senate Majority Leader Harry Reid, D-Nevada. The federal consumer financial watchdog agency was her idea, first broached in 2007. Her social activism, which includes an anti-bank agenda, is detailed in the Afterword.

p. xxii, According to the *Washington Post*: Jason Horowitz, "Financial crisis commission's report to bring book advance, cut of profit," *Washington Post*, August 9, 2010, http://www.washingtonpost.com/wp-dyn/content/article/2010/08/08/AR2010080802446.html.

p. xxiv, With a wave of subprime: Nonprime loans include so-called Alt-A loans for borrowers with marginally below-average credit scores and limited documentation, aka "liar loans." All loans with a FICO score below 660 are described as subprime, while those with loan-to-value ratios above 90 percent, or with certain loan features, such as negative amortization or interest-only payments, are described as Alt-A. Both types are considered riskier than prime loans.

p. xxiv, It is the mother of all bailouts: Steve Christ, "The Mother of All Bailouts: FRE and FNM: The Fiscal Deception Behind Freddie and Fannie," *Wealth Daily*, June 17, 2010, http://www.wealthdaily.com/articles/the-tab-for-fannie-mae-and-freddie-mac/2551.

## *Chapter 1: Prime Suspects*

p. 1, History should deal harshly: Timothy A. Canova, "The Legacy of the Clinton Bubble," *Dissent Magazine*, Summer 2008.

p. 1, As "the first black president,": Toni Morrison, "Clinton as the First Black President," *New York*, October 1998.

p. 2, To boost black homeownership: Bill Clinton, Remarks by the President at HUD Homeownership Event, in a press release dated June 5, 1995, http://clinton6.nara.gov/1995/06/1995-06-05-president-remarks-at-hud-homeownership-event.html.

p. 4, Meanwhile, the charming new: Claudia Cummins, "Fed video gives tips on avoiding loan bias; Federal Reserve Board recommendations for banks," *American Banker*, June 3, 1994, 3. The Federal Reserve Board issued the 23-minute training video for banks, titled "Closing the Gap: a Guide to Equal Opportunity Lending," on June 2, 1994.

p. 4, Subprime lending more than doubled: Timothy A. Canova, "The Legacy of the Clinton Bubble," *Dissent magazine*, Summer 2008.

p. 5, In 2000, the year . . . their share in 2000: Prepared statement of former Federal Reserve chairman Alan Greenspan, testimony before the Financial Crisis Inquiry Commission, Washington D.C., April 7, 2010.

p. 5, But by 2007, thanks: Ibid.

p. 5, The volume of CRA lending: Office of the Vice President, "Making the Dream of Homeownership a Reality: America Hits All-Time High Homeownership Rate," Clinton Presidential Center Web Site Online Archives, October 23, 1997, http://archives.clintonpresidentialcenter.org/?u=102397-vp-announces-record-homeownership-level.htm; Robert Litan, et al., "The Community Reinvestment Act After Financial Modernization: A Final Report," U.S. Department of Treasury, January 2001; "The 25th Anniversary of the Community Reinvestment Act: Access to Capital in an Evolving Financial Services System," Joint Center for Housing Studies, Harvard University, March 2002.

p. 5, Between 1995 and 2005: The Joint Center for Housing Studies' Web site offering download of *The State of the Nation's Housing 2006*, http://www.jchs.harvard.edu/publications/markets/son2006/index.htm, 15.

p. 5, Their "strong numerical gains,": Harvard University's Joint Center for Housing Studies, "The State of the Nation's Housing 2006—Part IV: Homeownership Trends," San Francisco Apartment Association Web site, November 2006, http://www.sfaa.org/0611harvard.html.

p. 7, The subprime and other weak mortgages: Peter J. Wallison, "Missing the Point: Lessons from *The Big Short*," in the American Enterprise Institute for Public Policy Research's "Financial Services Outlook," June 2010, http://www.aei.org/docLib/05-June-FSO-g.pdf.

p. 8, Adoption of these new: Mark Willis, "It's the Rating, Stupid: A Banker's Perspective on the CRA," *Revisiting the CRA: Perspectives on the Future of the Community Reinvestment Act Federal Reserve Bank of San Francisco* Web site, February 2009, http://www.frbsf.org/publications/community/cra/its_rating_stupid.pdf, p. 4.

p. 9, Widespread foreclosures have drained: Charlene Crowell, "Lost wealth $350 billion in 'Communities of Color,'" *Tri-State Defender Online*, July 1, 2010, http://tri-statedefenderonline.com/articlelive/articles/5024/1/Lost-wealth-350-billion-in-Communities-of-Color/Page1.html; "Foreclosures by Race and Ethnicity: The Demographics of a Crisis" (report), Center for Responsible Lending, June 18, 2010.

p. 9, And they will have to wait years: Even though some inner-city borrowers on the verge of default may be saved by loan modifications, their credit rating's will still suffer as much as 100-point drops as soon as the credit bureaus are notified that they signed up for the government's mortgage assistance. That makes it harder to get a loan and can present a problem when applying for a new job. And those who lose their homes to foreclosure will have their access to a new mortgage denied for several years. A foreclosure drags down a homeowner's credit score by 150 points or more on a scale of 300 to 850—and the stain of foreclosure stays on credit reports for seven years. Interestingly, the majority of borrowers who received loan modifications on delinquent mortgages—something the administration has pushed banks into doing—have defaulted again after nine months, according to a federal report. It is plain from high re-default rates that government-imposed repayment leniency is merely spreading out the foreclosure crisis.

p. 9, With the coming tsunami: Letter from Robert G. Rowe III, vice president and senior counsel, American Bankers Association, to Robert D. Feldman, executive secretary, FDIC, et al, "Re: Community Reinvestment Act Regulation Hearings," by electronic delivery, September 24, 2010, 4.

p. 9, Thanks to the subprime-led: V. Dion Haynes, "Blacks hit hard by economy's punch," *Washington Post*, November 24, 2009.

p. 11, This all started because: This clip can be viewed at http://www.thedailyshow.com/watch/tue-september-23-2008/bill-clinton-pt—1. Clinton also has offered the dot-com bust as an excuse. He says that when stocks went south, the only game in town was real estate. Only, the real estate bubble developed years before the Internet-led stock crash of 2000.

p. 12, When I was president: Transcript of remarks by former President William J. Clinton to the National Partnership for Women and Families, Washington D.C., June 15, 2007.

p. 13, As a result, Clinton's: Though, as the text states, the original page bearing this quote no longer exists, this entire quote appears on Yahoo! Message Board, at http://messages.finance.yahoo.com/Stocks_%28A_to_Z%29/Stocks_C/threadview?m=tm&bn=4476&tid=5261904&mid=5261912&tof=5&off=1. Obviously, I am not the only person who has seen it.

p. 13, Though this law has: Ibid.

p. 14, Discrimination in mortgage lending: "HUD's Regulation of the Federal National Mortgage Association (Fannie Mae) and the Federal Home Loan Mortgage Corporation (Freddie Mac): A Rule by the Housing and Urban Development Department, *Federal Register*, 31 October 2000, 65,094.

p. 14, HUD told them, "You . . .": Testimony of Alfred Pollard, general counsel, Federal Housing Finance Agency, before the U.S. Commission on Civil Rights, Washington, March 20, 2009.

p. 14, Cuomo, with Clinton's blessing: U.S. Department of Housing and Urban Development, "Cuomo Announces Action to Provide $2.4 Trillion in Mortgages for Affordable Housing for 28.1 Million Families" (HUD No. 99-131), HUD Archives: News Releases, July 29, 1999, http://archives.hud.gov/news/1999/pr99-131.html.

p. 14, These new regulations will: Ibid., "HUD Announces New Regulations to Provide $2.4 Trillion in Mortgages for Affordable Housing for 28.1 Million Families," (HUD No. 00-317), HUD Archives: News Releases, October 31, 2000, http://archives.hud.gov/news/2000/pr00-317.html.

p. 15, With the housing goals: Testimony of Alfred Pollard, general counsel, Federal Housing Finance Agency, before the U.S. Commission on Civil Rights, Washington, 20 March 2009.

p. 15, Fannie and Freddie "began buying . . .": Testimony of John Weicher, former HUD assistant secretary, before the U.S. Commission on Civil Rights, Washington, March 20, 2009.

p. 16, If you look at first-year defaults: Ibid.

p. 16, In its own 2004 report: "Rules and Regulations," Federal Register, Vol. 69, no. 211, November 2, 2004, 63,670–71.

p. 17, Plunging Fannie and Freddie: Peter J. Wallison, "The Price for Fannie and Freddie Keeps Going Up," *Wall Street Journal*, December 29, 2009, http://online.wsj.com/article/SB10001424052748703278604574624681873427574.html.

p. 17. That the [HUD] housing: Dwight M. Jaffe, "The Role of the GSEs and Housing Policy in the Financial Crisis," report prepared for the Financial Crisis Inquiry Commission, February 25, 2010, 16.

p. 17, "The housing goals," the: Live Leak, "The Subprime Cover-Up," http://www.liveleak.com/view?i=94c_1267800048&c=1.

p. 17, The higher goals "forced . . .": Carol Leonnig, "How HUD Mortgage Policy Fed the Crisis," *Washington Post*, June 10, 2008, http://www.washingtonpost.com/wp-dyn/content/article/2008/06/09/AR2008060902626.html.

p. 17, We had to absorb: "Fannie Mae Strategic Plan: 2007–2011," Fannie Mae, 2007, 53. The 84-page report is stamped, "Proprietary and Confidential."

p. 18, Because the goals were set: Official transcript of testimony by former Fannie Mae executive vice president Robert J. Levin, Financial Crisis Inquiry Commission, Washington D.C., April 9, 2010. (Commissioner Wallison introduced the rare line of questioning, albeit briefly. Chairman Angelides stopped him, noting his time had run out.)

p. 18, The key role played: Prepared statement of Edward J. Pinto, testimony before the House Committee on Oversight and Government Reform, Washington D.C., December 9, 2008, 7.

p. 18, And he was determined: Transcript of HUD Secretary Andrew Cuomo's remarks at press conference in Washington D.C., carried live on C-SPAN, April 6, 1998. This sound bite can be viewed on the YouTube video titled "Andrew Cuomo: CRA Should Be Abused to Force Banks to Give Risky Loans," at http://www.youtube.com/watch?v=PFlYmLAMbrw.

p. 18, I'm sure there'll be: Ibid.

p. 19, We can't hide from: Peter J. Wallison, interview with author by e-mail, October 19, 2009.

p. 20, It is a stretch: Vern McKinley, "Community Reinvestment Act: Ensuring

Credit Adequacy or Enforcing Credit Allocation?" Regulation, no. 4 (1994): 33, 34.

p. 20, Reno and her diversity cops: "A.G. Reno Backs Disparate Impact Test; Involves U.S. Attorneys in Housing Enforcement," National Fair Housing Advocate Online Web site, http://www.fairhousing.com/index.cfm?method=page.display&pagename=January-February_1994_Page2.

p. 21, Reno's "witch hunt," as: Claudia Cummins, "Regulators Cancel Plan to Join with Justice Dept. for Bias Probes," *American Banker*, June 4, 1993.

p. 21, The lack of profitability at: Willis, "It's the Rating, Stupid," 8.

p. 23, Her staff's widely distributed guidebook: Federal Reserve Bank of Boston, *Closing the Gap: A Guide to Equal Opportunity Lending*, http://www.bos.frb.org/commdev/commaff/closingt.pdf, p. 14.

p. 24, The underwriting guidebook also: Ibid., 15.

p. 24, It further advised loan: Ibid., 16.

p. 24, Today's wave of mortgage: Stan Liebowitz, "The Real Scandal: How Feds Invited the Mortgage Mess," *New York Post*, February 5, 2008, http://www.nypost.com/p/news/opinion/opedcolumnists/item_Qjl08vDbysbe6LWDxcq03J.

p. 25, Under the nation's first black attorney general: Consent Order, U.S. v. AIG Federal Savings Bank, et al, U.S. District Court for the District of Delaware, 19 March 2010, Appendix A, 18. Defendant banks are required to "post and prominently display in each location where loan applications are received" the following notice: "We do business in accordance with federal fair lending laws. UNDER THE EQUAL CREDIT OPPORTUNITY ACT, IT IS ILLEGAL TO DISCRIMINATE IN ANY CREDIT TRANSACTION: On the basis of race, color, national origin, religion, sex, marital status, or age; because income is from public assistance; or because a right has been exercised under the federal consumer credit protection laws. IF YOU BELIEVE YOU HAVE BEEN DISCRIMINATED AGAINST, YOU SHOULD SEND A COMPLAINT TO: Office of Thrift Supervision OR U.S. Department of Justice, Washington DC 20530, Tel: 1-800-896-7743."

p. 25, As a result, independent mortgage: Jeffery W. Gunther, Kelly Klemme, and Kenneth J. Robinson, "Redlining or Red Herring?" Federal Reserve Bank of Dallas, May/June 1999, Issue 3.

## Chapter 2: Returning to the Scene of the Crime

p. 27, We will require lenders: Thomas Perez, Remarks on Fair Lending and Fair Housing at the Brookings Institution (Washington, D.C.), June 23, 2010, United States Department of Justice Web site, http://www.justice.gov/crt/opa/pr/speeches/2010/crt-speech-100623.html.

p. 28, We believe that there are: Arnold King, "The Roots of the Freddie-Fannie Bailout," Library of Economics and Liberty Web site, August 18, 2008, http://econlog.econlib.org/archives/2008/08/the_roots_of_th.html.

p. 28, Trasviña's passion for ending: "HUD Official Promises Broader Effort on Affirmatively Affirming Fair Housing," Anti-Discrimination Center Web Site, January 21, 2010, http://www.antibiaslaw.com/news/hud-official-promises-broader-effort-affirmatively-furthering-fair-housing.

p. 28, In 2009, in his: John D. Trasviña, HUD assistant secretary for fair housing and equal opportunity, written statement presented with testimony before Subcommittee on Housing and Community Opportunity, House Financial Services Committee, January 20, 2010.

p. 29, He was her top: *U.S. v. Chevy Chase Federal Savings Bank, and B.F. Saul Mortgage Company*, http://www.justice.gov/crt/housing/documents/chevychasesettle.php.

p. 29, Holder accused its management: Ibid.

p. 29, Now the nation's first: Remarks by Attorney General Eric Holder to the National Association of Attorneys General, Washington D.C., March 2, 2009.

p. 29, Calling enforcement of housing: Barack Obama, *The Audacity of Hope* (New York: Three Rivers Press, 2006), 242, 243.

p. 29, He has warned that: Ibid., 244.

p. 30, He has quadrupled the: Transcript of testimony of Attorney General Eric Holder, Financial Crisis Inquiry Commission, Washington D.C., January 14, 2010.

p. 30, In his larger role today: Thomas Perez, "60-Day Progress Report," American Constitution Society, National Press Club, Washington DC, 18 December 2009.

p. 30, Like his mentor, he: Wes Vernon, Renew America Web site, "Thomas Perez: Obama's One-Man Gestapo," September 13, 2010, http://www.renewamerica.com/columns/vernon/100913.

p. 30, Perez is going to depend: Glen Fest, "Fair Warning on Fair Lending," *U.S. Banker*, August 2010.

p. 31, The program must offer: Agreed Order for Resolution, *U.S. v. First United Security Bank*, U.S. District Court for the Southern District of Alabama, 18 November 2009, 15.

p. 31, The division also required: Ibid, 10.

p. 31, In a March 2010 consent: Consent Order, *U.S. v. AIG Federal Savings Bank, et. al*, U.S. District Court for the District of Delaware, March 19, 2010, 8.

p. 32, Industry analysts argue such action: In a move that will likely have a chilling effect on lending, the Federal Financial Institutions Examining Council has expanded its CRA exam guidelines for banks to include "pricing discrimination," the improper steering of borrowers with good credit to loans with higher prices and fees even though such borrowers pose little risk to lenders of defaulting on loans—a practice also known as "reverse redlining." The administration wants examiners to curb aggressive marketing of subprime and other high-cost loans to minority neighborhoods—a practice inner-city "greenlining" advocates welcomed until it led to a rash of defaults and foreclosures in such neighborhoods. At the same time, however, it wants regulators to continue pressuring banks to make loans to low-income minorities who otherwise wouldn't qualify for prime loans. So now, lenders are damned if they do, damned if they don't. The result may be fewer loans of any kind—or worse, greater subsidization of housing and even greater risk and moral hazard in the financial sector.

p. 32, We are doing business: Perez, "60-Day Progress Report."

p. 32, That includes holding the: Perez, "Remarks on Fair Lending and Fair Housing."

p. 32, That is the charge I have: Perez, "60-Day Progress Report."

p. 32, He adds that the: Perez, "Remarks on Fair Lending and Fair Housing"; Remarks at the Rainbow PUSH Coalition – Annual Wall Street Conference, January 14, 2010, http://www.justice.gov/crt/speeches/tp_rainbow_push.pdf, 5.

p. 32, Indeed, thanks to one: Perez, "60-Day Progress Report."

p. 32, The nearly 15 percent boost: Perez, "Remarks on Fair Lending and Fair Housing."

p. 33, The unit "will address . . .": Ibid.

p. 33, As of the summer of 2010: Perez, "Remarks on Fair Lending and Fair Housing."

p. 33., Perez is building a "pipeline": Ibid.

p. 33, He also is working in: Ibid.

p. 33, In fact, the agency is: One such outside testing group, the nonprofit National Community Reinvestment Coalition, maintains its own "civil rights enforcement division," which engages in what it calls "mystery shopping." This involves NCRC staffers, both black and white, going into banks and posing as loan seekers. Their goal essentially is to entrap mortgage loan officers and brokers into making discriminatory statements or decisions.

p. 33, Perez is a longtime: Perez, "Remarks on Fair Lending and Fair Housing.

p. 33, The 1960s struggle, he: Ibid.

p. 34, Though more subtle, this: Perez, Remarks at the Rainbow PUSH Coalition – Annual Wall Street Conference, January 14, 2010, http://www.justice.gov/crt/speeches/tp_rainbow_push.pdf.

p. 34, In cracking down on: Perez, "Remarks on Fair Lending and Fair Housing."

p. 34, When we bring a lawsuit: Ibid.

p. 34, We will require lenders to: Ibid.

p. 34, In a little-noticed act: "Who's Thomas Saenz?" editorial, *Investor's Business* Daily, March 5, 2009. "Obama Flinches on Immigration," editorial, *New York Times*, March 24, 2009, A26. Saenz, who opposes Border Patrol enforcement and advocates amnesty for illegal immigrants, is now president and chief counsel for MALDEF, which was founded by three self-described "radical" Chicanos, according to the *San Antonio Express-News*. One of them is Mexican-American Mario Obledo, who in 1998 made the following racist statement on a Los Angeles radio show, as confirmed by Snopes.com: "We're going to take over all the political institutions of California. California is going to become a Hispanic state, and if anyone doesn't like it, they should leave. They ought to go back to Europe." That same year, MALDEF honored Obledo at a California banquet celebrating his years of leadership.

p. 35, Like his boss, Emanuel: "I have spent twenty years championing progressive politics and candidates, starting with my work as a field organizer for the Illinois Public Action Council," Emanuel said in his official 2004 congressional questionnaire (http://www.iviipo.org/questionnaires/CD5D_RahmEmanuel.pdf). Illinois Public Action Council, or IPAC, is another radical Alinsky group in Chicago that, among other things, has agitated for inner-city mortgages. Emanuel was IPAC's finance director in the early 1980s, the same time Obama got his start in Chicago organizing. In 2004, Bob Creamer was convicted of kiting checks and bank fraud while serving as IPAC's executive director. His wife, U.S. Congresswoman Jan Schakowsky, D-IL, was an IPAC board member and program director. She and Emanuel worked together there.

p. 35, In his final year: As Freddie's vice president for corporate relations, Robinson, a former top Clinton appointee at HUD, negotiated a 2000 deal to grant $1,050,000 to Jesse Jackson's Rainbow/PUSH organization, after Jackson publicly charged Freddie with racist lending. Freddie also pledged to buy "up to $1 billion worth of mortgage loans made to minority families" through Bank of America and Rainbow/PUSH (Kenneth R. Timmerman, "Freddie Mac, Verizon made Jesse's hit list; the powerful Federal Home Mortgage Corp. and Verizon Communications Inc. shared their wealth after the reverend's attacks, 2000 tax returns show," Insight on the News, May 27, 2002). Emanuel and Ickes were on Freddie's board at the time. Later, as a member of the U.S. House of Representatives, Emanuel hauled in $51,750 from Freddie and Fannie. In fact, he ranks 13th among top recipients of Fannie and Freddie campaign cash in Congress.

p. 36, After his tenure at: According to congressional financial disclosure statements, Emanuel made at least $320,000 in compensation from his time at Freddie, not including up to $250,000 from the sale of Freddie stock. Upon leaving Freddie, he took a job as an investment banker back in Chicago. After just over two years with Dresdner Kleinwort Wasserstein, Emanuel walked away with a cool $18 million while working merger deals that resulted in thousands of layoffs. His firm also funded subprime loans, yet Emanuel now has the temerity to blame Wall Street "greed" and the "anything goes," "right-wing" free "market" ideology of Republicans for setting "the house on fire." "We're paying a big price for ideology run amok," he said during the 2008 bank bailout talks. "That's what's happening here" (Steve Berg, "Difficult vote, but perhaps little choice, in Wall Street mess," September 29, 2008, *MinnPost*, http://www.minnpost.com/stories/2008/09/29/3687/.

## *Chapter 3: Obama's Fingerprints*

p. 37, With a former organizer: "A People's Platform for Social and Economic Justice," *National People's Action*, Chicago, 2009, 18.

p. 38, Like Alinsky, McKnight presupposes: "The Gamaliel Foundation's Faith and Democracy Platform," 2008, http://www.gamaliel.org/platform.htm. McKnight also is a director of Chicago-based Gamaliel, a radical community organizing group that agitates against redlining and "spatial racism."

p. 38, The last person there . . . in 1983 and 1984: Transcript of remarks by NPA's John McKnight speaking to a group of organizers at a Chicago training seminar, August 1, 2008.

p. 38, Toward the end . . . to do that: Ibid. With respect to having one of his protégés in the Oval Office, McKnight gushed to the trainees, "We are at the heart of one of the most important movements in all of this work." McKnight also is a longtime board member of the radical Alinsky group the Gamaliel Foundation in Chicago.

p. 39, I think he didn't . . . a letter: Ibid.

p. 39, With a former organizer: "A People's Platform."

p. 39, The NPA network will . . . financial institutions: Ibid.

p. 40, The work we're doing: Don Dodson, "Champaign's Rev. Barnes attends signing of financial reform legislation," *News-Gazette* (East Central IL), July 23, 2010.

p. 40, Alinsky identified banks as: Heidi Przybyla, "Obama Seen as Anti-Business by 77% of U.S. Investors," *Bloomberg News*, January 22, 2010.

p. 40, The target, therefore, should: Saul D. Alinsky, *Rules for Radicals*, Vintage Books ed. (New York: Vintage Books, 1989), 162.

p. 40, "The real enemy," Kellman: Barack Obama, *Dreams from My Father: A Story of Race and Inheritance*, (New York: Three Rivers Press, 1995), 150.

p. 40, Join us on them: Will McCahill, "Don't Fight Reform, Obama Warns Wall St. at NYC Dinner," *newser*, September 14, 2010, http://www.newser.com/story/72168/dont-fight-reform-obama-warns-wall-st-at-nyc-dinner.html.

p. 40, The Financial Services Roundtable: "Obama seeks tighter limits on banks' reach," Associated Press, January 21, 2010.

p. 41, Obama said that while: UPI, "Obama: reform would prevent 'meltdown,'" ArcaMax Publishing, December 12, 2009, http://www.arcamax.com/newsheadlines/s-663407-354383.

p. 41, The new law also: Under Title V of the Dodd-Frank Act, the Federal Insurance Office (originally proposed as the Office of National Insurance) will be set up within the U.S. Department of Treasury, and "shall have the authority to monitor the extent to which traditionally underserved communities and consumers, minorities, and low- and moderate-income persons have access to affordable insurance products regarding all lines of insurance, except health insurance." Inner-city activists argue that monitoring insurance rates is an important check on "unjustified" premiums. They liken insurance to a public utility, claiming that it is just as essential to life as water and electrical power.

p. 42, The new regulatory regime: Testimony of Michael Calhoun, Center for Responsible Lending Before the U.S. House of Representatives Committee on Financial Services, April 23, 2009, http://www.house.gov/apps/list/hearing/financialsvcs_dem/crl_-_calhoun.pdf.

p. 42, Far from mitigating risk: Sec. 1411, Ability to Repay, Subtitle B—Minimum Standards for Mortgages, Dodd-Frank Wall Street Reform and Consumer Protection Act of 2010.

p. 42, CRA activists are also: Prepared statement of Orson Aguilar, executive director of the Greenlining Institute, in testimony before the House Committee on Financial Services, September 16, 2009.

p. 43, Among other changes, it: Sec. 919, Remittance Transfers, Subtitle G—Regulatory Improvements, Dodd-Frank Wall Street Reform and Consumer Protection Act of 2010.

p. 43, Meanwhile, the activist Obama: Perez, "Remarks on Fair Lending and Fair Housing."

p. 43, Over at the Department: Cass R. Sunstein, *The Second Bill of Rights: FDR's Unfinished Revolution and Why We Need It More Than Eve*r (New York: Basic Books, 2006), 13.

p. 43, The appropriate response to: Joseph Lawler, "CRA Is Back," *American Spectator* AmSpec blog, June 18, 2009, quoting the white paper on the new regulations for the financial sector, http://spectator.org/blog/2009/06/18/cra-is-back.

p. 43, Never mind that the: Brian S. Wesbury, "Feds Spin Wheels on Finanical Regulation," First Trust Economics Blog, June 28, 2010, http://www.ftportfolios.com/Blogs/EconBlog/2010/6/27.

p. 44, They want CRA regulators: "Redline the CRA," staff editorial, *Investor's Business Daily*, August 19, 2010.

p. 44, He already has ordered: "Son of CRA: The Scandal Lives On 7.20.10," *Investor's Business Daily*, July 20, 2010, available for oral review on the OutloudOpinion Podcast, http://www.outloudopinion.com/2010/07/20/son-of-cra-the-scandal-lives-on-7-20-10/.

p. 44, The four federal agencies: OCC: Community Affairs – Neighborhood Stabilization Web site, http://www.occ.treas.gov/cdd/neighborstabilization.htm.

p. 44, The idea of imposing . . . created the crisis: Peter J. Wallison, Financial Crisis Inquiry Commission, author interview, October 5, 2009.

p. 44, CRA regulators will be assisted: Stephen F. Ornstein, Matthew S. Yoon, Matthew Dyckman, and John P. Holahan, "United States: Financial Regulatory Reform – Bureau of Consumer Financial Protection," September 6, 2010, Mondaq Web site, Finance and Banking, http://www.mondaq.com/unitedstates/article.asp?articleid=109154&rss=2.

p. 45, The consumer watchdog agency: Sec. 1013, Title X, Dodd-Frank Wall Street Reform and Consumer Protection Act of 2010.

p. 45, It will be staffed: Ibid.

p. 45, Providing this much power: Tom Petruno, "How New Consumer Agency Might Work," *Baltimore Sun*, June 18, 2009, http://articles.baltimoresun.com/2009-06-18/news/0906170119_1_consumer-protection-financial-products-financial-protection-agency.

p. 46, According to her amendment: Richard Spencer, "'Diversification' on Wall Street," July 29, 2010, *Alternative Right*, http://www.alternativeright.com/main/blogs/malinvestments/diversification-on-wall-street/.

p. 46, The CRA serves its: Ellen Seidman, testimony, Future of Housing Finance conference, U.S. Department of Treasury, Washington D.C., 17 August 2010.

p. 46, The secondary market needs: Ibid.

p. 47, In previous testimony: Testimony of Shaun Donovan, Secretary of U.S. Department of Housing and Urban Development Hearing Before the U.S. House Committee on Financial Services: "Housing Finance—What Should the New System Be Able to Do? Part II – Government and Stakeholder Perspectives," April 14, 2010, U.S. Department of Housing and Urban Development Web site, http://portal.hud.gov/portal/page/portal/HUD/press/speeches_remarks_statements/2010/Speech_0414a2010.

p. 47, This provided many of: Ibid.

p. 47, Donovan asserted that "ensuring . . .": Ibid.

p. 47, Non-CRA covered credit unions: Written testimony of NCRC president John Taylor, presented at Community Reinvestment Act hearings, William Seidman Center, FDIC, Washington D.C., July 19, 2010, 25.

p. 47, In the meantime, he: Ibid.

p. 48, With these changes, the: Eugene Ludwig, et al., "The Community Reinvestment Act: Past Successes and Future Opportunities," *Revisiting the CRA: Perspectives on the Future of the Community Reinvestment Act*, a joint publication of the Federal Reserve Banks of Boston and San Francisco, February 2009, 104.

p. 48, He wants the government: Transcript of speech by Eugene A. Ludwig at Adelphi University in New York, October 3, 2008.

p. 49, Some banks have felt: Mark Willis, "It's the Rating, Stupid: A Banker's Perspective on the CRA," *Revisiting the CRA*, 3.

p. 49, Indeed, he adds: Ibid.

p. 50, Wall Street owes a: "Regulators Must Fulfill Spirit and Intent of Bill," press release, National Community Reinvestment Coalition, Washington D.C., January 22, 2010.

## *Chapter 4: The Heist*

p. 51, Why did Jesse James: "Acorn holds summer summit with banks and thrifts," *ABA Banking Journal*, October 1992, 7.

p. 51, When I was president: Transcript of remarks by former President William J. Clinton to the National Partnership for Women and Families, Washington D.C., June 15, 2007.

p. 52, It will be socially: Jeffrey Krasner, "Fed to probe local lending," *Boston Herald*, January 28, 1992, 27; Michael Weinstein, "A hot summer in Boston: Temperatures and tempers may both overheat when two reports on low-income lending are delivered," *American Ban*ker, March 28, 1989.

p. 52, "This is discrimination," Munnell: Mitchell Zuckoff, "Study shows racial bias in lending; Gap cited in Boston-area banks," *Boston Globe*, October 9, 1992, A1.

p. 52, Maybe you can explain . . . you cannot: Jeffrey Krasner, "34% of all black mortgage requests rejected; Hub KO rate highest in U.S.," *Boston Herald*, October 22, 1991, 1.

p. 52, There's a natural tendency: Zuckoff, "Study shows racial bias in lending."

p. 52, In fact, her study: Dunham's report, based on preliminary loan data and titled, "Expanding the Potential of the Community Reinvestment Act: The Case for Affordable Housing in Boston," was never released to the public.

p. 52, We've got the most: Krasner, "34% of all black mortgage requests rejected."

p. 53, The Feds said the: Zuckoff, "Study shows racial bias in lending."

p. 53, In Washington, the top: "The Politically Correct Housing Bubble," *The Trumpet*, www.thetrumpet.com/index.php?q=5575.3886.0.0 (no longer accessible).

p. 53, Now, demanded ACORN legislative: Joel Glenn Brenner, "Blacks denied mortgages twice as often, study says," *Chicago Sun-Times*, October 28, 1992, 28.

p. 54, In addition to finding: The Boston Fed data were badly mangled. Of the 3,000 mortgages studied, according to an analysis by University of Texas economist Stan Liebowitz, 50 of the loans supposedly had the banks paying interest to the borrowers; 500 of them were not even in the data set from which the data was supposedly obtained; and some mortgages were supposedly approved for individuals who had negative net worth in the millions of dollars. Correcting for the myriad errors showed no evidence of discrimination.

p. 54, "In fact," noted Emory: George Benston, "It's Time to Repeal the Community Reinvestment Act," September 28, 1999, Cato Institute Web site, http://www.cato.org/pub_display.php?pub_id=4976.

p. 54, He also pointed out: Ibid.

p. 54, In April 1993, six: Federal Reserve Bank of Boston, "Closing the Gap: A Guide to Equal Opportunity Lending", http://www.bos.frb.org/commdev/commaff/closingt.pdf, 26.

p. 54, The 27-page booklet: Ibid., 16.

p. 55, In evaluating such customers: Ibid., 14–16.

p. 55, The widely distributed federal: Ibid., 15.

p. 55, The feds argued that: Ibid., 14.

p. 55, Even the most determined . . . Special care should be taken: Ibid.

p. 56, The guidebook listed penalties: Ibid., 27.

p. 56, To spread the word: Lawrence B. Lindsey, "A balanced response," *Mortgage Banking*, http://www.allbusiness.com/legal/laws/403398-1.html.

p. 56, Banks have a responsibility: Ibid., emphasis added.

p. 56, It featured an introduction: Jeff Bater, "Fed steps up fight for fair lending," UPI, June 2, 1994. The video shared the title of the guidelines published earlier: "Closing the Gap: A Guide to Equal Opportunity Lending." Regarding Greenspan, throughout his tenure as Fed chief, he was repeatedly targeted by anti-redlining groups like ACORN and National People's Action, who protested outside his offices and his residence.

p. 57, When they are put: Claudia Cummins, "Fed video gives tips on avoiding loan bias," *American Banker*, June 3, 1994, 3.

p. 57, Policies regarding applicants with: Jeff Bater, "Fed steps up fight for fair lending."

p. 57, He said if lenders: Lindsey, "A balanced response."

p. 58, Munnell became his assistant: Dunham now works as an economist for the U.S. Comptroller of the Currency, one of the federal agencies regulating banks for CRA compliance.

p. 58, No loan is . . . For those who: Glenn Beck, "Bank bust—Who's to blame?" Current Events & Politics Web site, September 18, 2008, http://www.glennbeck.com/content/articles/article/198/15375/?ck=1.

p. 58, We don't want banks . . . just not so: Remarks by Attorney General Janet Reno, news conference, U.S. Justice Department, Washington D.C., August 22, 1994.

p. 59, We're going through the: Claudia Cummins, "Regulators Cancel Plan to Join with Justice Dept. for Bias Probes," *American Banker*, June 4, 1993.

p. 59, One of Obama's clients: *Selma S. Buycks-Roberson, et al, v. Citibank Federal Savings Bank*, United States District Court for the Northern District of Illinois, Eastern Division, Case Summary, June 30, 1995 (docketed), 4–6.

p. 60, In its 1995 briefing: "Federal Law Prohibiting Lending Discrimination and the Department of Justice Lending Discrimination Enforcement Program," report prepared by Skadden, Arps, Slate, Meagher & Flom for American Bankers Association, Washington D.C., February 1995, 88.

p. 60, In sum, DOJ [Department . . . ]: Ibid, 105. Author's use by permission.

p. 60, The Clinton administration is . . . these changes: "ABA offers free 'toolbox for the future,'" Bank Marketing, December 1994, Vol. 26, No. 12, 76.

p. 61, Our concern is that . . . very vigorously: Claudia Cummins, "HUD draws fire for initiatives that seek to enforce bias laws," American Banker, April 15, 1994.

p. 62, We are working with: Roberta Achtenberg, interview with Chester Hartman, Shelterforce Online, http://www.nhi.org/policy/achtenberg.html.

p. 62, Among other things, MBA: PRNewswire, "HUD and Mortgage Bakers [*sic*] Execute Fair Lending Agreements," October 10, 1994. Available for viewing online at the Free Library by Farlex, http://www.thefreelibrary.com/HUD+AND+MORTGAGE+BAKERS+EXECUTE+FAIR+LENDING+AGREEMENTS-a015793333.

p. 63, Explaining the crackdown, comptroller: Robert Stowe England, "Assault on the mortgage lenders: in the name of racial justice, the Clintonites want the power to decide who gets a home of his own – efforts to impose regulations on banks to make loans even if applicants are not creditworthy," National Review, December 27, 1993.

p. 63, He vowed to eliminate: Vern McKinley, "Community Reinvestment Act: Ensuring Credit Adequacy or Enforcing Credit Allocation?" *Regulation*, no. 4 (1994): 30.

p. 63, Bhargava asked for "aggressive . . .": Paul Starobin, "The greening of ACORN's top lobbyist," National Journal 25, no. 29 (July 17, 1993): 1,826.

p. 63, "With CRA," Bhargava said: Barbara A. Rehm, "Activists warn banks that campaign to ease CRA rules might backfire," *American Banker*, June 29, 1992.

p. 64, When government regulators bark . . . Banks begin to: Stan J. Liebowitz, "Anatomy of a Train Wreck: Causes of the Mortgage Meltdown," *Housing America: Building Out of a Crisis* (New Brunswick, NJ: Transaction Publishers, 2008), 11.

p. 64, Of course, the new: Steven Malanga, "How the Fed, Media and Academia Aided and Abetted Lending Debacle," *Investor's Business Daily*, October 1, 2008.

p. 64, The most important fact . . . Once these standards: Peter J. Wallison, "Cause and Effect: Government Policies and the Financial Crisis," November 2008, AEI Online, http://www.aei.org/outlook/29015.

p. 64, Standards were loosened across: Stan J. Liebowitz, "Anatomy of a Train Wreck: Causes of the Mortgage Meltdown," August 22, 2008, http://www.scribd.com/doc/14435743/Anatomy-of-a-Train-Wreck. According to that site, "Anatomy of a Train Wreck" at the time was soon to be a forthcoming chapter in *Housing America: Building out of a Crisis*, eds. Benjamin Powell and Randall Holcomb (New Brunswick, NJ: Transaction Publishers, 2009). The abstract of this chapter can be downloaded from the Web site of the Social Science Research Network at http://papers.ssrn.com/sol3/papers.cfm?abstract_id=1211822.

p. 66, The "affordable mortgages" backing: "First Union Capital Markets Corp., Bear, Stearns & Co. Price Securities Offering Backed By Affordable Mortgages: Unique Transaction To Benefit Underserved Housing Market," press release, October 20, 1997.

p. 66, No, "CRA loans do . . .": Dale Westhoff (senior managing director of Bear Stearns), "Packaging CRA loans into securities," *Mortgage Banking*, May 1, 1998.

p. 67, Do we automatically exclude: Ibid.

p. 67, The media attributed the: Ronald Brownstein, "Minorities' Home Ownership Booms Under Clinton but Still Lags Whites,'" *Los Angeles Times*, May 31, 1999.

p. 67, Between 1993 and 1998: Robert E. Litan, "The Community Reinvestment Act After Financial Modernization: A Baseline Report," U.S. Department of the Treasury, April 2000.

p. 68, Astoundingly, half the growth: "The State of the Nation's Housing," Joint Center for Housing Studies, Harvard University, 2006, 15.

p. 68, In the 1990s, more: Edward Gramlich, "Subprime Mortgages," Urban Institute Press, 2007.

p. 69, The sudden entry of: Les Picker, "Origins of the Current Mortgage Problems," *NBER Digest*, April/May 2008, 1, http://www.nber.org/digest/may08/may08.pdf.

p. 69, This "would not have . . .": Atif Mian, et. al, "The Consequence of Mortgage Credit Expansion: Evidence from the 2007 Mortgage Default Crisis," National Bureau of Economic Research, January 2008, 24.

p. 69, According to Chicago economist: Brian S. Wesbury and Robert Stein, "Don't Forget Government Failure," First Trust Web site, Monday Morning Outlook, July 14, 2008, http://www.ftportfolios.com/Commentary/EconomicResearch/2008/7/14/dont_forget_government_failure.

p. 69, By 1998, the share: http://ffiec.gov/craratings/Rtg_spec.aspx.

p. 70, Washington Mutual eventually received: Washington Mutual, Inc., "Washington Mutual wins 2003 CRA Community Impact Award," CSR press release, November 3, 2003, http://www.csrwire.com/press_releases/24193-Washington-Mutual-wins-2003-CRA-Community-Impact-Award.

p. 70, As "the pressure from . . .": Mark Willis, "It's the Rating, Stupid: A Banker's Perspective on the CRA," *Revisiting the CRA: Perspectives on the Future of the Community Reinvestment Act Federal Reserve Bank of San Francis*co Web site, February 2009, http://www.frbsf.org/publications/community/cra/its_rating_stupid.pdf, p. 4.

p. 70, The policy "encouraged the . . .": Ibid., 5.

p. 71, I want to see . . . covers off: Remarks by Jesse Jackson of Rainbow Coalition, press conference regarding Community Reinvestment Act, National Press Club, Washington D.C., October 15, 1999.

p. 71, After the warm and: Stan Liebowitz, "The Real Scandal: How Feds Invited the Mortgage Mess," February 5, 2008, *New York Post*; Liebowitz, *Housing America: Building out of a Crisis* (New Brunswick, NJ: Transaction Publishers, 2008), 3.

p. 72, If the economy turns . . . amount at risk: Patrice Hill, "Risks feared as banks ease credit to woo minorities," *Washington Times*, September 25, 1999, A1.

p. 72, The effort to reduce: Peter J. Wallison, "The True Origins of This Financial Crisis," On the Issues, AEI, February 2009, 2.

p. 72, The higher goals will: U.S. Department of Housing and Urban Development,

"Cuomo Announces Action to Provide $2.4 Trillion in Mortgages for Affordable Housing for 28.1 Million Families" (HUD No. 99-131), HUD Archives: News Releases, July 29, 1999, http://archives.hud.gov/news/1999/pr99-131.html.

p. 72, To hit these sharply: "HUD's Regulation of the Federal National Mortgage Association (Fannie Mae) and the Federal Home Loan Mortgage Corporation (Freddie Mac): A Rule by the Housing and Urban Development Department," *Federal Register*, October 31, 2000, 65,106.

p. 73, He announced in a: Ibid.

p. 73, We have not been: Ibid.; Brian Collins, "Fannie, Freddie defend track record on blacks," *National Mortgage News*, March 6, 2000, 1. HUD was not the only one leaning heavily on Fannie and Freddie at the time. In 1998, Jesse Jackson held a press conference at the National Press Club in Washington to demand that Freddie Mac "end its racially discriminatory practices," while urging its shareholders to divest from the firm until it underwrote more minority mortgages. Less than two years later, Freddie pledged to buy as much as $1 billion in mortgage loans for minority families through Bank of America and Jackson's Rainbow/PUSH organization. Jackson, who called redlining "economic apartheid," also shook down Citibank and other New York banks as part of his so-called Wall Street Project. Leaders from the Congressional Black Caucus, moreover, pressed Fannie and Freddie officials in 2001 to add 1 million new minority households to the ranks of America's home owners over the following five years.

p. 73, He offered that half: Ibid.

p. 73, Cuomo envisioned the government-sponsored: "HUD's Regulation of the Federal National Mortgage Association (Fannie Mae) and the Federal Home Loan Mortgage Corporation (Freddie Mac)": 65,106.

p. 74, If everybody felt "more . . .": Ibid.

p. 74, Purchasing these loans could: Ibid., 65,053.

p. 74, Cuomo insisted that providing: Ibid, 65,094.

p. 74, Fannie's and Freddie's "guidelines . . .": Ibid, 65,135.

p. 74, Their chief regulator insisted: Ibid., 65,125.

p. 75, Even lenders who do: Ibid, 65,129.

p. 75, In fact, Cuomo wished: Ibid., 65,106. Cuomo's call for blurring subprime with prime apparently was heeded. The enormous size of subprime securities by Fannie and Freddie in 2003 and 2004 was not revealed until Fannie Mae in September 2009 reclassified a large part of its securities portfolio of prime mortgages properly as subprime.

p. 75, Under Raines's leadership, Fannie: Phil Gramm, "Deregulation and the Financial Panic," *Wall Street Journal*, Opinion, February 20, 2009, http://online.wsj.com/article/SB123509667125829243.html.

p. 76, Countrywide chief Angelo Mozilo: Eric Englund, "Countrywide Financial Corporation and the Failure of Mortgage Socialism," http://www.lewrockwell.com/englund/englund43.html.

p. 76, They "relaxed their . . . in 2003": John C. Weicher, "For the GSEs, the Goal Was Always Profit," *National Review Online*, November 17, 2008, http://hudson.org/index.cfm?fuseaction=publication_details&id=5876.

p. 76, In 1998, 57 percent: Justin Fox, "Subprime's Silver Lining," *Time*, April 2, 2007, 53.

p. 77, These types of statements: Written statement of Edward J. Pinto, testimony before the U.S. House Committee on Oversight and Government Reform, Washington D.C., December 9, 2008, 12. Freddie Mac also dove into the Alt-A mortgage market, thanks to pressure from HUD. In an October 6, 2004, e-mail from Freddie executive Mike May to Freddie CEO Dick Syron, May advised: "The Alt-A business makes a contribution to our HUD goals."

p. 77, By 2008, after making: Ibid., 3.

p. 77, Fannie and Freddie abandoned: Ibid.

p. 77, With the encouragement of: Ibid., 7.

p. 77, They increased their risk . . . after 2004: Testimony of former HUD Assistant Secretary John Weicher before the U.S. Commission on Civil Rights, Washington D.C., March 23, 2009.

p. 78, Our homeownership strategy will . . . bureaucracy: Bill Clinton, Remarks by the President at HUD Homeownership Event, in a press release dated June 5, 1995, http://clinton6.nara.gov/1995/06/1995-06-05-president-remarks-at-hud-home-ownership-event.html.

p. 79, Federal data show that: "HUD's Regulation of the Federal National Mortgage Association (Fannie Mae) and the Federal Home Loan Mortgage Corporation (Freddie Mac): A Rule by the Housing and Urban Development Department," *Federal Register*, October 31, 2000, 65,105.

p. 79, Growth in the sub-prime: Ellen Seidman, "CRA in the 21st Century: Community Reinvestment Act still motivates mortgage bankers," *Mortgage Banking*, October 1, 1999, http://www.thefreelibrary.com/CRA+in+the+21st+Century.-a063825220.

p. 79, Spurred by the threat: Ibid; David Listokin, et al., "The Potential and Limitations of Mortgage Innovation in Fostering Homeownership in the United States," Fannie Mae Foundation, 2002.

p. 79, Seidman, who has suggested: Ellen Seidman, testimony before the House Financial Services Committee, June 24, 2009, New America Foundation Web site, http://www.newamerica.net/publications/resources/2009/testimony_ellen_seidman.

p. 80, She argues that they: Seidman, "CRA in the 21st Century."

p. 80, The 1995 revisions to . . . not have developed: Ibid.

p. 80, Even though mortgage companies . . . all time high: Ibid.

p. 81, Lower-income and minority families: "HUD's Affordable Housing Goals for Fannie Mae and Freddie Mac," Issue Brief No. V, Office of Policy Development and Research, HUD, January 2001, 6.

p. 81, Lenders have listened . . . have increased: Janet Reno, remarks to the National

Community Reinvestment Coalition (Washington, DC), March 20, 1998, http://www.justice.gov/archive/ag/speeches/1998/0320_agcom.htm.

p. 81, Several years ago . . . access to credit: Gary Gensler, remarks to the House Banking and Financial Services Committee, May 24, 2000 (LS-659), http://www.ustreas.gov/press/releases/ls659.htm.

p. 82, We've had great success . . . that are underserved: Bill Clinton, speech to the Granoff Forum, February 24, 2000, http://archives.clintonpresidentialcenter.org/?u=022400-speech-by-president-to-granoff-forum.htm.

p. 83, Last June, I issued . . . down payment: George W. Bush, Remarks at the White House Conference on Minority Homeownership, October 15, 2002, http://fdsys.gpo.gov/fdsys/pkg/WCPD-2002-10-21/html/WCPD-2002-10-21-Pg1772.htm.

p. 84, Bush also praised Freddie . . . home ownership loans: Ibid.

p. 84, NCRC's Taylor, by now: John Taylor, et. al, letter to Regulations Division of HUD, July 16, 2004, 2.

p. 85, Prosecutors that year, for . . . and practices: Rick Rothacker, "Merger opposed over race issues," *Charlotte Observer*, November 1, 2007, D1. The "totality" language was identical to language used in Reno's consent decree over a decade earlier in the Chevy Chase Bank case.

p. 85, The number and percentage of: Transcript of opening statement of commissioner Peter J. Wallison, Financial Crisis Inquiry Commission, Washington D.C., September 17, 2009.

p. 86, It looks to me: Peter J. Wallison, author interview by e-mail, October 5, 2009.

p. 86, He is the ACORN: Starobin, "The Greening of ACORN's Top Lobbyist."

p. 87, He said their credit: H. Jane Lehman, et. al, "From housing activist to head of bank board," *Chicago Tribune*, November 3, 1991, W1.

p. 87, He sneered at bankers: Joanna Sullivan, "Merger mania killing Baltimore's bank industry," *Baltimore Business Journal*, July 8, 1994, 16.

p. 87, ACORN kind of grew: Robert M. Garsson, "Banks' Foes Have Clinton Connections, Too," *American Banker*, February 8, 1993.

p. 87, "I'm quite pleased," with . . . top-priority issue: Robert M. Garsson, "Clinton Taps Industry Critic as Policy Aide," American Banker, January 19, 1993.

p. 88, During the transition . . . have input: Transcript of remarks by Barack Obama, Heartland Democratic Presidential Forum, organized by the Center for Community Change, Des Moines, Iowa, December 1, 2007.

p. 88, Like Clinton before him: "The First Black President?" *Michigan Chronicle*, May 9, 2007–May 15, 2007, A1.

p. 89, A genuinely progressive movement . . . stealthy: Deepak Bhargava, "Realizing the Promise: The Meaning of This Moment," Center for Community Change, November 7, 2008, 3; Transcript of remarks by Deepak Bhargava at *The Nation* magazine's forum in Washington D.C., April 2009.

p. 93, Bush directs HUD secretary: George W. Bush, comments from a 2002 speech, in "George W. Bush Caused the Market Meltdown?" September 25, 2008, Crime & Federalism Web site, http://federalism.typepad.com/crime_federalism/2008/09/george-w-bush-c.html.

p. 93, Adopting Clinton's goal of: "HUD's Proposed Housing Goal Rule – 2004," http://www.alta.org/govt/issues/04/hud_gse_sum0407.pdf, p. 5.

## Chapter 5: The Next Hold-up

p. 95, Less than 1 percent: Paul Sperry, "O's latest biz-killer," *New York Post*, August 12, 2010, http://www.nypost.com/f/print/news/opinion/opedcolumnists/latest_biz_killer_k0WV67V5K8i8nq4pPGXJHM.

p. 95, I consistently believe that: "Obama notes 'tragic' U.S. past," (Honolulu) starbulletin.com, July 28, 2008.

p. 96, Artificial lines of race: Sheryll D. Cashin, "Shall We Overcome? Transcending Race, Class, and Ideology Through Interest Convergence," *St. John's Law Review*, April 1, 2005, http://www.allbusiness.com/legal/918333-1.html.

p. 96, Racism is masked and: The Gamaliel Foundation, "The Gamaliel Foundation's Faith and Democracy Platform," http://www.gamaliel.org/Printshop/FaithAndDemocracyPlatform2page.pdf.

p. 96, Claiming in his memoir: Barack Obama, *The Audacity of Hope* (New York: Crown, 2006; New York: Vintage, 2008), 302. Citations are to the First Vintage Edition.

p. 96, So many of the disparities . . . fixed them: Norman Solomon, "The Media Can Learn from Obama," Creators.com, 2008, http://www.creators.com/opinion/norman-solomon/the-media-can-learn-from-obama.html.

p. 97, Even if it were: Paul Sperry, "Obama's Stealth Reparations," FrontPageMagazine.com, October 28, 2008.

p. 97, As an Illinois state . . . still suffer from that: Quoted from the transcript of Senator Obama's interview for the *Odyssey* radio program on WBEZ 91.5 FM, at http://www.thenewamerican.com/usnews/election/457.

p. 98, In laying out his: Tom Petruno, "How New Consumer Agency Might Work," *Baltimore Sun*, June 18, 2009, http://articles.baltimoresun.com/2009-06-18/news/0906170119_1_consumer-protection-financial-products-financial-protection-agency.

p. 98, This federal statute gives: David H. Carpenter, The Dodd-Frank Wall Street Reform and Consumer Protection Act: Title X, The Consumer Financial Protection Bureau (Congressional Research Service, July 21, 2010), http://www.llsdc.org/attachments/files/224/CRS-R41338.pdf, p. 2.

p. 98, And the muscular new: Sec. 1013, Title X, Dodd-Frank Wall Street Reform and Consumer Protection Act.

p. 99, According to the text: U.S. Code 12, § 4520. Minority and women inclusion; diversity requirements (b), Cornell University Law School Web site, http://

www.law.cornell.edu/uscode/html/uscode12/usc_sec_12_00004520----000-.html.

p. 99, With the new financial . . . female or minority: Diana Furchtgott-Roth, "Racial, Gender Quotas in the Financial Bill," RealClearMarkets Web site, July 8, 2010, http://www.realclearmarkets.com/articles/2010/07/08/diversity_in_the_financial_sector_98562.html.

p. 100, Bank examiners will use: Sec. 1071., Small Business Loan Data Collection, Subtitle G—Regulatory Improvements, Dodd-Frank Wall Street Reform and Consumer Protection Act of 2010. "(a) PURPOSE.—The purpose of this section is to facilitate enforcement of fair lending laws." Lenders will report data to the newly formed Consumer Financial Protection Bureau, which will compile and aggregate the data for the federal regulatory agencies enforcing the CRA. Currently the CRA small business data lacks information on the race of small business owners. But the Dodd-Frank Act effectively overturns the Federal Reserve's so-called Regulation B, which prohibits lenders from collecting such loan data. This marks a major victory for NCRC, the Greenlining Institute, and other CRA lobbyists, who for years have complained the data ban limited regulators' ability to identify discrimination in non-mortgage lending. In 1994, Greenlining took out a full-page ad in the *New York Times* trashing the Greenspan Fed for keeping Regulation B in place, arguing it posed a "major obstacle to fair lending." At the time, U.S. Rep. Nancy Pelosi, D-Calif., openly backed San Francisco-based Greenlining's campaign against the prohibition. But as speaker of the House, Pelosi praised Rep. Barney Frank, D-Mass., for removing the roadblock and orchestrating other banking "reforms" as head of the House Financial Services Committee, even nicknaming him the "maestro." Greenlining envisions the data being used to "set specific minority small business lending targets." "The existing federal regulators should coordinate with the Consumer Financial Protection Bureau to make good use of the new small business lending data that will be collected," testified Greenlining spokeswoman Preeti Vissa during CRA hearings before the Federal Reserve Bank of San Francisco in August 2010.

p. 100, And as noted previously: "Financial Regulatory Reform A New Foundation: Rebuilding Financial Supervision and Regulation," U.S. Department of Treasury, June 17, 2009.

p. 100, NCRC's Taylor, who works: Written testimony of NCRC president John Taylor, presented at Community Reinvestment Act hearings, William Seidman Center, FDIC, Washington D.C., 19 July 2010, 25.

p. 101, Less than 1 percent: Transcript of remarks by Barack Obama, Hampton University, Hampton, Virginia, June 5, 2007.

p. 101, But that overlooks the: David G. Blanchflower, et al, "Discrimination in the Small-Business Credit Market," *Review of Economics and Statistics*, November 2003, 933.

p. 101, In the 2009 case: Agreed Order for Resolution, *U.S. v. First United Security*

*Bank*, U.S. District Court for the Southern District of Alabama, November 18, 2009, 14–16.

p. 102, There has been no factual: Ibid., 2.

p. 102, We have identified large: Assistant Attorney General Thomas E. Perez, transcript of speech, "Remarks on Fair Lending and Fair Housing," Brookings Institution, Washington D.C., June 23, 2010, http://www.justice.gov/crt/opa/pr/speeches/2010/crt-speech-100623.html.

p. 103, Yet business loans to: Sperry, "O's latest biz-killer."

p. 103, Under Dodd-Frank, [Obama] . . . economy will suffer: "Will Washington's Failures Lead To Second American Revolution?" July 30, 2010, http://www.investors.com/NewsAndAnalysis/ArticlePrint.aspx?id=542171.

p. 104, As we emerge from: Perez, Remarks on Fair Lending.

## Chapter 6: The Bank Robbers: Top 10 Most Wanted

p. 105, We believe that there: Kathleen Day, "HUD says mortgage policies hurt blacks; home loan giants cited," *Washington Post*, March 2, 2000, A01.

p. 106, Reno warned that she: Remarks by Attorney General Janet Reno, news conference, Department of Justice, August 22, 1994.

p. 107, Reno even cited the: Ibid.

p. 109, Such tactics amount to . . . adverse publicity: Vern McKinley, "Community Reinvestment Act: Ensuring Credit Adequacy or Enforcing Credit Allocation?"

p. 110, But where cooperation fails: Jerry Reynolds, "CRA Conference spotlights Indian country," *Indian Country Today* (*Lakota Times*), February 16, 1994.

p. 110, No loan is exempt . . . enforce the law: Ibid.

p. 110, Bankers, she said, were . . . in this nation: United States Department of Justice, Remarks of the Honorable Janet Reno, Attorney General of the United States, to the National Community Reinvestment Coalition (Marriott Hotel, Washington, DC), March 20, 1998, http://www.justice.gov/archive/ag/speeches/1998/0320_agcom.htm.

p. 111, The end game appears to: In fact, Reno's ally NCRC president John Taylor has intimated as much, arguing in a recent paper that he wants banks "affirmatively making loans to minorities," regardless of whether they are discriminated against. "A bank can employ non-discriminatory policies," he revealed in prepared testimony on July 19, 2010, "but still make relatively few loans to minorities because it does not market to minority communities."

p. 112, Two of these homes . . . look at them: Transcript of remarks by deputy attorney general Eric Holder, news conference, Department of Justice, Washington D.C., August 22, 1994.

p. 113, Later, Holder acknowledged that: Transcript of speech by Attorney General Eric Holder, Department of Justice, Washington D.C., February 18, 2009.

p. 113, This nation has still . . . padlocked suburbs: Attorney General Eric Holder at the Department of Justice African American History Month Program, *Justice News* (United States Department of Justice Web site), February 18, 2009, http://www.justice.gov/ag/speeches/2009/ag-speech-090218.html.

p. 114, I want Eric Holder: "Barack Obama interview Dec. 10, 2008" (edited transcript of interview), *Chicago Tribune*, December 10, 2008, http://www.chicagotribune.com/news/chi-obama-transcript_10dec10%2C0%2C2925275%2Cfull.story.

p. 115, Mortgage lending discrimination is: Claudia Cummins, "Justice Dept. vows pursuit of bias in home loans," American Banker, June 30, 1993, 1.

p. 115, There is no evidence that: Steve Cocheo, "Justice Department sues tiny South Dakota town for loan bias," *ABA Banking Journal*, January 1, 1994.

p. 116, The bank no longer: ibid.

p. 116, So it agreed to: "Federal Law Prohibiting Lending Discrimination and the Department of Justice Lending Discrimination Enforcement Program," report by Skadden Arps Slate Meagher and Flom (for American Bankers Association), February 1995, appendix.

p. 117, We want to get the word: Bunty Anquoe, "Settlement reached with banks discriminating against minorities: rejected applicants may be eligible for compensation," *Indian Country Today* (*Lakota Times*), January 26, 1994, 1.

p. 117, Small banks shouldn't feel: Cocheo, "Justice Department sues tiny South Dakota town for loan bias."

p. 117, We must continue to enforce: Federal News Service, "The State of the Union: Clinton Text: There's Much Work Ahead, He Says" (text from Bill Clinton's State of the Union address), January 26, 1994, *Los Angeles Times* Article Collections, http://articles.latimes.com/1994-01-26/news/mn-15502_1_hard-working-people/5.

p. 117, He turned to her: Kim I. Eisler, "Say Uncle," *Washingtonian*, July 1995.

p. 117, If we go back to: Charles Wisniowski, "Dream of Home Ownership Turning into a Nightmare," *Mortgage Banking*, October 1, 2007.

p. 118, It is very troubling . . . of an organization: Ken Harney, "No bias is found in credit scores," *Baltimore Sun*, August 31, 2007, E1.

p. 118, Though the balding, button-down: Eugene Ludwig, "Extending Credit to Lower Income Americans Safely and Fairly," keynote remarks at Moving Forward: The Future of Consumer Credit And Mortgage Finance, hosted by The Joint Center for Housing Studies of Harvard University, February 19, 2010.

p. 119, The CRA is about . . . a better world: Testimony of Eugene Ludwig before the Senate Banking Committee, Washington D.C., October 16, 2008.

p. 119, "At a minimum," he . . . targeted neighborhoods: Eugene A. Ludwig, "The Community Reinvestment Act: Past Successes and Future Opportunities," *Revisiting the CRA: Perspectives on the Future of the Community Reinvestment Act: A Joint Publication of the Federal Reserve Banks of Boston and San Francisco*, February 2009, 102.

p. 120, To help enforce the: Ibid., 103.

p. 120, Corporate America that is . . . social responsibilities: Transcript of speech by Eugene A. Ludwig at Adelphi University, New York, September 23, 2008.

p. 122, I don't want to . . . and luck: David R. Francis, "Economists Suggest More Taxes on Rich," *Christian Science Monitor*, April 23, 1992, 15.

p. 122, The time may have: Alicia H. Munnell, "Current taxation of qualified pension plans: has the time come?" *New England Economic Review*, March–April 1992.

p. 123, It is difficult to: Jaret Selberg, "Front-runner for Fed makes banks see red," *American Banker*, May 11, 1995, 1.

p. 123, The point of that: Justin Fox, "Subprime's Silver Lining: Yeah, people got bad mortgages, but others were able to finally buy a home," *Time*, March 22, 2007, http://www.time.com/time/magazine/article/0,9171,1601838,00.html.

p. 123, Suck it up: Ashlea Ebeling, "Pink Slips Replace Gold Watches," *Forbes.com*, April 30, 2009, http://www.forbes.com/2009/04/29/older-workers-layoffs-personal-finance-retirement-job-hunting-tips.html.

p. 124, Cuomo encouraged Fannie . . . and wealth: "HUD's Regulation of the Federal National Mortgage Association (Fannie Mae) and the Federal Home Loan Mortgage Corporation (Freddie Mac): A Rule by the Housing and Urban Development Department."

p. 125, Housing discrimination is much: "Cuomo Announces Groundbreaking Nationwide Audit of Housing Discrimination Around Nation" (HUD No. 98-600), U.S Department of Housing and Urban Development, http://archives.hud.gov/news/1998/pr98-600.html.

p. 125, There are a lot: Day, "HUD says mortgage policies hurt blacks."

p. 125, It was a mistake: Carol Leonnig, "How HUD Mortgage Policy Fed the Crisis," June 10, 2008, *Washington Post*, 3, http://www.washingtonpost.com/wp-dyn/content/article/2008/06/09/AR2008060902626_3.html.

p. 126, Congress should . . . consider expanding: William C. Apgar and Mark Duda, "The Twenty-fifth Anniversary of the Community Reinvestment Act: Past Accomplishments and Future Regulatory Challenges," *Economic Policy Review*, June 2003, 187.

p. 126, The night before [the]: Judith Havemann, "A Critic Takes on FHA's Case; Apgar Champions Low-Income Buyers," *Washington Post*, June 8, 1999, A17.

p. 127, Apgar is himself a: *Los Angeles Times*, January 18, 1988, http://articles.latimes.com/1988-01-18/business/fi-24547_1_housing-industry.

p. 127, She, too, thinks housing: Angela D. Chatman, "Fair Housing Optimism Is Infectious at Summit," *Cleveland Plain Dealer*, January 30, 1994.

p. 127, Citing Munnell's spurious work: Roberta Achtenberg, interview by Chester Hartman, *Shelterforce*, issue 79, January/February 1995, http://www.nhi.org/online/issues/79/achtenberg.html.

p. 128, I did get a presidential: Joe Eskenazi, "That 'Damn Lesbian' Roberta Achtenberg Thinks Now May Finally Be the Time for Executive Order

Barring Sexual Discrimination," *SF Weekly*, April 13, 2009, http://blogs.sfweekly.com/thesnitch/2009/04/that_damn_lesbian_roberta_acht.php.

p. 128, Working with the NAACP: "Achtenberg Pledges to Get Title VIII House in Order," The Advocate, National Fair Housing Alliance, July/August 1993.

p. 128, In fact, she joined: PR Newswire, "HUD and Mortgage Bankers Execute Fair Lending Agreement," October 10, 1994, http://www.thefreelibrary.com/HUD+AND+MORTGAGE+BAKERS+EXECUTE+FAIR+LENDING+AGREEMENTS-a015793333.

p. 129, Liberalizing lending policies in: Achtenberg, interview by Chester Hartman.

p. 129, As for Achtenberg's own: Peter Schweizer, *Architects of Ruin: How Big Government Liberals Wrecked the Global Economy—And How They Will Do It Again If No One Stops Them* (New York: HarperCollins, 2009), 54.

p. 130, She will bring an: Richard C. Paddock, "Likely Nominee a Strong Voice for Gays," January 29, 1993, *Los Angeles Times*, http://articles.latimes.com/1993-01-29/news/mn-2022_1_san-francisco-gay-community/2.

p. 131, They chose not to: Leonnig, "How HUD Mortgage Policy Fed the Crisis."

p. 131, The administration strongly supports: Mel Martinez, Statement before the U.S. Senate Committee on Banking, Housing, and Urban Affairs, October 16, 2003, http://banking.senate.gov/public/_files/martinez.pdf.

## Chapter 7: The Bank "Terrorists"

p. 133, Who's on your hit list: Michelle Malkin, "A closer look at left-wing thuggery," *Free Republic*, March 31, 2004, http://freerepublic.com/focus/f-news/1108799/posts.

p. 133, In 1999, as chairman of: Marcy Gordon, "Gramm makes banking reform a top priority," *Journal Record* (Oklahoma City, OK), January 13, 1999, http://findarticles.com/p/articles/mi_qn4182/is_19990113/ai_n10126392/.

p. 134, A proviso Clinton added: ibid.

p. 134, But in its 2004: Mark Willis, "It's the Rating, Stupid: A Banker's Perspective on the CRA," *Revisiting the CRA: Perspectives on the Future of the Community Reinvestment Act*, Federal Reserve Bank of San Francisco Web site, February 2009, http://www.frbsf.org/publications/community/cra/its_rating_stupid.pdf, p. 4.

p. 134, All told, community organizers: John Taylor, et al, "The Community Reinvestment Act: 30 Years of Wealth Building and What We Must Do to Finish the Job," *Revisiting the CRA: Perspectives on the Future of the Community Reinvestment Act*, a joint publication of the Federal Reserve Banks of Boston and San Francisco, February 2009, 149.

p., 135, But the largest banks: At least two of the largest banks, Bank of America and Wells Fargo, are now close to the 10 percent deposit cap. In other words, each of them owns about 10 percent of the nation's deposits, meaning they cannot legally acquire other banks without divesting branches.

p. 135, Most bankers have learned . . . to adapt: Transcript of remarks by Janet Lamkin, "Celebrating 30 Years of CRA," video posted on Greenlining Institute Web site, 2007.

p. 136, Commonly known as NACA: "The Bank Terrorist," editorial, *Investor's Business Daily*, November 19, 2008, http://www.investors.com/NewsAndAnalysis/Article/450547/200811191722/The-Bank-Terrorist.aspx.

p. 136, NACA founder Bruce Marks: ibid.

p. 136, Bruce has a Messiah complex: Neil Swidey, "Guarding the House," NACA Web site, December 30, 2007, https://www.naca.com/press/globe20071230.jsp.

p. 136, The angry "pit bull": Ibid.

p. 137, Then Bank of America CEO: NACA, "Bank of America – The Making of a Model Partnership," https://www.naca.com/about_naca/boa.jsp.

p. 137, Their pained looks told: Sam Ali, "Activist bringing Fleet fight to N.J.," *Star-Ledger* Archive, November 12, 2000, https://www.naca.com/press/pressClipShow.jsp?txtMode=pressClipShow&keyID=814.

p. 137, Marks considers such underwriting: "The Bank Terrorist."

p. 137, He boasts that 99: Ibid.

p. 137, Listen to NACA's pitch: Remarks by Bruce Marks, "Bank of America and NACA Announce Historic $6 billion Nationwide Mortgage Commitment," NACA press release, January 12, 2004, 2.

p. 137, Come to NACA, and: "Bank of America and NACA Announce Historic $6 Billion Nationwide Mortgage Commitment" (press release), January 12, 2004, http://www.naca.com/press/pr/2004/2004_01_12.pbl.

p. 137, These are the ['liberal underwriting']: "The Bank Terrorist."

p. 138, In 2007, the year: Carl F. Horowitz, "Leveraging Fannie and Freddie," *American Spectator*, August 4, 2008.

p. 138, Marks, a former union: "The Bank Terrorist."

p. 138, Marks will not disclose: Marks claimed in an interview with the *Boston Globe* that only 1.15 percent of mortgages in NACA's portfolio are late by 90 days or more, compared with the national rate of 2.95 percent. But that was in 2007, before the market crashed. And he did not reveal data for 30- or 60-day delinquencies. Marks refuses to open his books up to independent audit and publicly disclose his performance data, leading many to suspect he's hiding bad numbers.

p. 138, And NACA bails delinquent: Marks said in the same interview that 6.32 percent of NACA's borrowers have taken advantage of the fund. Again, this was in 2007, before the crash.

p. 138, Marks insists that regulators: "The Bank Terrorist."

p. 139, As usual, the bullying: "The Bank Terrorist."

p. 139, Now Marks, flush with: "Accountability Campaign," https://www.naca.com/index_main.jsp.

p. 139, Every aspect of their: https://www.naca.com/economicJustice/currentCampaign.jsp.

p. 140, For future underwriting practices: "The Bank Terrorist."

p. 140, Who's on your hit list: Malkin, "A closer look."

p. 141, Anything to appease such: "The Cycle of Organizing: Revitalizing Old Campaigns with New Strategies," *Disclosure*, October 31, 2002.

p. 141, It's also worth noting: http://www.abcdinstitute.org/faculty/.

p. 141, With a fellow community: "Our Moment is Now," National Training and Information Center/NPA Organizers Conference, 2009.

p. 141, As a result of: "A People's Platform for Social and Economic Justice," National People's Action, 2008, 1–4.

p. 141, Next up: Ibid., 26.

p. 142, The HUD-funded NPA: National People's Action's Facebook page, http://www.facebook.com/pages/National-Peoples-Action/144454682234042.

p. 142, Among its accomplishments, NPA: http://www.npa-us.org/history.html.

p. 143, The nonprofit group states: National Community Reinvestment Coalition, PowerPoint presentation by David Berenbaum, for MBA's Subprime Lending and Alternative Products Conference, Best Practices Workshop, May 12–14, 2004, slides 2 and 3, http://www.mortgagebankers.org/files/present2004/SUBPRIME/MBABPBerenbaumPowerpoint.ppt.ppt.

p. 143, Among other things, he . . . for everything: NCRC Anti-Predatory Lending Toolkit.

p. 145, This helps us spot: "More is better in his version of CRA grades," *American Banker*, October 27, 2000, 1.

p. 145, Echoing Greenlining's battle cry: "Impact of CRA," September 22, 1999, *Los Angeles Times*, http://articles.latimes.com/1999/sep/22/local/me-12988.

p. 145, He remarked that banks: "State Treasurer Angelides Pledges New Partnership with Community Banks," PR Newswire, May 3, 1999.

p. 147, For every dollar of wealth: "Greenlining Tells Fed: Communities of Color are 'Canaries in the Coal Mine' of Economic Crisis," August 17, 2010, http://www.commondreams.org/newswire/2010/08/17-8.

p. 147, Expanding the CRA is: "Greenlining to Push Improvements to Community Reinvestment Act at Fed Hearing in L.A. Tuesday" (press release), August 16, 2010, Greenlining Institute, http://www.greenlining.org/news/category/press-release; "Greenlining Tells Fed: Communities of Color . . ."

p. 147, We also urge that: Testimony of Orson Aguilar, Executive Director, The Greenlining Institute, Hearing of the House Financial Services Committee: "Proposals to Enhance the Community Reinvestment Act," September 16, 2009, http://www.house.gov/apps/list/hearing/financialsvcs_dem/orson_aguilar.pdf.

p. 148, Aguilar says the CRA's: ibid.

p. 148, For over two decades: http://www.acorn.org/index.php?id=754.

p. 149, Why reward this racist: Transcript of Public Meeting Regarding Norwest Corporation and Wells Fargo & Company (transcript of panel 3), September 17, 1998, Federal Reserve Board Web site, http://www.federalreserve.gov/events/publicmeeting/19980917/panel3.htm.

p. 149, ACORN knows that corporate: Sol Stern, "ACORN's Nutty Regime for Cities," *City Journal* (Spring 2003), http://www.city-journal.org/html/13_2_acorns_nutty_regime.html.

p. 150, There is not a shred: Amilda Dymi, "Activists protests at exec's home during conference," *Origination News* magazine, August 2000, 35.

p. 150, The bank said the group: Wells Fargo, "Wells Fargo Senior Executive Says Activist Group Distorts, Misrepresents Company's Record" (news release), June 28, 2004, https://www.wellsfargo.com/press/ActivistResponse.

p. 150, Pricing for consumer loans: Ibid.

p. 151, Barack has proven himself: Hank De Zutter, "What Makes Obama Run?" *Chicago Reader*, December 7, 1995, 8.

p. 151, We accept and respect: Ibid. A.; J. Linn Allen, "Home mortgage gap starts with bank lack," Chicago Tribune, September 1, 1992, C8.

p. 153, Fannie alone has donated: Horowitz, "Leveraging Fannie and Freddie."

p. 153, What has ACORN accomplished . . . threat reappears: ACORN, Acorn Accomplishments (Web page), no longer accessible.

## Chapter 8: Myth of the Racist White Lender

p. 155, The picture for Asians: Robert B. Avery, et al, "Higher-Priced Home Lending and the 2005 HMDA Data," *Federal Reserve Bulletin*, 2006, A159.

p. 155, As subprime mortgage foreclosures: American Bankrutcy Institute, Edwards-Clinton-Obama debate transcript, January 15, 2008, http://www.abiworld.org/pdfs/Democratdebatetranscriptonbankruptcy1-15-08.pdf, p. 3.

p. 156, The reality in our country: Testimony of John Taylor, President and CEO, National Community Reinvestment Coalition Before the Oversight and Investigations Subcommittee of the House Financial Services Committee: Rooting Out Discrimination in Mortgage Lending: Using HMDA as a Tool for Fair Lending Enforcement, July 25, 2007, http://financialservices.house.gov/hearing110/httaylor072507.pdf, p. 2.

p. 156, Whereas statistics are touted . . . vis-a-vis Asians: Transcript of remarks by Andrew Sandler during interview with NPR's "Talk of the Nation," Washington D.C., September 30, 1997.

p. 157, The picture for Asians: Avery et. al, "Higher-Priced Home Lending," A159.

p. 157, In 2007, as the number: Michael Powell and Janet Roberts, "Minorities Hit Hardest as New York Foreclosures Rise," *New York Times*, May 16, 2009; Jennifer Lee, "Study Notes Fewer Loans to Hispanic and Blacks," New York Times, October 28, 2008, A26.

p. 158, Lost in all the: "Bad credit is pervasive among blacks, survey says," Associated Press, September 22, 1999.

p. 158, Such institutions have come: McKinley, "Community Reinvestment Act."

p. 158, Federal statistics show that: In addition to the Federal Reserve Board study, University of Tennessee finance professor Harold Black found that black-owned banks are more likely to turn down black applicants than their white-owned counterparts. He also found that black-owned banks are less likely to lend in the ghetto—a practice known (when white-owned banks are accused of doing it) as racist "redlining."

p. 159, While black-owned firms are: David G. Blanchflower, et al, "Discrimination in the Small-Business Credit Markets," *The Review of Economics and Statistics*, November 2003, 933.

p. 160, Black-owned firms were: Ibid., 932.

p. 160, Blacks have been disadvantaged: Cindy Loose, "Racial Disparity Found in Credit Rating," *Washington Post*, September 21, 1999, A01.

p. 161, Slightly more than 1: "Bad credit is pervasive among blacks, survey says."

p. 162, On average, Asian-Americans were: "New Information Reported under HMDA and Its Application in Fair Lending Enforcement," Federal Reserve Board, 2005, 377.

p. 163, According to LaTanya M.: Jodi Nirode and Stephanie Brenowitz, "Home Inequity: A dream denied; Even with high incomes, blacks face a tough time getting home mortgages," *Columbus Dispatch*, June 3, 2001.

p. 164, Blacks spend more money: Cassandra George-Sturges, "Economic freedom remains a goal for African Americans, entrepreneur says," *Michigan Citizen*, October 10, 1998, 8.

p. 164, Even the poorest Asians: "Consumer Credit Survey," Federal Home Loan Mortgage Corporation, 1999. The $1.3 million comprehensive national survey, which included a 12-page questionnaire completed by 12,140 respondents (from a universe of 80,000), ages 20 to 40, was conducted for Freddie Mac by Market Facts. Individual credit data was provided by Experian and included FICO score data. Individuals with "bad" credit were defined as those who had a record of delinquency or a bankruptcy or who had been 90 days late on a payment in the previous two years or 30 days late on a payment more than once in the previous two years. The survey of blacks was aided by five historically black colleges and universities. The Urban League and NAACP accepted the survey results, and they worked with Freddie Mac on a related education program. However, that was not good enough for Rep. Waters, D-Calif., who dismissed the findings as "incomplete, dishonest, and racist." She added in a September 30, 1999, press release: "'Bad credit' as defined by whom or determined by whom?—the same lenders who have been found to discriminate against African-Americans. . . . I am very disturbed by the tone of the accusation." Waters is best known for fanning the flames of the deadly 1992 Rodney King riots in her South Central Los Angeles district, earning her the sobriquet "Kerosene Maxine."

p. 165, The media, wedded as: The liberal media have perpetuated the myth. Case in point: The *Charlotte Observer* in the run-up to the financial crisis ran a series on "racist lending," which strongly suggested that bank bias is the reason more blacks get subprime loans than whites. Problem is, it glossed over the key factor behind the trend: lower credit scores among African-Americans. The newspaper's veteran business editor, Glenn Burkins, acknowledged in an e-mail that the paper lacked "credit score information," but he decided to go with the series anyway. It also left out the Asian cohort in its analysis of high-cost loans by race, even though the data were available. Of course, including Asian borrowers would have muddied the picture that the liberal McLatchy Co.–owned paper was trying to present—that banks are run by racist white men. If it had introduced the Asian wild card, it would have had to suggest white lenders were discriminating against whites in favor of Asians, which does not fit the progressive narrative of racist white America. Still, the Pulitzer Prize Committee named the *Observer* a 2008 finalist in Public Service for its coverage of the mortgage crisis, in part because it resulted in "changes" in local lending practices involving minorities (Charlotte is headquarters to Bank of America and Wachovia, among other major banks). The panel called the series "illuminating." Indeed, it revealed a lot—mostly about the media's bias in covering the banking industry. Burkins, who is black, recently left the *Observer* to start a Web site focusing on news exclusively for African-Americans. Explaining his move, he said that the "mainstream media does a good job of writing about the African American community, but not for them—there's a difference" ("The Online Migration: Ex-Observer staffers David Boraks and Glen [sic] Burkins have launched hyperlocal Web sites; Welcome to the future of news," *Charlotte* magazine, August 2009, 62). Now you know a little more about the personal bias of those who allege bank bias.

p. 165, The technical validity of: Testimony of John Taylor Before the Oversight and Investigations Subcommittee of the House Financial Services Committee, July 25, 2007, http://financialservices.house.gov/hearing110/httaylor072507.pdf, p. 6.

p. 165, Our pricing is automated: Sue Kirchhoff, "Borrowing Patterns Fall Along Racial Lines," *Arizona News*, December 6, 2004, http://aznews.us/borrowing_patterns_fall_along_racial_lines.htm.

p. 166, We consider each applicant: Joanne Morrison, "Banks extend pricier loans to minorities: study," Reuters, April 7, 2008, http://www.reuters.com/article/idUSN0758544920080407.

p. 166, For starters, the head of: Thomas E. Perez, transcript of speech, "Remarks on Fair Lending and Fair Housing," Brookings Institution, Washington D.C., June 23, 2010, http://www.justice.gov/crt/opa/pr/speeches/2010/crt-speech-100623.html.

p. 166, Also, the financial overhaul law: Sec. 1403, Prohibition on Steering Incentives, Title XIV—Mortgage Reform and Anti-Predatory Lending Act, Dodd-Frank Wall Street Reform and Consumer Protection Act of 2010.

p. 166, The newly formed federal: Sec. 1078, Study and Report on Credit Scores, Subtitle G—Regulatory Improvements, Dodd-Frank Wall Street Reform and Consumer Protection Act of 2010.

p. 167, Many American blacks falsely: "The Best Quotes from Larry Elder's The Ten Things You Can't Say in America," *Right Wing News*, http://www.righ-twingnews.com/quotes/elder10.php.

p. 167, As recent Census Bureau: "Poor in Judgment," *Investor's Business Daily*, August 31, 2005.

p. 168, If there is a "dual lending . . .": Testimony of John Taylor, p. 2.

## Chapter 9: Deadbeat Borrowers in Black and White

p. 169, I will crack down: Associated Press, "Obama Mocks McCain in Nevada Stops," September 17, 2008, 8 News Now (Las Vegas, NV), http://www.8newsnow.com/global/story.asp?s=8999386&nav=168xs3j8.

p. 170, Subprime mortgages and the brokers: Mark Whitehouse, "A DAY OF RECKONING: Subprime Aftermath: Losing the Family Home," *Wall Street Journal*, 30 May 2007, A1. In his July 25, 2007, testimony before a House Financial Services subcommittee, National Community Reinvestment Coalition president John Taylor made a point of citing the Journal article to back his charge that "predatory lenders" were preying on black communities. "The *Wall Street Journal*, for example, recently wrote a poignant and detailed article describing widespread foreclosures due to predatory lending in Detroit's middle-income African-American communities," Taylor said. (In fact, it lacked critical details.) Interestingly, longtime *Wall Street Journal* managing editor Paul Steiger, a dyed-in-the-wool liberal (yes, liberal), left not long after the story ran to start up a "public-interest" investigative journalism project—Pro Publica—underwritten by the Sandler Family Supporting Foundation, a far left charity that supports among other "progressive causes" the "fight against predatory lending." Grant records show the foundation has given ACORN at least $525,000. FEC records show Pro Publica chairman Herbert Sandler has shelled out hundreds of thousands of dollars in campaign donations to Democrats; and in 2004 alone, he pumped an eye-popping $2.5 million into the coffers of the leftist group MoveOn.org.

p. 172, In effect, she had: Edward Ericson Jr., "Victim Mentality," *Baltimore City Paper*, July 30, 2008.

p. 172, Holding herself up as: David Montgomery, "The Foreclosees Protest an American Dream Turned Nightmare," *Washington Post*, October 2, 2008.

p. 172, We've come to a heck: Ibid.

p. 172, The couple fell behind on: Binyamin Appelbaum, "THE HARD TRUTH IN LENDING: A 10% loan, a job loss, their first home gone; couple: mortgage rate a big factor," *Charlotte Observer*, August 28, 2005, A12.

p. 173, Bias looks to play: "Truth in lending: Bias looks to play a role, as blacks pay higher mortgage rates" (editorial), *Charlotte Observer*, August 28, 2005, p. 2.

p. 173, I try my best to: Appelbaum, "THE HARD TRUTH IN LENDING."

p. 174, In their case, they had: The National Community Reinvestment Coalition is not satisfied with the disclosure law. In its "Anti-Predatory Lending Toolkit," the NCRC suggests that HUD settlement statements cannot be "reasonably comprehended" by African-Americans, even with the additional reading time. Who's racist?

P. 174, Rick Maher moved his: Nancy Stancill, "Owners with unpaid dues risk losing their home: Residents are falling behind on association fees, and one family faces foreclosure," *Charlotte Observer*, September 23, 2008.

P. 175, Was I supposed to: Brian Carlton, "Taylor Glenn family must pay late dues by Oct. 8," *Union County Weekly*, October 3–9, 2008, 15.

P. 175, They have no scruples: "Mahers knew about fees" (letter to the editor), *Union County Weekly*, October 3–9, 2008, 14.

p. 175, We didn't feel that: Carlton, "Taylor Glenn family must pay late dues by Oct. 8."

p. 176, I can't help it: Ibid.

## *Chapter 10: Hannie Mae: Casas for Illegals*

p. 179, Espanol.hud.gov is another step: Maria Pia Tamburri, "Martinez Launches New Spanish-Language Website Espanol.hud.gov to Increase Housing Education and Homeownership Opportunities" (news release: HUD no. 03-074), United States Department of Housing and Urban Development, June 19, 2003, http://archives.hud.gov/news/2003/pr03-074.cfm.

p. 179, If Clinton was America's: Toni Morrison, "Talk of the Town: Comment," *The New Yorker*, October 1998.

p. 180, You can imagine somebody . . . home ownership loans: "George W. Bush Delivers Remarks at White House Conference on Increasing Minority Homeownership," FDCH Political Transcripts, Washington D.C., October 15, 2002.

p. 181, To reach this growing population: Tamburri, "Martinez Launches New Spanish-Language Website."

p. 181, Changing demographics will create: "HUD's Proposed Housing Goal Rule – 2004," http://www.alta.org/govt/issues/04/hud_gse_sum0407.pdf, p. 4.

p. 181, The HUD proposal also: Ibid., 5.

p. 181, It is compassionate to . . . to realize the dream: George W. Bush, "President Highlights Compassionate Conservative Agenda" (news release containing transcript of a speech at the Playhouse Square Center, Cleveland, OH, July 1, 2002), http://georgewbush-whitehouse.archives.gov/news/releases/2002/07/20020701-1.html.

p. 181, More Hispanics in America: Steve Bousquet, "Martinez Defends Study Decision," *St. Petersburg Times*, October 3, 2004, http://schakowsky.house.gov/index.php?option=com_content&task=view&id=1775&Itemid=17.

p. 182, NAHREP maintains that California: Alejandro Becerra, "The Potential of Hispanic Homeownership: Challenges and Opportunities," report published by the National Association of Hispanic Real Estate Professionals, 2007, 21.

p. 183, Giving new meaning to: "Mortgage Lending Crisis and Its Impact on Hispanic Community" at http://www.consumer-action.org/radar/articles/mortgage_lending_crisis_and_its_impact_on_hispanic_community.

p. 183, According to a recent: Kenneth R. Harney, "Fed Examines Credit Scores, Finds No Bias," *Washington Post*, September 1, 2007, http://www.washingtonpost.com/wp-dyn/content/article/2007/08/31/AR2007083100769.html.

p. 184, NAHREP currently estimates that: Becerra, "The Potential of Hispanic Homeownership," 26.

p. 184, By law, banks do: FDIC says TIN mortgage lending is perfectly legal, even though immigration code states that it is a crime to aid or abet illegal immigrants for financial gain.

p. 185, We have to go . . . rent to their landlords: Transcript of remarks by Mark Doyle on Chicago Public Radio, as reported by Ashley Gross in "Mortgages to Illegal Immigrants Come Under Fire," on WBEZ 91.5's City Room Web site, October 16, 2007, http://www.chicagopublicradio.org/Content.aspx?audioID=14015.

p. 186, Flagrant examples include Gerardo . . . their loan: Anthony Ha, "Minorities Hit Hard by Foreclosure Crunch," *Hollister* [CA] *Free Lance*," May 3, 2007.

p. 187, So much for Bush's: Bush, "President Highlights Compassionate Conservative Agenda."

p. 187, The lower [Hispanic homeownership]: Steven Malanga, "Obsessive Housing Disorder," *City Journal* 19, no. 2 (Spring 2009), http://www.city-journal.org/2009/19_2_homeownership.html.

p. 187, In fact, President Obama's: Stanton R. Koppel, (1)(e), "Report on Feasibility of and Impediments to Use of Remittance History in Calculation of Credit Score," Sec. 919, "Remittance Transfers," Subtitle G, "Regulatory Improvements," Dodd-Frank Wall Street Reform and Consumer Protection Act.

p. 188, In the case of: Becerra, "The Potential of Hispanic Homeownership," 23.

p. 188, Congressman Baca remains equally: Steven Malanga, "Our Real Estate Obsession Endures," Real Clear Markets, March 11, 2009, Manhattan Institute for Policy Research Web site, http://www.manhattan-institute.org/html/miarticle.htm?id=4160.

## *Chapter 11: Red Herrings*

p. 189, Redlining may have become: Federal Reserve Bank of Dallas, "Redlining or Red Herring," *Southwest Economy* (May/June 1999), http://dallasfed.org/research/swe/1999/swe9903b.pdf, p. 8.

p. 190, Because the Community Reinvestment: "Financial Regulatory Reform: A New Foundation: Rebuilding Financial Supervision and Regulation," U.S. Department of Treasury, 17 June 2009, http://www.financialstability.gov/docs/regs/FinalReport_web.pdf, p. 69. CRA lobbyists are even more disingenuous in defending the law's role in the crisis. Consider a November 24, 2008, briefing paper the Greenlining Institute put out to deflect growing criticism. Like the Obama administration, it argued that "the explosive growth in subprime lending occurred more than two decades" after the CRA was enacted in 1977. But then the paper, titled "CRA Myth vs. Fact," added, "No major changes to CRA were enacted during this time" (http://www.expandcra.org/about-cra/cra-myth-vs.-fact/). The operative word is "enacted." Of course nothing was enacted by Congress. Clinton bypassed legislation and overhauled the CRA through executive order. But Greenlining knows this, since it offered input during the proposal phase.

p. 190, As banks bent their: "HUD's Regulation of the Federal National Mortgage Association (Fannie Mae) and the Federal Home Loan Mortgage Corporation (Freddie Mac): A Rule by the Housing and Urban Development Department," *Federal Register*, October 31, 2000.

p. 190, Secondary-market innovations have: David Listokin et al, "The Potential and Limitations of Mortgage Innovation in Fostering Homeownership in the United States"(Fannie Mae foundation, 2002), as noted in Stan J. Liebowitz, "Anatomy of a Train Wreck: Causes of the Mortgage Meltdown," August 22, 2008, http://www.scribd.com/doc/14435743/Anatomy-of-a-Train-Wreck. According to that site, "Anatomy of a Train Wreck" at the time was a forthcoming chapter in *Housing America: Building out of a Crisis*, eds. Benjamin Powell and Randall Holcomb (New Brunswick, NJ: Transaction Publishers, 2009). The book has since been published. The abstract of this chapter can be downloaded from the Web site of the Social Science Research Network, at http://papers.ssrn.com/sol3/papers.cfm?abstract_id=1211822. The footnoted quote is found on page 7 of this PDF.

p. 190, Former Federal Reserve chairman . . . dimensions that it did: Transcript of testimony by former Federal Reserve chairman Alan Greenspan before the U.S. House Committee on Oversight and Government Reform, Washington D.C., October 23, 2008.

p. 191, The worst abuses were: "Financial Regulatory Reform: A New Foundation, 69.

p. 191, subprime loans made by: Mortgage lenders are sometimes owned by holding companies or other financial institutions. Some mortgage companies are owned by bank depository institutions, and are therefore subsidiaries of a bank regulated under the CRA. Others are owned by holding companies that also own a bank and are therefore affiliates of a bank covered by the CRA. Mortgage companies that are not a subsidiary or affiliate of a bank depository institution are called *independent mortgage companies*. Banks do not have to report the lending records of subprime subsidiaries and affiliates on CRA exams.

p. 192, They also gave them credit: CRAFund is managed by Community Capital Management, which happens to be chaired by the CRA's top lobbyist in

Washington—NCRC's John Taylor. His fund does the legwork for banks in search of CRA credits.

p. 192, The Federal Reserve estimates: Glenn Canner and Neil Bhutta, in a Federal Reserve Board of Governors summary titled "Staff Analysis of the Relationship between the CRA and the Subprime Crisis," to Sandra Braunstein, director of the Consumer & Community Affairs Division, November 21, 2008 http://www.federalreserve.gov/newsevents/speech/20081203_analysis.pdf, p. 3.

p. 193, The Clinton HUD . . . discriminatory matter: PR Newswire, "HUD and Mortgage Bankers Execute Fair Lending Agreement," October 10, 1994, http://www.thefreelibrary.com/HUD+AND+MORTGAGE+BAKERS+EXECUTE+FAIR+LENDING+AGREEMENTS-a015793333.

p. 193, In a little-noticed report: Robert E. Litan et al, *The Community Reinvestment Act After Financial Modernization: A Baseline Report* (United States Department of Treasury, April 2000); available online at http://www.butera-andrews.com/legislative-updates/directory/Background-Reports/Treasury%20CRA%20Report.pdf. (The quote referenced can be found on page 20 of this PDF).

p. 193, The CRA does not: "The Community Reinvestment Act and the Mortgage Crisis," preliminary staff report, Financial Crisis Inquiry Commission," April 7, 2010, 4.

p. 194, The safety and soundness: Jeffrey W. Gunther, "Should CRA stand for 'Community Redundancy Act'? *Regulation* 23, no. 3, 2000, 60.

p. 194, Yes, Clinton's 1995 revision: See the Federal Deposit Insurance Corporation document at http://edocket.access.gpo.gov/cfr_2003/pdf/12cfr345.22.pdf.

p. 194, Even former Federal Reserve: Lawrence B. Lindsey, "The CRA as a Means to Provide Public Goods," *Revisiting the CRA: Perspectives on the Future of the Community Reinvestment Act: A Joint Publication of the Federal Reserve Banks of Boston and San Francisco*, February 2009, 164.

p. 194, CRA loans . . . purchased by Fannie or Freddie: "HUD's Regulation of the Federal National Mortgage Association (Fannie Mae) and the Federal Home Loan Mortgage Corporation (Freddie Mac)," 65,104. At least a third of CRA loans can be classified as subprime or worse, with FICO credit scores below 660 and a disproportionately large share below 620. The remaining share of CRA portfolios consist of Alt-A and other nonprime loans.

p. 194, Purchasing these loans could: *Federal Register* 65, no. 211, Part II, Department of Housing and Urban Development 24 Part 81 CFR, HUD's Regulation of the Federal National Mortgage Association (Fannie Mae) and the Federal Home Loan Mortgage Corporation (Freddie Mac); Final Rule, "Rules and Regulations" (October 31, 2000): 65053, http://www.novoco.com/low_income_housing/resource_files/hud_data/GSEs.pdf.

p. 195, CRA-mandated loans have: "The Community Reinvestment Act and the Mortgage Crisis," preliminary staff report, Financial Crisis Inquiry Commission, April 7, 2010, 6.

p. 195, A Federal Reserve study: "The Performance and Profitability of CRA-Related Lending," report by the Board of Governors of the Federal Reserve System submitted to Congress, July 2000, 49.

p. 195, Another Federal Reserve study: Testimony of Howard Husock, Manhattan Institute scholar, U.S. Commission on Civil Rights, Washington D.C., March 23, 2009.

p. 195, The situation was nearly: Transcript of remarks by Bank of America CFO Joe L. Price, earnings call, April 20, 2009.

p. 195, The process of justifying: Mark Willis, "It's the Rating, Stupid: A Banker's Perspective on the CRA," *Revisiting the CRA: Perspectives on the Future of the Community Reinvestment Act*, Federal Reserve Bank of San Francisco Web site, February 2009, http://www.frbsf.org/publications/community/cra/its_rating_stupid.pdf, p. 6.

p. 195, "To be sure," says: "The Community Reinvestment Act and the Mortgage Crisis," preliminary staff report, Financial Crisis Inquiry Commission, April 7, 2010, 7.

p. 196, In its current efforts: Board of Governors of the Federal Reserve System et al, "Agencies Announce Public Hearings on Community Reinvestment Act Regulations" joint release, June 17, 2010, http://www.ffiec.gov/cra/pdf/hearingspr.pdf.

p. 196, And a study of . . . by 2005: Ellen Schloemer, et al, *Losing Ground*, Center for Responsible Lending, December 2006, 13.

p. 197, Though generally discouraged as: Wayne Barrett, "Andrew Cuomo and Fannie and Freddie," *Village Voice*, August 5, 2008.

p. 197, We should be careful: "Fannie's And Freddie's Fakeover," staff editorial, *Investor's Business Daily*, August 17, 2010.

p. 198, As detailed in earlier: "HUD's Regulation of the Federal National Mortgage Association (Fannie Mae) and the Federal Home Loan Mortgage Corporation (Freddie Mac)," 65,106.

p. 198, Two years later, the: Kenneth Temkin, et al, "Subprime Markets, the Role of GSEs, and Risk-Based Pricing," report prepared for HUD by the Urban Institute, March 2002.

p. 198, In 2004, furthermore, HUD: "Rules and Regulations," *Federal Register* 69, no. 211, November 2, 2004, 63,670–71.

p. 198, In the 2000 GSE: "HUD's Regulation of the Federal National Mortgage Association (Fannie Mae) and the Federal Home Loan Mortgage Corporation (Freddie Mac)."

p. 199, I joined the board: Glenn Thrush, "Clinton campaign head made $200,000 with subprime lender," (New York) *Newsday*, March 30, 2008.

p. 200, It wasn't the CRA: Barney Frank, "The Great Economic Hole" (speech, on floor of House of Representatives, April 2, 2009), http://www.house.gov/frank/speeches/2009/04-02-09-great-economic-hole.html.

p. 200, Senate Banking Committee chairman: Peter Urban, "Dodd reacts to financial crisis," *Connecticut Post Online* (Bridgeport, CT), September 16, 2008.

p. 200, I do believe that . . . to do that: Testimony of Marsha Courchane, former Office of the Comptroller of the Currency official during the late 1990s, before the U.S. Commission on Civil Rights, Washington D.C., March 23, 2009.

p. 200, This was the Bush, "The Great Economic Hole."

p. 201, In a 2004 report: "Rules and Regulations," 63,670–71.

p. 201, Nor did prior easing: "The State of the Nation's Housing," Joint Center for Housing Studies, Harvard University, 2006, 15.

p. 202, As Obama maintains, the: Barack Obama, "Obama's Weekly Address: Financial Reform," December 12, 2009, http://www.realclearpolitics.com/articles/2009/12/12/obamas_weekly_address_financial_reform_99538.html.

p. 202, More precisely, Washington accounts: Peter J. Wallison, "Going Cold Turkey: Three Ways to End Fannie and Freddie without Slicing Up the Taxpayers," *Financial Services Outlook*, September 2010, 3.

p. 203, Think of this as: Barney Frank, "Last Stand of the Deregulators," address at the Harvard Institute of Politics, April 6, 2009), http://www.house.gov/frank/speeches/2009/04-06-09-last-stand-of-deregulators.html. Fighting for his political life in a tough congressional race, Frank the following year gave an evening interview with Fox News host Neil Cavuto in which he appeared to admit that he, too, pushed Fannie and Freddie to make risky loans based on social policy. "It was a great mistake to push lower-income people into housing they couldn't afford and couldn't really handle once they had it," he said. But the fast-talking veteran Boston politician was not blaming himself. He was blaming, once again, "Bush," a transcript of the full interview reveals. Frank only admitted being "too sanguine" about the financial health of Fannie and Freddie (as he himself pushed them to make more affordable-housing loans in 2003, when he argued, "Fannie Mae and Freddie Mac are not facing any kind of financial crisis [and] the more people exaggerate these problems, the less we will see in terms of affordable housing"). In the same August 17, 2010, interview with Fox, Frank also appeared to call for ending their affordable housing mission. "I hope by next year we'll have abolished Fannie and Freddie," he said. This, anyway, was the quote that was played up in the conservative media. But the full transcript shows that Frank quickly added: "The only question is what do you put in their place? You can't tear down the old jail until you build a new one . . . I am for doing some housing help . . . If we want to subsidize housing then we could do it up front and let the budget be clear about that." In other words, he hopes taxpayers will *directly* fund affordable housing through a substitute government agency instead of indirectly through a failed public-private entity such as Fannie or Freddie. Bottom line: Frank has not reformed his position. If his interview was a *mea culpa*, it was a *mea* kinda *culpa*. Frank's stubborn bias can be found in the text of his financial reform legislation. Tacked on at the end of the Dodd-Frank Act, in the

"Miscellaneous" findings section, Frank highlights the Bush administration's 2004 increase to Fannie's and Freddie's affordable housing goals while completely omitting the Clinton administration's much larger 2000 hike. It is historic revisionism writ large.

p. 204, The conservative view is . . . help poor people: Ibid.

## *Afterword*

p. 205, In America, we have this: Frank De Zutter, "What Makes Obama Run?" *Chicago Reader*, December 7, 1995, http://www.chicagoreader.com/chicago/what-makes-obama-run/Content?oid=889221.

p. 205, The late, great economist: Joseph Schumpeter, *Capitalism, Socialism, and Democracy* (New York: Harper & Row, 1947); Roger L. Ransom, *Coping with Capitalism: The Economic Transformation of the United States, 1776–1980* (Englewood Cliffs, NJ: Prentice-Hall Inc., 1981), 22.

p. 206, President Obama, for one: Paul Kengor, "Obama and the Call for 'Economic Justice,'" *American Thinker*, September 15, 2010, http://www.americanthinker.com/2010/07/obama_and_the_call_for_economi.html.

p. 207, Hoover Institution fellow . . . as individuals: Shelby Steele, "The High-Wire Act of Barack Obama," *Hoover Digest*, no. 1 (2008), http://www.hoover.org/publications/hoover-digest/article/5713.

p. 207, In America, we have this: De Zutter, "What Makes Obama Run?"

p. 208, We claim the value: Gamaliel Foundation Vision Statement, http://www.gamaliel.org/Foundation/vision.htm.

p. 208, Every community organizer that: Ward Connerly, "The Artful Dodger," *FrontPage Magazine*, June 25, 2008, http://archive.frontpagemag.com/readArticle.aspx?ARTID=31452.

p. 210, African-Americans and Latinos: Testimony of the National Community Reinvestment Coalition David Berenbaum, Executive Vice President Before the Senate Committee on Banking, Sub-Committee on Housing, Transportation and Community Development Ending Mortgage Abuse: Safeguarding Homebuyers Tuesday, June 26, 2007 (on behalf of John Taylor), http://banking.senate.gov/public/_files/berenbaum.pdf.

p. 212, There is no evidence that: George Benston, "It's Time to Repeal the Community Reinvestment Act," September 28, 1999, Cato Institute Web site, http://www.cato.org/pub_display.php?pub_id=4976.

p. 212, The fact that government: Jeffrey A. Miron, "Commentary: Bankruptcy, not bailout, is the right answer," *CNN.com*, September 29, 2008, http://articles.cnn.com/2008-09-29/politics/miron.bailout_1_bailout-subprime-lending-bankruptcy?_s=PM:POLITICS, p. 1.

p. 213, This means, at a general: Ibid., 2.

p. 213, The CRA should be repealed: "CRA Is Politicized Credit Allocation, *Regulation* Says," *CATO Policy Report*, March/April 1995, Cato Institute Web site, http://www.cato.org/pubs/policy_report/pr-ma-cr.html.

p. 213, This is another thrift: Steven A Holmes, "Fannie Mae Eases Credit to Aid Mortgage Lending," *New York Times*, September 30, 1999.

p. 213, [Instead] it sends the: Howard Husock, "The Trillion-Dollar Bank Shakedown That Bodes Ill for Cities," *City Journal*, Winter 2000, http://www.city-journal.org/html/10_1_the_trillion_dollar.html.

p. 216, The bill does not respond: Randall Smith, et al, "Impact to Reach Beyond Wall Street: Key Questions Unresolved for Businesses and Consumers Until Bill Takes Effect," *Wall Street Journal*, July 16, 2010.

p. 217, By not addressing Fannie: Brian S. Wesbury and Bob Stein, "Fictitious Financial Reform," *Forbes*, June 29, 2010, http://www.forbes.com/2010/06/28/finance-reform-economy-obama-opinions-columnists-wesbury-stein_2.html, p. 2.

p. 218, We should be careful: Posted by Kaslin, "Fannie and Freddie's Fakeover," *IBD* Editorials, August 17, 2010, http://www.freerepublic.com/focus/f-news/2572649/posts.

p. 219, Seidman, who headed Fannie's: Remarks by Ellen Seidman, Conference on the Future of Housing Finance, U.S. Treasury Department, Washington D.C., August 17, 2010.

p. 219, The private sector will not: "Fannie's and Freddie's Fakeover," staff editorial, *Investor's Business Daily*, August 17, 2010.

p. 219, Echoing Seidman, Geithner asserted: Rebecca Christie and Lorraine Woellert, "Geithner says Fannie Mae, Freddie Mac need overhaul," *Washington Post*, August 17, 2010, http://www.washingtonpost.com/wp-dyn/content/article/2010/08/17/AR2010081701768.html?hpid=topnews.

p. 220, Wells Fargo, for one: "Fannie and Freddie's Takeover."

p. 221, Raines, a Clinton appointee: Elizabeth Omara-Otunnu, "Fannie Mae Bending Financial System to Create Homeowners, Says Raines," *Advance* (Univ. of CT), October 30, 2000, http://www.advance.uconn.edu/2000/001030/00103004.htm.

p. 221, We have come to: Ibid.

p. 222, The financial crisis was: Peter J. Wallison, "Grading the Bill," sidebar to main story by Damian Paletta and Aaron Lucchetti, "Law Remakes U.S. Financial Landscape, *Wall Street Journal*, July 16, 2010.

# ACKNOWLEDGMENTS

It goes without saying that this book could not have been written without the assistance of many others. But ultimately nobody is responsible for anything in this book but me. I wish I could thank my "assistants," or at least one "researcher," but alas, I do not have any. I do, however, have a patient publisher in Joel Miller of Thomas Nelson, and a patient agent in Andrew Stuart, who put this deal together, and then, with extraordinary forbearance and grace, watched me break deadline after deadline as I dealt with a crashed hard drive, followed by a particularly insidious computer virus, as well as a chronic pinched cervical nerve from prolonged periods sitting at my desk, typing (and retyping).

I also want to give props to Renée Chavez, a copy editor who is both fast and fastidious, as well as the consummate professional. The manuscript was in good hands with her.

Thank you to friends and family for their prayers, not just for me but for my long-suffering "book widow" and children. They have endured too much for too long. I apologize for my absence. Thank you for your loving patience. I will make it up to you, I promise.

As usual, my parents were very supportive, both interested in their own way in my latest book project. My father, Joe, an individual investor and financial news hound, kept a steady stream of financial newsletters and articles coming into my in-box even before the market entered its 2008 death spiral. My mother, Nancy, meanwhile, wondered when she would next see me on TV.

Finally, I want to acknowledge Wes Mann, my editor at *Investor's Business Daily*, who let me vent my spleen on this subject on his Pulitzer-winning editorial pages. Wes, a veteran newsman, is one of the best minds in the business.

To all of the above, I owe an enormous debt of gratitude.

# ABOUT THE AUTHOR

Veteran newsman Paul Sperry is former Washington bureau chief for *Investor's Business Daily* and a regular contributor to the national newspaper's Pulitzer Prize–winning editorial pages. A media fellow at Stanford University's Hoover Institution, he is the best-selling author of three previous books, including the highly acclaimed *Infiltration: How Muslim Spies and Subversives Have Penetrated Washington*, which is being used by top law enforcement agencies across the country, as well as the U.S. Department of Defense and CIA. In addition to IBD, Sperry's work has been featured in the *New York Times*, *Wall Street Journal*, *New York Post*, *Houston Chronicle*, *American Spectator*, and *Reason*, among other publications. He has broken a number of major news stories on economic and domestic policy, as well as other national issues, that have been cited and credited by the *Washington Post*, *USA*

*Today*, *ABC News*, UPI, the Associated Press, and CNBC, among others. Sperry has appeared on *Fox News*, CNN, C-SPAN, and the *NBC Nightly News*. He lives near Washington with his wife and children.

# INDEX

## C

## D



## E



## F